GOULD's MILLIONS

By Richard O'Connor

GOULD's MILLIONS

RICHARD O'CONNOR

DOUBLEDAY & COMPANY, INC.

GARDEN CITY, NEW YORK

1962

Library of Congress Catalog Card Number 62-7669
Copyright © 1962 by Richard O'Connor
All Rights Reserved
Printed in the United States of America
First Edition

CONTENTS

PART ONE

PRODIGY

1. "BUT I'M ON TOP, AIN'T I?"

A THIRD of the way through the last century were born two men whose lives and works, though strikingly dissimilar, were to imprint themselves deeply on American society.

Without them, the Success Story, the greatest of all the American legends, ranking even the saga of the frontier, would have been much less compelling. It would have lacked its Aesop. It would also have been deprived of its most fascinating villain.

Horatio Alger (1834–1899), born in a Unitarian parsonage in Revere, Massachusetts, and himself a graduate of the Harvard Divinity School, went to New York and was everlastingly impressed by the tales of poor boys who thrust their way out of city or rural slums, sink-or-swim, onward-and-upward, and through luck-and-pluck made their fortunes. "Holy Horatio," as he was known in his earnest youth, left a more indelible mark on the American character than many superior writers through his fables of ragged newsboys and clean-living young clerks who stopped runaway horses, rescuing worthy merchants, acquiring better jobs, and marrying the worthies' daughters. All you had to do was wash your face, memorize *Poor Richard's Almanack*, and keep an eye out for lively steeds. Few boys, until quite recently, escaped Holy Horatio's admonitions—and fewer still were not impressed by them. Alger gave most of his money away and died a poor man.

Jay Gould (1836–1892) also came to the big city impressed

by the possibilities of rising from low rank through diligence
and clean living. He first appeared on the streets of New York
with a mousetrap, a better mousetrap it may be presumed,
and beat a path to the world. Up to a point little Jay Gould
might have served as the model of an Horatio Alger hero. He
was young, poor, energetic and ambitious. But he was also
damnably dishonest, and there he parted company with the
Alger boys. His life and career, in fact, became the ultimate
perversion of the Alger legend. He was a certifiable crook by
the time he reached voting age. He never took his eye off the
main chance. Before he died he was worth approximately a
hundred million dollars, which he acquired along with the
title of the most hated man in America.

As representations of the American Success Story whose
lustiest phase was the period between the Civil War and the
turn of the century, the days of the "Robber Barons," the
"wizards" and "wolves" of Wall Street, the plunderbund which
built an empire in the process of enriching themselves, Alger
created the pious legend but Gould was the bitter reality. Poor
boys who made good, and better than good, were necessarily
dehumanized in the process, but it took later generations to
recognize the self-made man for what he was. Despite Alger,
the million 're who rose from the gutters of the metropolis
was no great-hearted man eager to give a leg up to other
climbers toward the summit of great wealth. He wanted
wealth and power without limit for himself and everlasting
security and unassailable social position for his family. Of all
those nineteenth century climbers, parvenus and adventurers,
including the early Astors and Vanderbilts, Sage, Hill, Field,
Rockefeller, Harriman, and Mills, Jay Gould was undoubtedly
the most perfect specimen; frail and tubercular, he went the
farthest on the slenderest resources; friendless throughout his
life, he was able to afford the most enemies; abhorring violence, he found the "splendid courage of the mongoose"[1] to

[1] The phrase is Julius Grodinsky's, in his scholarly and precise *Jay
Gould: His Business Career.*

surmount personal assaults, lynch mobs, industrial wars and riotous strikes.

If ever Napoleonic command was developed in the field of American finance, it was embodied in Jay Gould. Between the Civil War and 1892, the year of his death, he conducted a brilliant if reprehensible campaign against his fellow financiers, speculators and incidental empire builders, the American government, its servants and its people, in which he lost a few skirmishes but never a battle. Through the manipulation of railroad and telegraph systems he came close to engorging the American West. None of his contemporaries quite approached his genius for trickery and thimblerigging, his boldness in corruption and subornation, his talent for strategic betrayal, his mastery over stock and bond rigging, his daring in looting a company and defrauding its stockholders. Daniel Drew warned that his touch was death, and James Keene, another ex-collaborator who came to grief operating against Gould, declared him "the worst man on earth since the beginning of the Christian era." His skill at dealing and trading was so notorious that even the sophisticated financiers of Europe feared to join in any of his schemes. Once on a brief visit to the continent he sent in his calling card to one of the Rothschilds. It was returned with the scrawled comment: "Europe is not for sale."

Gould, of course, flourished in a remarkably fertile time for a man of his talents and accomplishments. Individual enterprise then was seldom checked by any governmental controls. The Securities and Exchange Commission was many happy years in the future, as were the antitrust laws and most of the interstate commerce regulations. Plentiful capital was available for investment. There was a large and cheap supply of labor, largely immigrant, with no union protection. There were no taxes on excess profits and only the most negligible levy on income. Breath-taking gambles could be taken on Wall Street, with only a ten percent margin required. Those were capitalism's days of wine and roses.

Yet Gould, more than any of his contemporaries, would have been a remarkable man in any age or circumstances. In all his operations, murky though many of their details were, the manifestations of genius shone through. If he was as ruthless, treacherous and antihuman as his enemies contended, he also possessed the qualities of imagination, vision and daring, and an unparalleled grasp of the complexities of corporate operations that enabled him to keep the books of a dozen companies in his head, that marked a master in the field of finance. And no matter what his angry contemporaries said about him, there were one or two clearly admirable traits to his character. He was never a hypocrite, never fell in with the credo of the nineteenth century capitalist that wealth was sanctified by God, that a man who acquired millions necessarily was guided by a Divine Will. He never deceived himself. He had the true gambler's flair for taking risks coolly and facing ruin calmly. If he went to hell the day on which Wall Street rejoiced at the news of his death, he surely arrived at his destination without any bleating of *mea culpas* to annoy his host.

A child psychologist probably could have unearthed the seeds of Jay Gould's extraordinary ambition, his need to compensate for physical inferiority through the exercise of wit and cunning, in his far from placid childhood. His mother died when he was five years old, and his upbringing was largely left to his five older sisters. The boy was eager for his father's approval, but the senior Gould, a hard-pressed farmer who looked for brawn rather than brains in his son, was openly disappointed by his frailty. It was not a loveless home, with five sisters to lavish their affection on a younger brother, but the parental indifference the boy experienced was reflected in the almost excessive affection and tolerance which he gave his own children.

Jason Gould, his given name early shortened to Jay, was born on May 27, 1836 at West Settlement, a small farming community just down the valley from Roxbury, New York, in the lower pastoral ranges of the Catskills. His mother was Mary Moore, of Scottish descent, little of whose character survives except that her only interest outside of her family, it was said, lay in the Yellow Meeting House, a "hardshell Baptist" congregation located at Hardscrabble and West Settlement Roads.

On his father's side, the boy was descended from a long line of proud and distinguished Connecticut aristocrats and Puritans, of Burrs and Bradleys and Talcotts, as well as Goulds. The Goulds, who migrated to Connecticut in 1647 from Bury St. Edmund in England, changed their name from Gold, leading to the frequent allegation that the family was originally Jewish. Henry Adams, in his autobiography, referred to Gould as "a complex Jew," and it was the unattractive fashion of his times to attribute his acquisitive tendencies to whatever fraction of Jewish ancestry might have been mingled with all those proud (and indisputably Aryan) Burrs, Talcotts and Bradleys, not to mention his mother's Scots' blood, which formed his lineage. The best efforts of the genealogists have succeeded only in establishing that the first Gold—whatever his religion—to set foot in America was Nathan, who became chief military officer for Fairfield County, deputy governor, and chief justice of the Supreme Court of Connecticut. Jay's great-grandfather was Colonel Abraham Gold, a Revolutionary War militia commander, and his grandfather, Captain Abraham Gold, "grim, earnest and honest," was one of half a dozen Connecticut men who settled in Delaware County, in the Catskill foothills, some time in the 1780s. It was Captain Gold, in 1806, who changed the family name to Gould.

Prominent as his family had been in settling the country while it was still under the manorial influence of Dutch patroons and English patent holders, the Gould patrimony had dwindled by the time Jay was born. His father, John Burr Gould, operated a dairy farm on 150 acres of hillside land.

It was a hard-scrabble life, bringing up a large family on the proceeds of a small dairy, but the Goulds, despite the legend fostered by earlier biographers, were, by comparison with their despairing neighbors, among the more prosperous and conservative families in the region. They owned the only cider press in the neighborhood, lived in an ample two-story frame house, and made no secret of the fact that they considered themselves a cut or two above the other West Settlement farmers.

Until he was fourteen, Jay attended the nearby Beechwood Seminary, where he was an unwilling, unpopular and occasionally rebellious pupil. The boy had a passion for acquiring knowledge which he regarded as necessary to his future career, such as mathematics, but he rebelled at learning by rote what a mere country schoolmaster decided was proper. Being undersized and scrawny, he was bullied by the bigger and stronger boys in the schoolyard. Most boys endure such barbarities in silence. Jay, however, had to have his revenge. He unashamedly tattled to the teacher, though this was regarded as contemptible by his fellows, no matter what the provocation. It later years his schoolmates would recall the delighted grin on his small, sallow face when the schoolmaster would take the hickory switch to his tormentors. Already he had learned to defy public opinion, rather than forfeit self-satisfaction.

One day he balked at going to school, and his exasperated father locked him in the cellar. The elder Gould promptly forgot all about him. Late that night his sisters, frantic with worry over their brother's disappearance, somehow managed to communicate their concern to the preoccupied father. Jay was missing? Let's see, where'd he put that boy? After a short struggle with his memory, Gould senior recalled locking him in the cellar, and Jay was released to the tearful custody of his sisters.

Jay also was oppressed by the several chores that fell his lot on the farm, though they were inconsiderable compared to those imposed on most farm boys. Morning and evening, he had to tend the family herd, driving the cows out to their hilly pastures in the morning and driving them back to the barn just before sundown. He also had to help his sisters with the milking. Testifying before a United States Senate investigating committee in 1869, by which time he had succeeded in milking the American gold market for millions of dollars, he recalled in a plaintive and quavering voice how, as a barefooted boy, the thistles had scratched him while he performed his humble chores. Actually, his fond sisters shielded him from too harsh an acquaintance with physical labor. Jay's father considered him "not worth much" around the farm, as Jay frankly admitted in later years. Even as a boy in short pants, Jay was certain that hornyhanded toil would never be his lot in life; his sense of direction was unerring.

Perhaps the best outside authority on Jay Gould's boyhood was John Burroughs, one of ten children born to a tenant farmer a few miles from the Gould home, who was his schoolmate and closest acquaintance. In later years Burroughs became a world-famous naturalist and essayist, a latter-day Thoreau of upstate New York. Legend credits Burroughs, in fact, with arousing Gould's interest in the beauties of nature. Burroughs himself doubted it. In maturity Gould raised orchids by the thousand and delighted in his formal gardens, but his passion was contained in these narrow limits rather than the whole cruel and varied range of nature. His naturalistic bent extended only to what he could own and control.

As a very old man John Burroughs confided to his biographer[2] that he and Jay "played and wrestled together, swapped slate pencils, traded knives and marbles, helped each other out of scrapes and into them, and went home with each other nights; or rather John sometimes went home with Jay, not Jay with John . . . The Goulds were very prosperous, and naturally stiff-necked; and they lived in a little better style than

[2] Dr. Clara Barrus, in *John Burroughs: Boy and Man.*

the other farmers." As he remembered Jay's sisters, Betty was "stern, with the Gould pride," Sally was much like Betty, Annie was "beautiful, modest and gentle," Nancy and Mary "very sweet." Jay also had a younger half brother, Abraham, the issue of the elder Gould's second marriage.

In their wrestling matches, Burroughs recalled, Jay showed a trickiness which was to be the hallmark of his future business dealings. When John got the better of Jay, who was smaller and lighter but a year older in time and a century in guile, Jay would cheat by employing an illegal hold and wriggling out of his difficulty. In reply to John's indignant protests, Jay would triumphantly point out:

"But I'm on top, ain't I?"

In that ungrammatical boast, Jay the boy summed up what was to be the philosophy of his life.

His cleverness and quickness of wit were what John Burroughs remembered best about him. Once, as punishment for misbehavior in class, John was ordered by the teacher to write twelve lines of verse before leaving school that afternoon. Jay did not want to be deprived of his company on the way home, so he swiftly dashed off the lines and slipped them to his friend. This was Jay Gould's only known attempt at poetry:

> *Time is flying past,*
> *Night is coming fast,*
> *I, minus two as you all know,*
> *But what is more*
> *I must hand over*
> *Twelve lines by night*
> *Or stay and write.*
> *Just eight I've got*
> *But you know that's not*
> *Enough lacking four;*
> *But to have twelve*
> *It wants no more."*

The teacher overlooked the impudent essay in poetic short measure and let John go on his way.

Biographical legend insisted that Burroughs and Gould continued their boyhood relationship and became lifelong friends, but long after Gould's death the great naturalist made it plain that this was a lot of nonsense. Burroughs said that he never spoke to Gould after their school days, when their paths so widely diverged. Burroughs began working for the Treasury Department in Washington during the Civil War. Like many writers of the time, he found a bread-and-butter job in the federal bureaucracy while working on the essays which first brought him to the attention of the literary world.

One day while he was working as a Treasury clerk his superior asked him to show a group of New York bankers and speculators through the vault. Among them was Jay Gould, now a millionaire. "He did not recognize me, though I knew him instantly," Burroughs recalled. "I showed them the vault, but did not make myself known to Jay. Yes, one would think that I would have—there's a queer streak in me, I guess." The only other time Burroughs saw his boyhood friend was on Fifth Avenue in New York. They passed without speaking. It was probable that Gould, never a snob, simply failed to recognize his old friend.

In that undramatic way, unneeded though it may have been to the solitary and preoccupied Gould, passed the only disinterested friendship of his life.

The most fearful and exciting events of his childhood centered around the antirent war which raged through his native Delaware and surrounding counties in 1844, when Jay was only eight years old. Perhaps it was during that rural turbulence that he learned, despite his frailty, timidity and hatred of physical violence, to stand up against the proletarian mob; to hold in contempt the have-nots, the failed and feckless, the eternal commoners; to identify himself with those who took what they wanted and held onto it no matter what clamor was raised against them.

An oppressive manorial system then prevailed in the Delaware River country, a near-feudal survival of the days when most of upstate New York was held as an absolute fief by such patroon families as the Hardenburghs, Livingstons, Rensselaers, Bradts, and others. Under grants by the English throne before the American Revolution, the Hardenburgh family and its heirs were assigned forever a tract of 2,000,000 acres in Delaware County, and in 1751 the family improved its lot by buying the Indian tribal lands between the two branches of the Delaware. Settlers who came into the country were forced to agree to live under a leasehold system established by the absentee landlords and enforced by their almost equally hated agents. Some were granted "durable leases" to remain in force "as long as the grass grows and water flows," others worked their land under redemption, three-year or yearly leases. Most of the original leases provided that the lessee, after the first seven rent-free years, pay one shilling (twenty-four and a third cents) per acre annually on whatever land he farmed.

In 1844 the Equal Rights Association was organized to oppose the leasehold system, many of its members being tenant farmers who owed years of back rent. Those of their neighbors who refused to join the association or go along with its objective of nullifying the landlords' leases were called "uprenters" and "Tories." Among these more conservative and frugal farmers, many of them descendants of the first settlers, was John Burr Gould, Jay's father. The elder Gould continued to stand against his more radical and violent neighbors even when a night-riding activist branch emerged as an offshoot of the Equal Rights Association, determined to win by force what it might take longer to accomplish through legislation and public pressure on the state government. Armed bands calling themselves "Indians" and meeting in Tom Keater's boozing den in Roxbury began to terrorize those farmers who refused to join the association, applying tar and feathers to the holdouts. Many of the "Indians," righteous as their cause

may have been, were recruited from the wilder youths, mal-
contents, boozers and deadbeats of the Delaware country. To
strike terror into their enemies, they dressed in sheepshead
masks, calico robes, with horns fastened to their foreheads and
cow tails pinned to their rumps, and coursed over the hills
and through the valleys with a great blowing of horns. Before
the summer of 1844, a thousand men had joined these roving
bands to harass their dissident neighbors, without causing a
moment's distress to the faraway landowners who were the
real cause of their grievances.

On July 6, 1844, five of the "Indians" appeared at the
Gould farm, intent on coating the elder Gould in tar and
feathers, but he brandished his musket and drove them off.
The frustrated raiders, however, managed to tar and feather
several of Gould's like-minded neighbors.

Five days later, a band of fifteen of the "Indians" showed
up at the Gould place with "demon-like yells" and surrounded
the head of the family and his eight-year-old son. Jay never
forgot how his grim and self-contained father stood up to the
threatening gang.

This was Jay's description of that second encounter as he
recorded it in his *History of Delaware County,* published a
dozen years later:

". . . How bright a picture is still retained upon the memory
of the frightful appearance they presented as they surrounded
that parent with fifteen guns poised within a few feet of his
head, while the chief stood over him with fierce gesticulations,
and sword drawn. O, the agony of my youthful mind, as I
expected every moment to behold him prostrated a lifeless
corpse upon the ground. His doting care and parental love had
endeared him to his family. But he stood his ground firmly;
he never yielded an inch. Conscious of right, he shrank from
no sense of fear—and finally, when a few neighbors had
gathered together, a second time they were driven from the
premises and down the road in single file."

That was the last time the antirenters disturbed the peace

at the Gould farm. Elsewhere in Delaware County the war passed through the comic opera stage into something like a serious insurrection, with pitched battles between the sheriff's posses and the masked and horned partisans. Eighty of the sheriff's men under Deputy Sheriff Osman Steele clashed with 130 "Indians" in a woods near Roxbury that fall. Deputy Steele, grappling with one of the antirenters, ripped off his sheepshead mask and found that he had captured the town constable of Roxbury! A short time later, in the "Battle of Shacksville," even larger forces of the law and of the partisan bands fell upon each other in the fields. In that struggle, Deputy Steele was shot three times and died a few hours later.

That tore it: there was nothing for Governor Silas Wright to do, politically disastrous though it turned out to be, but to proclaim a state of emergency and raise a battalion of militia to restore order in Delaware County. More than a hundred men accused of leading the insurrection were arrested and held in two log stockades; some of the men were imprisoned at subsequent trials and two were hung as Deputy Steele's murderers. The antirent resistance movement was quelled in its more violent activities but it won out in the end, of course, as resentment of the manorial system spread and a new, anti-rent governor was elected. "So far as the validity of the manorial titles was brought in question," Jay Gould wrote in his *History of Delaware County*, despite his father's courageous stand against the masked intruders, "we have ever deemed it a privilege and a duty to raise our voice uniformly on the side of the oppressed versus the oppressor." A noble sentiment, but he was careful not to repeat it some years later when his railroad employes went on strike and were vigorously put down.

Even as a schoolboy trudging over the mountain road to the district school or driving his father's cows from their pastures at dusk, Jay was planning his future beyond the Catskill peaks, looking forward to the day when a quick mind and a tenacious will would make him the superior of every farm lout who bullied and tormented him on his way to school. He hated school, was impatient with its droning routine, but was eager for an education on his own terms and shaped to his own purposes. Without any outside assistance or encouragement, he studied mathematics, which fascinated him not so much as an intellectual realm in itself but as a means to an end. His eldest sister Betty later wrote of him, "He did not engage much in sports; he did not have much time. In winter he would sometimes ride down on a sled, perhaps once or twice, but he really didn't have any time for sports, because he was always either studying or reading. He never played baseball, checkers, or cards. When he was twelve or thirteen years old, he was studying geometry and logarithms and getting ready for surveying. He was thinking about building a railroad across the continent, so that California might be nearer to us."

To further his education, at the age of fourteen, he wanted to attend the select school in Hobart, eleven miles from his home, although his father told him the family could not afford it. Jay went ahead with his plans nevertheless, and arranged to have himself boarded by a blacksmith in Hobart in return for keeping that craftsman's books.

His father's attitude was one of complete indifference when Jay revealed his plan for attending the Hobart Academy. Jay later recalled that the elder Gould told him, with neither rancor nor regret, that "I was not worth much at home and I might go ahead."

Before he left the local school that spring of 1850, he submitted a composition titled "Honesty Is the Best Policy," a copy of which happily survives and provides a highly ironic side light on his subsequent career, which was grimly devoted to proving the opposite.

"To become honest," wrote Jay Gould at fourteen, "requires self-denial; it requires that we should not acquaint ourselves too much with the world; that we should not associate ourselves with those of vulgar habits; also, that we should obey the warnings of conscience.

"If we are about to perform a dishonest act, the warnings of conscience exert their utmost influence to persuade us that it is wrong, and we should not do it, and after we have performed the act this faithful agent upbraids us for it. This voice of conscience is not the voice of thunder, but a voice gentle and impressive; it does not force us to comply with its requests, while at the same time it reasons with us and brings forth arguments in favor of right.

"Since no theory of reason can be sustained without illustration, it will not be unbecoming for us to cite one of the many instances that have occurred, whose names stand high upon the scroll of fame, and whose names are recorded on the pages of history,—George Washington, the man who never told a lie in all his life. In youth he subdued his idle passions, cherished truth, obeyed the teaching of conscience, and 'never told a lie.' An anecdote which is much related and which occurred when he was a boy, goes to show his sincerity. Alexander Pope, in his 'Essay on Man,' says, 'An honest man is the noblest work of God.' . . ."

And so on.

It was the last indication he ever gave that he was aware of the "voice of conscience"; from then on all his senses were attuned to intercept the faint signals of opportunity.

2. ON HIS OWN AND ON HIS WAY

JAY GOULD's hopes for a sounder and more practical education at the Hobart Academy fell far short of the impatient youth's demands on his preceptors. He found that he had drilled himself more competently in mathematics than could be imparted in any classroom, and as for the rest of the curriculum, it held little interest for him. To Jay Gould, as he later explained, an education should elevate a young man to a position in which "he is capable of speaking and acting for himself without being bargained away and deceived by his more enlightened brothers"; it should also be a means of "controlling the human destiny in yielding happiness and enjoyment to its possessor." All else was dross and pretense. What use would Jay Gould have for the moral principles, the watered-down theology, the smattering of literature and philosophy that the faculty of Hobart Academy drummed into the heads of its pupils? What could be gained through further schooling by a young man who would be a leather magnate before he was twenty-one, a millionaire before he was thirty?

Even in his middle teens, tucked away in the backwoods hamlets of upstate New York, Gould could sense the sort of world in which he intended to make his mark, a world entirely unrelated to that pictured by the bearded innocents of the Hobart Academy faculty.

Mid-century America, already expanding and industrializing at a pace which would be the decisive factor in the coming Civil War, was characterized by the explosions of energy, the ruthlessness and exploitation which attend such manifestations of national growth. There was little room and less charity for the weak, the lazy, the foolish and the amiable. In every level of American society it was root-hog-or-die, as the anti-rent war of 1844 had shown even in the sleepy and backward Catskill country. The only alternatives presenting themselves to Jay Gould, with his frail body and a noticeable predisposition to chest and stomach ailments, were to develop a superior cunning or to submit to a form of slavery not much gentler than that imposed on the Negroes in the southern states. Unfit for harder and more remunerative work, he could look forward to a life of clerking in a country store for his bed, board and a few dollars a month, an existence terminated only by the inevitable journey to the county poorhouse. Life in the

America of a century ago was almost unbelievably harsh for the unsuccessful.

"As a young man what did Jay Gould see?" Gustavus Myers asked in his classic *History of the Great American Fortunes*. "He saw, in the first place, that society, as it was organized, had neither patience nor compassion for the very poverty its grotesque system created. Prate its higher classes might of the blessings of poverty; and they might spread broadcast their prolix homilies on the virtues of a useful life, 'rounded by an honorable poverty.' But all these teachings were, in one sense, chatter and nonsense; the very classes which so unctuously preached them were those who most strained themselves to acquire all of the wealth that they possibly could. In another sense, these teachings proved an effective agency in the infusing into the minds of the masses of established habits of thought calculated to render them easy and unresisting victims to the rapacity of their despoilers.

"From these upper classes proceeded the dictation of laws; and the laws showed that the real, unvarnished attitude of these fine, exhorting moralists was towards the poor. Poverty was described as a crime. The impoverished were regarded in law as paupers, and so repugnant a term of odium was that of pauper, so humiliating its significance and treatment, that great numbers of the destitute preferred to suffer and die in want and silence rather than avail themselves of the scanty and mortifying public aid obtainable only by acknowledging themselves paupers.

"Sickness, disability, old age and even normal life, in poverty were a terrifying prospect. The one sure way of escaping it was to get and hold wealth. The only guarantee of security was wealth, provided its possessor could keep it intact against the maraudings of his own class. . . . To get wealth he must not only exploit his fellow men, he found, but he must not be squeamish in his methods. This lesson was powerfully and energetically taught on every hand by the whole capitalist class."

Jay Gould's first full-time job taught him the meaning of exploitation. On leaving the Hobart Academy he went to work in the general store at Hobart, clerking, keeping the books, sweeping out and keeping the shelves stocked. In exchange for bed and board, he worked from six in the morning to ten at night, sixteen hours a day. Despite that work load, the boy got up at 3 A.M. every morning to put in three hours study of mathematics, surveying, and engineering until it was time to open the store.

Some months later Jay jumped at what seemed to be a sterling opportunity. An engineer was engaged in surveying and mapping Ulster County and was willing to hire Jay as one of his three young assistants. The wage would be twenty dollars a month plus his keep, a lordly sum for a boy his age, even considering his self-taught skills. If his first employer was an exploiter of child labor, his second was simply a cheat and a deadbeat. Immediately after going to work for the map maker (as he subsequently testified before a New York State Senate committee on the relations of capital and labor) "I learned that my employer's credit was not very good, and I was to obtain no money for my work until the map was completed." This meant that he would somehow have to pay for his own board and lodging while working on the survey.

There was still a little of the baby brother who had been spoiled and protected by his five doting sisters in Jay Gould. On hearing the news of his employer's insolvency, as he later recalled, "I came to a piece of woods where nobody could see me, and I had a good cry."

Almost as quickly as his tears dried, Jay came up with a plan to pay for his "running expenses" while working on the Ulster County map and survey. He would make "sun dials" for the farmers along the way at one dollar apiece, which would take care of his food and lodging. Actually these "sun dials" were what the farmers called "noon-marks," a line running north and south by which they could regulate their clocks, the sun being due south at noon. When the survey was

completed, Jay and the other two assistants were informed
that their employer was still bankrupt and they would have
to publish the survey themselves in place of their long-de-
ferred wages. Jay sold his interests in the project to the others
for $500. One of those associates, Oliver J. Tillson, recalled
in later years that "Gould was all business. Even at mealtimes
he was always talking maps. My father used to say, 'Look at
Gould! Isn't he a driver?'"

That $500 was the sixteen-year-old Jay's first capital, the
seedling from which one of the great American fortunes
sprouted.

Through various efforts during the next three years he was
able to increase that nest egg tenfold. He mapped and surveyed Albany and Ulster counties, wrote a history of Delaware County, surveyed the route for a plank road from Albany
to Shakers, and promoted a mousetrap. All of these ventures,
thanks to his industry and intelligence, were profitable and
successful, but he saw them only as steppingstones leading
toward greater achievement; already his attention was fixed
on New York and the financial market place. If ever a boy
set his mind on being a capitalist, at an age when most red
blooded young Americans fancied lustier careers than the
countinghouse, it was Jay Gould. His whole untypical being
was focused on money and ways of making it work for him.
He had little or no time for girls, none at all for whatever
rural dissipations might have led a less dedicated youth astray.
Whatever passion or emotional forces churned in him were
channeled into projects which would allow him to watch his
money grow.

In undertaking the survey of his native Delaware County,
he made certain in advance that the resulting maps would
find a market by soliciting subscribers before the work was
done, early in 1853. Already he understood the value of publicity, a somewhat cynical appreciation which was to result
years later in manipulating the editorial columns of a New
York newspaper to influence the stock market. It was char-

acteristic that he made use of the local paper, the Delaware
County *Mirror*, through a rather disingenuous application of
cold cash. On his seventeenth birthday, May 27, 1853, he sent
five dollars to S. B. Champion, the editor of the *Mirror*, ex-
plaining, "It is small indeed, but I promise to do better in
the future. By the way, I think the friends of our paper"—the
our was dropped in so casually—"ought to do something to
sustain the enlargement without an increase in price; you may
put me down for five dollars annually and during the political
campaign. I will send you a list of some of the poorer families
to have the *Mirror* sent to." As he distributed largess and subsidized local journalism, the young man obviously considered
himself a power in the community, naturally concerned with
politics (four years before he was old enough to vote) and
furnishing reading matter to the worthy poor.

Editor Champion was soon made aware of an underside to
the young man's generosity. In August, Jay wrote the editor
about the progress of his Delaware County survey, concluding, "Thus far in this State, without exception, these maps
have met with unbounded success, having been liberally and
some of them munificently countenanced by the Supervisors
and sometimes by individuals. In Delaware County the Supervisors ought to encourage it by having a map for each of
the school districts. I want you to give me an editorial to this
effect." Editor Champion complied.

At seventeen, Jay Gould had already decided that the role
of the promoter, rather than the performer, was likely to be
more profitable and certainly more congenial. Most of the
actual surveying on the project was undertaken by his several
assistants. Meanwhile Gould was devoting himself to securing the support of the county's more prominent citizens and
trying to interest Zadoc Pratt, one of the more imposing big-
wigs of neighboring Greene County, in surveying and mapping that district. Mr. Pratt, who was soon to loom largely on
the young man's expanding horizons, was promised that the
projected survey would include a drawing of Prattsville and

"views" of its finer residences, particularly those "whose pro-
prietors offer a proper remuneration."

Aside from these exertions, he had taken over promotion
of a mousetrap invented by his maternal grandfather, Alexander Moore, which he hoped would find a receptive market.
The World's Exhibition was being held in New York City that
summer. Jay decided to take the invention there in hope of
interesting some small manufacturer, which he did. His first
visit to the metropolis, with the mousetrap contained in a
mahogany case which testified to an appreciation of the value
of packaging, no matter how humble the product, was interesting chiefly for a misadventure which landed him in a police
station and the New York papers for the first time.

With his mousetrap and its expensive case under his arm,
Jay boarded one of the Sixth Avenue horsecars for the trip
downtown. Gawking at the sights, he presented himself as a
lovely target for the sneak thieves and pickpockets who
swarmed by the thousands through the New York streets. A
thief relieved him of the mahogany box and took to his heels
at the next stop. Jay followed him in full cry. A few hundred
feet away the boy succeeded in collaring the thief though he
was a "great strong fellow." As he later admitted to a reporter, "I really regretted I had done so and tried to let him
go, but the fact is one of my fingers caught in a button hole
of his coat and before I could get off there was a crowd
around us and a policeman." The thief insisted that the box
was his own property and that Jay was trying to rob him, so
the officer had no choice but to take both of them to the nearest precinct station.

Jay finally managed to convince the police that he was the
victim, not the perpetrator of the crime, when he suggested
that they open the box and find his mousetrap in it. When the
box was opened and the thief saw what he had stolen, Jay
said, the culprit's face "assumed such an expression of disgust
that I could not help laughing at him." The New York *Herald*
gave a half-column account of the "plucky visitor's" adven-

ture, which apparently attracted the attention of a small manufacturer who agreed to market his grandfather's mousetrap. Once again the value of publicity was impressed upon him.

As a by-product of his mapping and surveying project, Jay then decided to write a history of Delaware County, which he hoped would find a place in every respectable home. He published the work himself, seeing no reason why an author should not share more fully in the proceeds of his labors, an idea which, fortunately for the publishing industry, never became widespread, in partnership with a Roxbury printer named Keeny. For a boy in his teens, the 450-page work[1] was really a remarkable job, thorough, painstaking and apparently accurate, much of it gleaned from older residents who had lived through its events. Early in 1856 it came off the press: *History of Delaware County and the Border Wars of New York, Containing a Sketch of the Early Settlement of the County and a History of the Late Anti-Rent Difficulties, with Other Historical and Miscellaneous Matter Never Before Published.*

Its style was self-consciously literary and its manner a trifle overheated, but Jay did full justice to his subject matter. Indians were "cruel demons" or "tawny brethren," depending on whether they were massacring a settlement or selling their tribal lands for a pittance. The author paid enthusiastic tribute to "those Spartan sires, whose ashes are now mouldering in the tomb and whose tongues have become silent and speechless, palsied by death." There was a fairly sober account of the Six Nations which had once roamed the country, of the incursion of Dutch, English and German settlers, of the Revolutionary War veterans who came in the second wave of settlers. His descriptions of the terrain and of the natural beauty of the foothills and valleys of the country often were unassumingly poetic. But the boy author really let himself go when

[1] A surviving copy of which may be found in the New York Public Library's genealogy department.

it came to describing the border wars, the massacres, ambushes and atrocities which accompanied the settlement of the county. Wolf hunts were also recounted in vivid and gory detail. They revealed in the frail, sickly and undersized boy a certain fascination with violence and bloodshed which one would never have suspected from his gentle demeanor, a vicarious bloody-mindedness that would enable him to endure the sufferings of others without undue psychological stress.

The young author took care to wring every possible benefit from his work, in addition to whatever profits might accrue. Extravagant praise was laid on for the important and influential men of the Delaware country, upon whom Jay counted for a leg up in the world. The volume was dedicated to the Hon. Amasa Junius Parker, the judge who sentenced the antirent partisans to the gallows and prison. Mr. Zadoc Pratt, of Prattsville, though a resident of Greene County, was also mentioned in flattering terms. Pratt had turned Jay down on his proposed survey of Greene County, but the latter still had plans for him.

Shortly after his book was published, Jay came down with typhoid fever. Two years earlier he had survived an inflammation of the lungs. All his life he was to be a prey to illness —dyspepsia and neuralgia, later tuberculosis. Such experiences, however, did not inculcate any great respect for the medical profession. Jay preferred to be his own doctor; besides, he was convinced that any disease could be conquered through the exercise of will power, with which he was plentifully supplied. Nursed and pampered by his five loving sisters, he slowly recovered from the attack of typhoid. He wrote his friend Champion, the Roxbury newspaper editor, "The Doctor stands over my shoulder and criticizes every movement as an alarming symptom; his orders are for the present—live on soup made of shadows—to say the word map requires a portion of castor oil, and to think or transact any kind of business is equal to jumping into a mill pond in winter time; but I have dismissed their sympathies and regulate my own diet. I find health and strength to improve in consequence."

Convalescence was slow, but he used the time to decide on his future course of action. While his sisters fed him broth, he determined to consolidate his assets and make a deeper plunge in the business world. For this he would need a partner, at least temporarily, one with plenty of capital to invest. Mr. Pratt of Prattsville was very much on his mind; the problem was to cultivate his friendship and win his confidence, and to this project he would devote all the charm and tenacity of one of his more frivolous contemporaries wooing the belle of the neighborhood.

This peculiar charm, when he chose to exert it, was all the more remarkable in a youth of Jay's temperament. It must have taken great effort for one with his essentially cold and self-centered disposition, his secret arrogance and his well concealed contempt for the rest of humanity, to play the humble protégé, drinking in his patron's words of wisdom when he knew very well he was twice as smart as the deluded old duffer.

In his physical appearance alone, he could hardly have been impressive enough to gain the confidence of so many different men of substance, over whose shoulders he climbed to wealth and power. Then and all his life, he was thin, weedy, pallid. He was about five feet six inches tall, had black hair that began disappearing from his forehead rather early in life, and soon, by way of compensation, would grow a full beard that covered his face like an apron. Undoubtedly his most prepossessing feature was his black eyes, intensely sad eyes which gave him the look of a starving poet, which could be liquid with sympathy and comprehension, or on other occasions "searching, firm, cold and all but incapable of changing in any way that might betray his feelings." Their expression reflected, not what was happening in the mind behind them but what he wished other people to believe was happening. They were not the windows of his soul, as with a less complex personality, but a screen on which his dissemblances were artfully projected. Those dark, probing, fallen-angel eyes were what people always remembered best about Jay Gould.

And how they must have brimmed with worshipful attention when he breached Zadoc Pratt's defenses and cozened the old man into entering a partnership with him, a briefly doting relationship that was to cost Pratt exactly sixty thousand dollars in cash and much more in pride.

In addition to his winning ways and a scheme which promised to enrich both of them, Pratt was undoubtedly influenced in Gould's favor by that fact that, at twenty, Jay had managed to gather together a capital of $5000. Just after recovering from the typhoid, he sold all his interests in the Delaware and Albany County surveys and maps and the rights to his *History of Delaware County* which, with the proceeds from his mousetrap, made up the five thousand. It was an impressive sum, in those days, for a young man of his age to have scraped together, more than most men had after a lifetime of work. Thus Gould was able to present himself as a man of means as well as schemes.

Zadoc Pratt, fifty years senior to Gould, had retired after a long and illustrious career in business and politics. His tannery at Prattsville had been the largest in the state and enabled Pratt to boast that he had tanned more than a million hides of sole leather before selling out. He operated a 365-acre model farm on which new agricultural methods were introduced. For ten years he had served honestly and intelligently as his district's representative in the United States Congress. There was probably no more respected and honored man in western New York.

Pratt was content in retirement, yet the twenty-year-old Gould, who had never tanned a hide in his short life, was able to persuade him to go back into the leather business. He was so taken with the young man's energy, imagination and intelligence that some suspected Jay had hypnotized him with those black, narcotic eyes; certainly Pratt continued to trust him long after common sense dictated otherwise.

The opportunity which Jay so glowingly depicted was for the construction of a tannery in the Lehigh country across the Pennsylvania border. This section had just been opened up by the extension of the Delaware, Lackawanna and Western Railroad from New York to Scranton. There were large tracts of hemlock, the bark of which was used in the tanning process, available in the area; the farming regions of the state would be able to supply any amount of hides, and the leather market then was booming. Aside from Jay Gould's persuasive powers, the proposition was sound on its own merits. Pratt agreed to invest $120,000 to buy land, contract for cuttings of hemlock and construct the tannery. Gould's contribution was to include his $5000 plus his services, which was certainly a generous estimate of their worth, considering that they were entering into an equal partnership.

At the outset Gould lived up to the old man's expectations in full measure. He bought the timber rights to more than 10,000 acres of hemlock-forested land. Then, not far from Stroudsburg, he set up a sawmill and blacksmith's shop, hired from fifty to sixty laborers and began construction of the tannery and cottages to house his labor force.

Mr. Pratt insisted that the name of the village be Gouldsboro, to which Jay offered no objection. (It was later changed to Thornhurst, after the Gould name became opprobrious.) Gould also supervised the construction of a plank road from his tannery to Gouldsboro Station on the Delaware, Lackawanna and Western line. Within a few months the tannery was in operation; it was believed to be the largest in the country.

Viewed from Prattsville, with the complacency of the senior partner's faith in his protégé, everything was going swimmingly those first six months of operation. The tannery was in full production, the goods were moving smoothly to market, the product seemed to be first-rate.

At the year's end, however, Zadoc was an increasingly troubled old man. Business was booming, but the profits reported by Gould did not tally with the volume of sales. On top of that, rumors were reaching Pratt that Gould had been engaging in various ventures on the side, presumably with the firm's money.

One day late in January 1857, Pratt took the train to Gouldsboro Station and rode over the plank road to the tannery.

Gould, he found, was absent from the tannery's offices. Business, the clerks told Pratt, often took Mr. Gould to New York —much oftener than Pratt had suspected.

Considerably alarmed now, Pratt insisted on looking over the firm's books. He was not a bookkeeper but even so he could see that something was out of joint. He was "puzzled by their intricacies," as he later told a friend. An expert accountant himself, Gould had obviously cooked the books, and the only reason there could be for those "intricacies" was that he had been tapping the firm's funds. A little quiet investigation later that day revealed to Pratt that Gould had secretly established a private bank in nearby Stroudsburg, in his own name but with Pratt & Gould funds as his capital.

Grimly and perhaps sorrowfully, Pratt waited for Gould to return, which he did the next day, January 27, 1857.

Not yet twenty-one years old, Jay Gould faced his white-bearded and wrathful accuser with all the bland confidence of a veteran swindler.

Pratt charged him with diverting the company's funds for his own purposes and rigging the books to conceal it.

He waited for an explanation, but Gould favored him with only a sarcastic smile.

Pratt, somewhat disconcerted at the young man's effrontery, went on to say that he had financed this tannery proposition, not because he needed more money or diversion in his advanced years, but because he had regarded Gould as

worthy of a decent start in life. Didn't Gould think he owed
him an explanation at least?

Gould shrugged, but said nothing.

Then he didn't deny the charges?

Gould shook his head, still coolly smiling.

Zadoc Pratt then realized that for the first time in his life
he had come across a completely amoral specimen of humanity, a creature as remorseless as a weasel loose in a hen roost.

Now came a tricky moment for Jay Gould: his benefactor could close the tannery, call in the law and demand
that Gould be prosecuted. But Gould had gambled that he
wouldn't, a gamble based on a shrewd estimate of Pratt's character. The old boy would be so shocked at his partner's callous
indifference, so shaken by the betrayal of his confidence, that
his only recourse would be flight. And as he was usually to
be, Gould was completely accurate in judging his victim's
reaction.

Pratt, in fact, was so disgusted with Gould and even more
so with himself for having been diddled by a mere boy that he
offered him an amazingly advantageous deal on the spot.
Either Gould could buy him out or he would buy Gould out.
He was probably confident that Gould wouldn't be able to
accept the first alternative.

Why, said Gould, he wouldn't consider selling his interest
in a property he had labored so long and hard to develop.
How much did Pratt want for his share of the company?

Sixty thousand, Pratt told him, undoubtedly expecting him
to swoon in dismay.

But Gould surprised him by agreeing at once; the cash to
complete the transaction would be forthcoming in a few days.
That night Pratt returned to Prattsville with the realization
that befriending Gould had cost him exactly sixty thousand
dollars—but happily unaware that through his indulgence
there was loosed on the financial world, on the whole country
in fact, a mild-looking young monster to whom that sum
would soon be a pittance. . . .

Back in Gouldsboro, Jay was congratulating himself on a good day's work. Getting rid of Pratt for half of what he had invested in the company was a great though not unexpected stroke of fortune . . . and of careful planning. For some time Gould had been expecting Pratt to swoop down on the company's books. Either through information supplied by someone close to Pratt or at the prompting of his intuition, which was almost as acute as his perception of other men's character and motives, Gould knew almost to the day when Pratt would descend on him. On the day of Pratt's arrival, January 26, Gould had been concluding negotiations with two men who would enable him to buy Pratt out. Thus he returned to Gouldsboro, in a beautiful piece of timing, just when he acquired the financial resources to rid himself of an unwanted partner.

For some months Gould had been cultivating the acquaintance of the sharp traders in the New York leather market— "The Swamp," as it was then called. He had been cautiously speculating in hide futures, investigating all phases of the leather business, and preparing to branch out as a trader and speculator, if possible with someone else's money. When he became aware of Pratt's restiveness over the anemic profits shown by their ledgers, he hastened to find backers to take Pratt's place. Once again he was wise in choosing a man of known rectitude and substance, rather than one of the flashier operators in the leather market. The reaction of a respectable man to being trimmed was predictably less violent than that of a fellow sharper.

His new-found friend was Charles M. Leupp, one of the city's more prosperous leather merchants, who was known as "a merchant of the old school ever insistent on personal integrity." Until he met Gould, Leupp's career had been a solid succession of modest triumphs in the business world. He owned a $150,000 mansion at Madison Avenue and Twenty-fifth Street which was one of the showplaces of the East Side.

From all the evidence, Leupp trusted Gould as whole-

heartedly as Zadoc Pratt had done, and was equally impressed by the young man's mild and virtuous manner.

Somewhat less dazzled by Gould's personality was Leupp's
brother-in-law, David W. Lee, an attorney, who was to be the
third partner in the new firm of Gould, Leupp and Lee, when
funds were supplied by Leupp to buy out Zadoc Pratt. The
skeptical lawyer, though warning that Gould was a shade too
persuasive, had to concede that it seemed a sound business
proposition. For sixty thousand dollars they would acquire a
two-thirds interest in one of the country's largest tanneries.
Gould, Leupp and Lee each would be equal partners.[2] The
existence of the private bank in Stroudsburg, the drain down
which the tannery's corporate assets had a tendency to disap-
pear, obviously was not disclosed.

The new partnership proceeded smoothly for several
months as the tannery operated at its full productive capacity.
During the early months of 1857, a fever of speculation was
running its course. Trading in leather, as well as other commodities, was caught in the upsurge and prices were rising to
unprecedented levels.

Leupp himself was too conservative to be swept along in
the speculative frenzy, but Gould was secretly engaged in
gambling for both of them, with company funds but without
Leupp's or Lee's consent. Fascinated by the overnight profits
to be made in the leather market, Gould was spending more
time in "The Swamp" than in Gouldsboro. He had caught the
gambling fever. Using Leupp's name without his knowledge,
Gould was building a corner in the hide market. Just before
the frenzy ended, in fact, he had bought up all the hides on
the market plus all those to be delivered in the next six
months.

On paper, at least, he was a millionaire shortly after turning twenty-one.

[2] Details of Gould's partnership may be found in M. J. Martin's
pamphlet, *Jay Gould and His Tannery*, Scranton, 1945.

Then came the Panic of 1857, in which paper profits went up in smoke and Gould was caught short in his gamble on leather futures.

Gould took the news of the crash with a born gambler's cold nerve. Next time, he promised himself, he'd be smarter, get out quicker. Only fools hung on until the engineers of speculative raids cut the ground out from under them.

Meanwhile, Charles Leupp was learning that he had not only invested in the Gouldsboro tannery but his name and credit had been used to finance Gould's corner on the hide market. In addition, his other investments had taken a nose dive, and the position of his leather marketing firm was endangered.

Like his predecessor Pratt, Leupp undertook the worried journey to Gouldsboro, unwilling still to believe that he had been betrayed. Again a cool and unfeeling Gould confronted his victim. He admitted using the firm's money and Leupp's credit in his forays against "The Swamp," and conceded that for the time being both were probably in an undeclared state of bankruptcy.

On the trip back to New York, Leupp brooded over the ruin of a career which, through no fault of his own, except his blind trust in Gould, seemed certain to end in bankruptcy and disgrace. He went directly to his Madison Avenue mansion, locked himself in his library, placed the barrel of a revolver in his mouth, and fired a bullet into his brain.

Since it was not yet the fashion for ruined investors to jump out of windows or otherwise dispose of themselves, Leupp's suicide caused a great stir in the city. His relatives and friends naturally attributed it to Gould's operations. No proof to this effect could be offered at the inquest, however, and the coroner's jury decided that Leupp had killed himself while suffering from melancholia, a disorder that was going to afflict so many of Gould's associates.

The shot fired in Leupp's library was to have a long-ranging echo. A dozen years later, during a panic directly caused by

Gould, a half-demented crowd was to gather outside his
offices hopeful of hanging him to the nearest lamppost and
chanting:

"Who killed Leupp? Jay Gould!"

3. CAT IN THE CORNER

HIS speculative failures in the leather market and the suicide
of his partner, not to mention the calumnies heaped on him
by people who held him at least partly responsible for Leupp's
death, gave him hardly a moment's pause. Jay Gould was still
solvent. His business dealings before his major operations on
and against the stock market are still murky and obscure—
not only because he wanted to cover his tracks but because
he seldom committed the details to any record, preferring to
keep them filed away in his secretive brain—but it is apparent
that he came out of the Panic of 1857 in fairly good shape.
The money with which he had gambled was other men's. He
still had the tannery (though Leupp's heirs were contesting
him for its control), the private bank at Stroudsburg and certain investments which will be detailed below. Very early in
his career Gould had learned to keep a portion of his assets
safe from the storms of the market place. One might say that
this was the secret of his career: always to keep a cash reserve securely hidden, held for release at the last strategic
moment, just as a seasoned general would win a battle with
his last uncommitted battalion.

Thus he was able to pay for the agitation and litigation
necessary to keep control of his holdings as they came under
assault during the next three years.

In his surviving partner, David W. Lee, Leupp's brother-in-law and a first-rate lawyer, Gould was confronted by an opponent who could not be hoodwinked. Right from the beginning Lee had resisted the Gould blandishments and viewed him with suspicion; now he regarded him as little better than a thief and embezzler. His only concern, as he said, was to protect the interests of his two nieces, Leupp's daughters, in the tannery at Gouldsboro which constituted the bulk of their patrimony.

A partner like Lee, Gould recognized immediately, would be a positive handicap. Lee would be tracing every dollar that came into the firm. Therefore he began negotiations to buy out the Leupp and Lee interests. The attorney insisted on a price of sixty thousand dollars, the amount that had been invested, and he could not be beaten down.

Gould finally agreed, with the proviso that the sum be paid in $10,000 annual installments.

When the final papers were drawn up, however, Lee discovered that Gould had made no provision for paying interest on the unpaid balance of the sale price. With that Lee exploded; the deal was off; the matter would have to be decided by the courts.

Gould then proceeded to operate the tannery as though the clamorous Lee and the interests he represented didn't exist.

By March 1860, Lee realized that he would have to take direct action or the whole property would evaporate while Gould fought a delaying battle in the courts. He went to Scranton and raised a small force of unemployed miners, saloon idlers and assorted street corner toughs, who descended on Gouldsboro and occupied the tannery during the night. The next morning Gould found that he had been locked out, with plug-ugly faces staring from every window. He was not dismayed. In Gouldsboro he was not only the local tycoon and paymaster but had taken care to make himself a popular and benign figure whom a sinister New York lawyer was trying to dispossess. He also made it clear to the populace, then numbering about 300, with most of them on the tannery payroll, that their livelihood depended on his retaining control of the company.

After obtaining a small armory of rifles and muskets, he summoned the enraged citizens of Gouldsboro to a pre-battle banquet at the local hotel. Kegs of oysters were opened and barrels of whisky were tapped to inflame their fighting spirit. By the time Gould got up to address his private militia they were in a mood to take on the United States Army if necessary. He further inflamed the lumberjacks and tannery workers by pointing out the injustice of a gang of Scranton mercenaries, hired by a New York lawyer who skulked far from the scene of the coming battle, depriving them of their wages and causing suffering to their families.

His final remarks, as quoted in the New York *Herald*, were cagily phrased. "I do not want any violence or mistreatment of these men," he said, neglecting to explain what all those firearms were for, "but this tannery belongs to me and these persons have no right holding it from me or keeping it idle and keeping you men out of your jobs. If you can get possession peaceably it is right. Use no violence, but get the tannery." The phrasing indicated that Gould was well aware of the penalties for inciting to riot, and that once loosed on the tannery his followers would use their weapons as intended. Once again he had nimbly skirted the jagged edges of the law.

The next morning, at 10:30, supplemental rations of whisky having been issued with a generous hand, the "Battle of Gouldsboro" began.

Outnumbered at least ten to one, the Scranton men inside the tannery didn't have a chance. Only four of them were armed with revolvers, the rest with sticks and stones. Gould's men, on the other hand, were all equipped with firearms or axes. In a few minutes they had broken down the barricades, stormed into the tannery and quickly vanquished the defenders. Four of the latter suffered gunshot wounds, two of them were in serious condition, and the rest were badly beaten.

Gould's account of the fray recalled his stirring descriptions of Indian battles in his *History of Delaware County*, but was possibly less accurate:

"I quietly selected fifty men, commanding the reserve to keep aloof. I divided them into two companies, one of which I dispatched to the upper end of the building, directing them to take off the boards, while I headed the other one to open a large front door. I burst open the door and sprang in. I was immediately saluted with a shower of balls, forcing me to retire, and I brought them up a second or third time and pressed them into the building. By this time the company at the upper end of the tannery had succeeded in effecting an entrance, and the firing now became general on all sides and the bullets were whistling in every direction. After a hard-contested struggle on both sides, we became the victors, and our opponents went flying from the tannery, some of them making fearful leaps from the second story."

Gould's story of the battle differed materially from the less heroic but presumably more accurate account in the New York *Herald,* published March 16, 1860, under the headline TANNERY INSURRECTION IN PENNSYLVANIA. While Gould claimed the tannery had been seized by thirty to forty men, the *Herald* reported that they numbered fifteen. Four men armed with cap-and-ball pistols could hardly have loosed a "shower" of bullets. The *Herald* estimated Gould's force at 180 to 250 men, though he claimed only 150. Instead of making "fearful leaps" from second story windows, the Scranton men who offered resistance were thrown out bodily, according to the *Herald*. Oddly enough, too, the *Herald* man failed to observe Jay Gould valiantly leading his men in the assault, and one gathers that Gould, like any sensible general, directed operations from a headquarters well to the rear, where his meditations could not be disturbed by showers of lead and flying brickbats.

In any case, it turned out to be a tactical victory at best. The bloodshed led to a flurry of court orders which not only interfered with production but prevented Gould from finding a market for his finished hides. In a few months he had to close the tannery down, leaving Gouldsboro a ghost town with vivid memories of its founder. . . .

Legend had it that Gould, beaten but unbowed, had to scrounge around for railroad fare to make it to New York. Actually, if secretly, he was still well-heeled, in stocks and real estate if not in cash. In New York, he set himself up as "Jay Gould, Leather Merchant" at 39 Spruce Street, but this too was a blind; he was interested in more promising ventures than the leather business. His only connection with it and Pennsylvania was to dispose of his share of the Gouldsboro properties. The tannery was destroyed by fire—the circumstances of which might have been more thoroughly investigated—while the disputed ownership was still in the courts. He sold the last of the property in 1868. A more lucrative venture stemming from his several years in the Pennsylvania backwoods was his purchase of 800 acres of coal-bearing land from the Lackawanna Company for $125,000, which he later sold for $500,000.

All these transactions were peripheral, however. The immense possibilities of the railroads, which were then being extended throughout the civilized parts of the nation, were what really engaged his attention and inflamed his imagination. He was determined to get in on the ground floor of what was to be the biggest boom the country had ever seen. In those days, with small railroads being bought, sold and speculated on with abandon, it was possible for a daring fellow with small capital to buy his way into the game. With funds diverted from his former partners, Gould had already acquired a stake in railroading, and for the next several years he carefully tended to its multiplication.

His ambition to join the growing ranks of the railroad magnates was helped along by his meeting with a merchant who was then a member of the Erie board of directors.

During his brief bachelor days in New York, Gould stayed

at the Everett House. Almost across the street from the hotel was the substantial home of Daniel G. Miller, at 33 East Seventeenth Street. Miller was a partner in the produce firm of Lee, Dater and Miller, and speculated conservatively, on the side, in railroad ventures.

Somehow Gould met his daughter Helen. According to Henry Clews, in *Fifty Years in Wall Street,* "the merchant took him to his house to board and Mr. Gould fell in love with his handsome daughter." It seems unlikely that a prosperous merchant would be taking in boarders. The story that later circulated in New York society, which rarely neglected an opportunity to slander him, was that Gould accosted her on the street after learning who her father was. Gould in the role of a masher, shy and inexperienced as he was with the other sex, is almost as preposterous as the thought of Miss Helen Miller, reared in the rigorous social tradition of Murray Hill, allowing herself to be picked up on the street by a strange man. It is more likely that Gould somehow made the acquaintance of her father and thus insinuated himself into the family circle. He then became the modest, gentle, and retiring Helen's principal suitor.

Miller, who undoubtedly had more than an inkling of Gould's reputation as a businessman, was strongly opposed to the idea of acquiring him as a son-in-law, but eventually Gould got around him.

On January 27, 1863, then twenty-six years old, Gould married Helen Miller, who was three years younger, in a modest ceremony at her father's home. The marriage turned out to be long, happy, and fruitful. No matter how blemished was Gould's reputation in the market place, his domestic life was never shadowed for a moment by gossip or rumor.

In a sense Gould was to lead two totally different lives, that of the unscrupulous financier and speculator, builder and destroyer, who came to be regarded as capitalism's worst example and heaviest cross—and that of the devoted family man, an affectionate husband and a fond father who over-indulged his children.

Once he shut the door of his house behind him, he basked in the warmth and simplicity which formed his domestic atmosphere. The Wall Street tiger turned into a pussycat purring by the fireplace. Neither he nor his wife had social ambitions, except for their children, and both were content to leave the dining-out and theatergoing to others. Most men of his stamp, if we may believe the social chroniclers of the time, tended to relax over lobster and champagne suppers with their mistresses or attend purple-faced routs at which naked females burst from papier-mâché pies. Had he been lured to such an affair, Jay Gould would have fled at the first glimpse of a bare shoulder emerging from the pastry. He was tolerant enough with business associates who took their pleasure where they found it, but outside of business hours he was as moral, as strait-laced as any of his Yankee ancestors.

Socially, even in respectable company, Gould had always been something of a disaster. The graces of civilized inter-course were not acquired until his later years, and then only in scant measure. He was simply too preoccupied with making money to lend himself wholeheartedly to any occasion.

Henry Clews told the story of his first yachting trip, shortly after he established his "leather merchant" office in Spruce Street. A member of the Cruger family of Cruger-on-Hudson took pity on Gould's apparently lonely and friendless exist-ence and invited him for a cruise on the river.

Hardly had the pleasure jaunt began before Gould made himself unpopular with his hosts, fretting over whether the boat would return to its dock in time for him to catch his train back to New York. Their guest made himself so obnox-ious with his suggestions that they cut the cruise short and return to Cruger-on-Hudson that the Crugers decided to teach him a lesson. Returning to the dock, with Gould's train in sight just beyond it, they let the centerboard down and caused the yacht to run aground. Digging each other in the ribs, they told Gould that he'd have to swim for it if he hoped to catch his train.

The single-minded young man quickly removed his clothes and stripped down to "aggressively scarlet undergarments" while the ladies aboard "hid their blushes behind parasols." Holding his dry clothes over his head, he breasted the water and made his way ashore. The moment he was on dry land, the Crugers hauled up the centerboard and sailed close enough to the shore to yell raucous advice about a "warm mustard bath" and jeer at him. Which party displayed the worse manners was a moot question, but it was obvious that Jay Gould would enjoy few social triumphs.

For more than a year Gould and his bride shared her parents' home in East Seventeenth Street. Their first child, George Jay Gould, was born there on February 6, 1864. From his cradle onward young George was treated like a princeling, the designated successor to his father, who loved him and spoiled him and ruined him.

Five other children were born to the Goulds, Edwin in 1866, Helen in 1870, Howard in 1871, Anna in 1875, and Frank in 1877. With each of them Gould sought to make up for the emotional deficiencies of his own childhood. He was determined to give them everything he had lacked in the way of sympathy and affection as well as the more material comforts. Except for the echoes of his career of financial violence and the intense hatred he aroused, which must have penetrated even their early years, the children led the most sheltered of lives and were cushioned against any possible psychological upset.

Living with his in-laws turned out to be highly advantageous in that it brought Gould and the prosperous Mr. Miller closer together. Miller discovered that, whatever the state of his son-in-law's business morality, he had all the mental equipment of a commercial genius. Soon the merchant was assisting him in various ventures, and was never given cause to regret it; presumably Gould had too much respect for the integrity of the family to treat Miller as he had other men who trusted him.

Together they investigated the possibilities of expanding their holdings in railroad stocks. Gould had already taken the plunge. Using funds which Leupp believed he was investing in the tannery, just before his partner committed suicide in the belief that he was ruined, Gould was coolly taking advantage of the Panic of '57 and buying into the Rutland & Washington Railroad. The sixty-two-mile line ran from Troy, New York, to Rutland, Vermont. Always adept at fishing in troubled waters, Gould managed to buy a large block of the Rutland & Washington's first-mortgage bonds at ten cents on the dollar.

He held onto the bonds through the vicissitudes of fighting the Leupp estate for control of the tannery, for they constituted the opening wedge of his long-nurtured dream of breaking into the railroad game. Now, with his father-in-law's help, he was able to buy up a controlling interest in the road. He was determined to build up the line to the point where it would be worthy of consolidation with one of the larger New England railroads. So, at twenty-seven, Gould became a railroad president—and not only that but secretary, treasurer and superintendent of the line. After several months of his expert management, the line was sold, with an excellent profit, for a merger with the Rensselaer & Saratoga Railroad.

Once more Gould was to repeat his success with building up a small railroad in financial difficulty and then selling it to an expanding system. An acquaintance of his in the Street had bought control of the Cleveland & Pittsburgh but wanted to sell his shares to meet certain pressing obligations. The stock was worth $60 a share but the owner was willing to sell for $40. The offer seemed too good to be true, but Gould investigated and found it was worth snapping up with the proceeds of the Rutland & Washington sale. He now owned fifty-one percent of the Cleveland & Pittsburgh, and though it paid dividends from the start he began operations designed to attract a purchaser. The price of the stock was manipulated until it reached 120, three times what Gould had paid for his controlling interest. At that point, the Pennsylvania Railroad, which needed the Cleveland & Pittsburgh line to complete its western extension, offered to buy his majority shares. Gould agreed, and took a 200 percent profit.

In the meantime he had bought his way into partnership in a Wall Street brokerage, which became the firm of Smith, Gould & Martin. The office served him mainly as a base of operations; he already felt too confident of his money-making powers to concentrate on taking a modest percentage of other men's speculations. For his two partners, however, it was the worst move they ever made. Smith was caught short in one of Gould's early raiding operations. Martin died broke in an insane asylum.

During those first years in New York, while Jay Gould was marrying, juggling railroad stocks and carving out his foothold in Wall Street, the Civil War was reddening the sky and draining the lifeblood of the severed parts of the nation. The Union was in crisis, but Gould remained calm. The war was fought while he was between the ages of twenty-four and twenty-eight, but Gould managed to choke back his patriotic sentiments and opted for the comforts and privileges of civilian life. There was money to be made in war, and Gould meant to have his share, just like the Vanderbilts and Morgans and others who affected to look down on him as a vulgar moneygrubber in later years.

And the war money, the profits to be made out of patriotically supplying the Union armies, heroically driving up stock and bond prices, valiantly gambling on the market reaction to Union victories or defeats, flowed into New York like a mighty river. Many New Yorkers, particularly those who were making millions out of military contracts, were seriously advocating that New York declare itself a sort of neutral enclave which devoted itself to business rather than bloodshed. The

Democratic Mayor Fernando Wood, who was lukewarm toward the principles of the Union and much cooler toward the Republican Administration, thought it might not be a bad idea if New York joined in the secession movement. "Why should not New York City," he demanded, "instead of supporting, by her contributions in revenues, two-thirds of the expenses of the United States, become also equally independent?"

Wall Street's attitude toward the war was summed up by one of its current titans, Daniel Drew, who cozily ruminated, "Along with ordinary happenings, we fellows in Wall Street now have in addition the fortunes of war to speculate about, and that always makes great doings on a stock exchange. It's good fishing in troubled waters."

In the Gold Room at Broad Street and Exchange Place— the future scene of one of Gould's greatest coups—speculation in gold prices rose to record heights. Rocking the Treasury boat was detrimental to government securities at a time when the Administration was hard pressed to pay the bill for a huge war machine, but the brokers were undeterred. Business, after all, was business and must not be disturbed by patriotic considerations. Unsympathetic newspapers took to calling the Gold Room brokers "General Lee's left wing." Vengeance, however, was to be neither God's nor the government's but Jay Gould's.

Later the authorized (and subsidized) biographies of the leading financiers related how they patriotically threw all their energies and resources into the war effort. Actually, as subsequent Congressional investigations revealed, they made millions out of selling the government defective rifles from European armories, unseaworthy ships, shoddy uniforms, rotten foodstuffs and cardboard-soled shoes. Gustavus Myers concluded that "the craze for profits crushed every instinct of honor and humanity . . . the battlefields were not more deadly than the supplies" furnished by profiteering contractors. "Commodore" Cornelius Vanderbilt, whose descendants were so haughty about the "tainted" wealth of the Goulds and other parvenus, made millions out of equipping General Banks' expedition to New Orleans in 1862, a task with which he was carelessly charged by the War Department. Vanderbilt rescued rotting ships from their harbor graves to be loaded with Banks' troops, even though he knew they had to make the journey over the open sea. "In perfectly smooth weather," an Iowa senator later said, summing up testimony concerning one of the old hulks attached to the expedition, "the planks were ripped out of her and exhibited to the gaze of the indignant soldiers on board, showing that her timbers were rotten. The committee have in their committee room a large sample of one of the beams of this vessel to show that it has not the slightest capacity to hold a nail." Had the ramshackle fleet encountered a storm off Cape Hatteras, the whole expedition would probably have been lost at sea. Further testimony showed that Vanderbilt, working through an agent, demanded a slice of the purchase price on all ships bought for the expedition. Vanderbilt escaped prosecution, however, by throwing all the blame on his agent. The government, it was estimated, was swindled out of $25,000,000 by contractors dealing in ships which had to be condemned.

J. Pierpont Morgan, then a young man of Gould's age, made his first big killing on an arms deal so malodorous that even his fellow entrepreneurs were shocked. He also was clever enough to work through an agent. Five thousand Hall's carbines, which five years before had been condemned by army inspectors as obsolete and dangerous, were acquired at the rate of $3.50 a carbine. Morgan then sent the carbines to General Frémont's army headquarters at St. Louis, receiving $22 apiece for them. The whole lot had to be condemned when it was found that men firing the carbines got their thumbs blown off. Even so, Morgan demanded and received the full price for his merchandise.

This, of course, is only a quick sampling of the methods

by which Gould's colleagues enriched themselves at the expense of the nation.

To his eternal credit, it must be recorded that Gould did not engage in similar activities. Possibly this was through lack of opportunity rather than any excess of scruple, but no evidence can be found that he ever dealt in war supplies like Vanderbilt and Morgan. He was content, for the moment, with taking modest profits out of juggling railroad stocks and with keeping his frail form out of army blue. Either through paying for exemption from military service or hiring a substitute, he escaped being caught in the increasingly finer meshes of the Union draft. The Conscription Act of 1863, reflecting the Union's desperate need for new levies, provided that no man could claim exemption on the grounds that he was the sole support of his wife and children. He could, however, buy his way out for $300 or less. "Never before since the birth of the nation had the people been served notice so arrogantly that the privilege of dying in battle was reserved exclusively for them," the historian Hart Smith wrote; "that moneyed men owed no duty to the nation that could not be discharged with a trifling payment in cash, not even the primary obligation of defending it." In protest against the new conscription law, from 50,000 to 70,000 men came rioting out of the city's slum districts and for almost a week anarchy ruled the streets of New York. The police concentrated to protect Wall Street and its environs while regiments of the regular army poured in to restore order. The moneyed people organized a force called the Volunteer Specials to protect themselves and their property as the rioting took a toll of 2000 lives and millions in burned and looted homes, stores and offices. Gould, as usual, played cat in the corner. He saw to it that the clerks in his brokerage joined the Volunteer Specials but stayed out of the firing lines himself.

Gould's original genius displayed itself in just one phase of his wartime operations in the stock market. The newly proliferating electric telegraph, which was proving itself as a strategic instrument of warfare through its speed-up of communications both on the battlefield and between the armies in the field and the War Department, exercised an early fascination for Gould—an experimental itch which was to result one day in his owning most of the American telegraph system. Certain operators, Daniel Drew among them, were making killings in the market through inside information on how the Union cause was faring. Gould then was too minor a figure to be included in the manipulations of such pools. So he figured out a way to make himself an insider on his own. Exactly how he set up his private wire service was his own carefully kept secret, but somehow he obtained advance telegraphic information on Union victories and defeats, which enabled him to gamble successfully on the panicky fluctuations of the market. Probably the information was forwarded by some obscure but strategically placed clerk in the War Department or the Military Telegraph Bureau. One can hardly imagine a Union commander hastening from the smoking battle scene to tip off Jay Gould how to play the market the next day, although considering the post-military careers of such officers as Butterfield, Sickles and Babcock, all generals with an eye on the main chance, it was not utterly impossible.

Whispers of Gould's mysterious access to military information inevitably were wafted around Wall Street, where secrecy was as difficult to maintain as in a ladies' cloakroom. Appomattox silenced the guns before anyone else could appropriate Gould's scheme, but his enterprise redounded to his credit among other operators, who admired nothing so much as sharp practice. Obviously he was a man to be reckoned with; from boyhood on he had skinned everyone who fell under his sway, he had married wisely, had operated shrewdly on the Exchange and in railroads, and knew how to keep his mouth shut, not the least desirable of attributes among men whose maneuvers in the eternal guerrilla war of the bulls and the bears were necessarily clandestine.

In those first postwar years Gould thus won admittance to the "insiders," the speculative pools where the big money circulated, despite an inborn lone-wolfishness which made him uncomfortable as a member of any clique.

During those days when Wall Street was adjusting to the calamity of peace, Gould formed the alliance, first with Jim Fisk and then with Daniel Drew, which was to turn the normally bizarre world of railroad financing into a Walpurgis Night.

Fat and flamboyant Jim Fisk came billowing into Gould's orbit shortly after the end of the war. Their dissimilarities, fitting together to form the perfect whole for an operation which was to bluff, bulldoze, bludgeon, and blackmail the rest of the financial community for half a dozen years, were probably their greatest asset. Gould was small, sallow, and secretive, Fisk large, porcine, red-faced, blond and noisy—a typical bouncing extrovert who loved rich food, fast women, blaring bands and the excitement of the market place. "The difference between Jay and me," as Fisk once said, "is that I have more trouble to get my dinner than to digest it, and Jay has more trouble to digest it than to get it." One was ascetic, the other a riotous voluptuary who led, as one observer said, "a life of half-barbaric prodigality." They had little in common except a thirst for acquisition—though Fisk regarded money as something to spend and Gould as something to be converted into power—and a total lack of scruple about accomplishing their purpose. And they shared at least one negative virtue: neither pretended, as so many of their contemporaries did, that there was something inherently righteous about acquiring wealth. Even Horace Greeley's critical New York *Tribune* conceded that Fisk was never guilty of hypocrisy: "When he devoured the widow's substance he differed from so many of his associates in refraining from the pretense of long prayers."

The Vermont-born Fisk, son of a Vermont peddler, was two

years older than Gould. In his youth he had been a circus roustabout. Later, when he took over his father's peddling routes in New England, his wagons, red with yellow wheels and lashings of gilt looked like a circus caravan when he took to the road, and his jovial personality and waxed golden mustachios made a wonderful impression on the wizened housewives of New England. His success attracted the attention of the great Boston mercantile firm of Jordan, Marsh & Co., which not only bought him out but engaged him as a traveling salesman. When the Civil War came, Fisk showed great initiative in palming off the firm's shoddier merchandise, blankets and such, on the Union Army.

Cotton got scarce with the application of the Union blockade and Jordan, Marsh's mills were starved for the product. Fisk was sent to Memphis to remedy the situation, and there his peculiar talents truly blossomed. He made a deal with an actress to obtain passes through the Union lines from susceptible officers. Agents were sent to buy all the cotton they could, contraband though it was. Thus Jordan, Marsh's money helped to finance the Confederate war effort, but what price patriotism when the company's cotton mills needed raw material and the market for their product was booming. In one day, it was reported, Fisk managed to buy $800,000 worth of cotton. Once, one of his steamers headed for Boston went down with $350,000 worth of Jordan, Marsh cotton when ammunition on board exploded, but the loss was only a drop in the bucket. By 1864, however, Jordan, Marsh decided to dispense with his services, possibly because they were attracting too much attention from unbribable Union Army headquarters, and Fisk was handed $65,000 in severance pay.

Having acquired expensive tastes on the Boston firm's open-end expense accounts, Fisk had to cast about for some line of endeavor which would allow him to indulge a Falstaffian propensity for complaisant females, boned squab, champagne, jewelry, and finery. Military uniforms and ceremony had a boyish fascination for him, but he had come close enough to the battlefields to learn of their discomforts and deferred martial experience until peacetime, when it was possible to buy a regiment and its colonelcy for his amusement.

On returning north from his ventures in contraband, Fisk dabbled in textiles for a few months in Boston, then came to New York and opened a brokerage in Broad Street, less than a block from Gould's offices. Here he set up a bar and poured liberally for all who were willing to listen to his grandiose talk of how he was going to "clean up on the Street." He joined the bulls but was caught short in a bear uprising close to the end of the war, and it looked as though he might literally become a street cleaner. The surrender at Appomattox rescued him from the dilemma, when he and three other schemers rigged up a deal to sell Confederate bonds short on the London exchange the moment Lee and his army gave up, he and his colleagues having arranged to beat the news to England through an elaborate telegraph-steamer-courier setup. A few months later he lost his English winnings in Wall Street. His friends in Boston, including Eben Jordan, the senior partner of Jordan, Marsh, lent him enough money to get back in the game.

Twice in one year Fisk had been wiped out in Wall Street. Lesser men would have considered themselves "ruined"—then the direst word in the language, for a ruined woman had lost her virtue and a ruined man had lost his money, and it was hard to say which was worse. The hearty Fisk, "Jubilee Jim" as he liked to be called, laughed it off and ordered up another round of champagne. He'd beat 'em yet, as he was fond of telling his drinking companions. "If I don't make things squirm," he added, "I'll eat nothing but bone-button soup until Judgment Day."

It was during that comeback period that he and Jay Gould met, sized each other up, liked what they saw, and began the collaboration which their contemporaries declared unholy. Fisk admired Gould's grasp of the intricacies of finance.

Gould was awed by Fisk's energy, his exuberance and his ability to overwhelm people with his swashbuckling personality. To their coming partnership, as Meade Minnigerode wrote in *Certain Rich Men*, Gould would bring "the brains, the strategy and the cunning," Jim Fisk "the life, the force and brutality."

Gould, at thirty, with Fisk as his indispensable battering ram, was now ready for his assault on the heights of American finance.

PART TWO

FIVE COUPS, FIVE FORTUNES

Some meditations by Jay Gould on speculation, money-making and other diabolic arts:

"People will deal in chance. Your minister, doctor and barber all have the same interest in speculation. Would you not, if you stopped it, promote gambling?"

"All my life since I became of age, I have been dealing in railroads, and I have always considered their future and not their past. That is the way I have made my money."

"The perfect speculator, the perfect gambler, if you will, must know when to come in; more important, he must know when to stay out; and, most important, he must know when to get out once he is in."

"Stock doesn't always depend upon dividends altogether. I paid 750 for my Missouri Pacific—4,000 shares at that figure. You pay more for rubies than for diamonds and more for diamonds than for glass."

"My idea is that if capital and labor are let alone they will regulate each other."

"No man can control Wall Street. Wall Street is like an ocean . . . full of eddies and currents. The thing to do is to watch them, to exercise a little common sense, and on the wane of speculation to come in on the top."

"My theory of investments is this: To go into everything that promises profit. I believe in this country, its future. Unfortunately I do not always succeed. I have been in a score, a hundred speculations from which I would have gladly withdrawn."

(To his associates, in discussing a proposed transaction): "The procedure, gentlemen! The procedure! We need not hesitate about *dimensions!*"

4. THE ERIE BLED FOR TWELVE MILLION

ONE of Jim Fisk's initial attractions for Jay Gould undoubtedly was the fact that Fisk had wormed his way into Daniel Drew's acquaintance. Drew, in turn, fascinated Gould not only because he was then the most successful speculator in Wall Street, but was the controlling influence over the ludicrously miserable enterprise known as the Erie Railway.

Gould, always sensitive to the barometric pressure of rising opportunity, had become aware that the Erie was about to be plundered by a group of insiders.

To get inside that charmed circle, he needed Fisk's influence with Drew.

A country slicker come to the big city, David Harum outwitting the sophisticated New Yorkers in the best tradition of contemporary stage comedy, Drew was the most improbable figure ever to achieve a dominant position in American finance. He was then close to seventy and affected an ecclesiastical manner to cloak an eminently carnivorous disposition. Lank and lantern-jawed, he loved to sing hymns and went to church every Sunday but gave up at least six-sevenths of his time to worshiping Mammon.

Born in upstate New York, he had become a cattle drover after serving an apprenticeship, like Jim Fisk, as a circus roustabout. Once he drove a lean and stringy herd to the New York market, only to learn that the butchers would buy nothing but fat cattle. That night, in their Harlem pasture, he fed his cows all the salt they wanted; next morning he herded them downtown, where he allowed them to quench their thirst. John Jacob Astor's brother, a butcher, came over to inspect Drew's stock, now sleek and bulging on their diet of salt and water. He paid a top price for the cattle, only to be disillusioned by nightfall by the sudden shrinkage of his animals. This, according to Wall Street legend, was the inception of the term "watered stock," a commodity in which Drew was to become a specialist.

Drew subsequently branched out as a drovers' banker and operator of a steamboat line. Later he opened a brokerage, was aroused by the possibilities of the railroads, and began buying control of the Erie Railway, thus setting himself up as a rival of the hardheaded Commodore Vanderbilt, who was extending his Hudson River (later the New York Central) Railroad in the same direction. Both were given to salty phrasemaking. Vanderbilt: "Law? What do I care about the law? Hain't I got the power?" Drew: "If a cat would eat fish, she must be willing to wet her feet." Both liked to eat fish, and neither hesitated to wet his feet.

The Erie, which its engineers characterized as "two thin streaks of rust," could have been a great money-maker if it had been properly managed and its huge debt reduced. Its main line ran from the west bank of the Hudson, across the river from Manhattan, to Buffalo, and plans were being made to extend it to Chicago. Two million passengers and more than three million tons of freight were hauled every year by its 370 locomotives. With honest management it could have rivaled the Pennsylvania and the New York Central as a principal link between New York and the prospering hinterland. But almost since its founding in 1833 it had been milked of its profits, and its maintenance was a bad joke among railroaders. Its trains were constantly colliding; travel on the Erie was almost as hazardous as a trip around Cape Horn, and mere derailments were almost a daily occurrence. Yet there were those who loved her. English investors, through some insular quirk, were loyal despite her tribulations. And a young housewife of Oswego, New York made herself the heroine of an upstate legend when, a tree having fallen across the tracks near her home, she stripped off her red flannel underdrawers and flagged down an oncoming train.

Drew flagged down the whole railroad by a somewhat more complex maneuver. In his role as the "great bear" of Wall Street he hammered Erie's stock down from 63 to 33, then offered to lend the road $1,500,000 on condition that he be elected to its board of directors. Subsequently Drew took over as treasurer of the line and was soon running it to suit himself. His management was so flagrantly corrupt that Erie became known as the "Scarlet Woman of Wall Street." As chief pimp, Drew was making millions through manipulating its stock and tapping its cash reserve of $16,000,000. "I got to be a millionaire afore I knowed it, hardly," was the way Drew told it.

Jim Fisk eased his way into Drew's confidence—or at least his company—by reminiscing with the tricky septuagenarian about their mutual experiences in the circus world. Since he needed cash to tighten his hold on Erie, Drew commissioned Fisk to sell his Long Island Sound steamship line. Fisk also came in handy as one of the brokers through whom Drew staged a bear raid on his own company's stock, and was now regarded as one of Uncle Dan'l's closest confederates. He then introduced Gould to Drew, who, like many less shrewd men, was charmed by the former's expressive eyes and murmuring, confidential voice. Soon all three were sitting on Erie's board of directors, cozy as bugs in a rug.

That year of 1867 Erie was the center of a three-cornered fight for control. The first war party was headed by Drew, with Fisk and Gould among his lieutenants. The second was a group of Boston financiers, headed by John S. Eldridge and Eben Jordan, the latter Fisk's old sponsor, who owned the heavily mortgaged Boston, Hartford & Erie Railway, which they intended to merge with the Erie road of New York. The third faction was Commodore Vanderbilt's. As owner of a competing line he hoped to gain control of Erie and put her out of her misery.

The odds in Wall Street naturally favored Vanderbilt, with his thirty millions and his unmatched reputation as a corporate infighter. Vanderbilt's ruthlessness extended outward from the family circle. He had once cheated his son on a ferrying contract just to teach him to keep his guard up at all times. When his sorely oppressed wife Sofia found the courage to object to his plans for a new home, he had her committed to an asylum until she came around to his way of thinking. At seventy-two the Commodore was well accustomed to having his own way, usually in a cloud of blasphemous expletives.

Obviously, in this three-cornered fight for control of Erie, one faction was liable to be combined against by the other two and frozen out of the game. Not unexpectedly, perhaps, the Bostonians persuaded Vanderbilt to throw in with them, Drew being the more dangerous adversary and having recently nicked Vanderbilt for several million in his bear raid. Eldridge was elected president of Erie, and Drew was kicked off the board of directors, though Fisk and Gould were allowed to remain. Then the Commodore had second thoughts about Drew, his old whist-playing crony. Drew, with his large stock holdings, might be more dangerous off the board than on, so he was restored to membership over the bitter objections of Eldridge and the other Bostonians. In no time at all, there was another change of alignment. The Bostonians, embittered by the way Vanderbilt had broken the agreement to ditch Drew, now were persuaded to ally themselves with the latter. The new alliance was kept secret, and Vanderbilt was allowed to think that he was presiding over Erie's destinies through a docile board of directors. Thus while trains crashed and rails rusted away, the Erie was being governed by three conflicting theories of mismanagement: Vanderbilt's (kill it off), the Bostonians' (merge it with their own foundering line) and Drew's (milk it for all it's worth).

The Commodore learned that the Drew and Boston factions had combined against him when he suggested that the Erie, along with the New York Central and the Pennsylvania, stop cutting their freight rates, charge shippers all the traffic would bear, and pool their earnings from the freight carried out of New York City. Erie's directorate turned the proposal down, serving notice on the Commodore that he would have to fight for the road's control.

Vanderbilt responded with all the vigor which had built his empire from one leaky Staten Island ferry. Through his tame judge, George G. Barnard of the Supreme Court, he obtained injunctions restraining Drew from using for speculative purposes 58,000 shares of Erie stock which Drew had secretly converted from bonds, and Erie from paying Drew any interest or principal on money he had loaned the company. Meanwhile, he issued the order to his brokers—"Buy Erie, and keep on buying it"—by which he intended to seize a controlling interest in the railroad and dictate the election of a new board in March 1868.

Drew was ready for these new maneuvers, by which the Commodore thought he could crush the opposition under the weight of his thirty millions. How fortunate, he must have thought, to have two such bright, loyal, quick-witted young men as Gould and Fisk as his henchmen. Gould for his brains, Fisk for his brass, his boldness in directing the Drew operations on the stock exchange. Wily and mistrustful of the rest of humanity as he was, Drew was apparently gulled, for the first time in his life, by the two young men who were throwing all their energy and resources into fighting for old Uncle Dan'l. It was almost frightening, in fact, considering how cautious Drew had always been in the past where the legalities were concerned, the way the pair of them had talked him into running up the Jolly Roger.

For Fisk and Gould had discovered a strategic weapon in the cellars of the Erie offices—a printing press. With it, ostensibly on Drew's behalf, they planned to whip up a paper storm that would turn Wall Street upside down and capsize the Commodore before he knew what was happening to him.

"If this damned printing press doesn't break down, we'll give the old hog all he wants of Erie," was the way Fisk put it.

Until now, the Wall Street operators had played the game according to a rather elastic set of rules. It could not be called a code of honor, but there was some respect for the rights of one's fellows, at least a pretense of protecting the investing public. All this went out the window with the advent of the Drew-Fisk-Gould combine, as Charles F. Adams, Jr. observed in *Chapters of Erie:* "It was something new to see a knot of adventurers, men of broken fortune, without character and without credit, possess themselves of an artery of commerce more important than was ever the Appian Way, and make levies, not only upon it for their own emolument, but, through it, upon the whole business of a nation."

Obviously the most dangerous of this trio was Gould. His character, it seemed to Adams, was "strongly marked by his disposition for silent intrigue. . . . There was a reminiscence of a spider in his nature. He spun huge webs, in corners and in the dark, which were seldom strong enough to resist a serious strain at the critical moment. His disposition to this subtlety and elaboration of intrigue was irresistible. . . . Mr. Gould was probably as honest as the mass of his fellows, according to the moral standard of the Street; but without entering upon technical questions of roguery, it is enough to say that he was an uncommonly fine and unscrupulous intriguer, skilled in all the processes of stock gambling, and passably indifferent to the praise or censure of society."

Gould, Fisk, and Drew now proceeded to flood the market with watered stock.

The device they used to lend a faint shadow of legality to their printing project was to request the Erie board of directors for permission to issue $10,000,000 worth of convertible bonds. With perfectly straight faces they explained that the bond issue was needed to purchase steel rails and new equipment for the ramshackle line, citing its superintendent's report that there was hardly a mile stretch between Jersey City and Buffalo "where it is safe to run a train at the ordinary passenger-train speed," that the trains had to crawl along at twelve to fifteen miles an hour and "broken wheels, rails, engines, and trains off the track have been of daily, almost hourly, occurrence for the last two months."

All too true, but the bemused superintendent never saw a dime of that bond issue for repairs.

Gould and Fisk set their presses whirring in the Erie basement, and ran off the ten million in bonds, which were promptly converted to 100,000 shares of stock and thrown on the market. They were undeterred by a new Vanderbilt injunction ordering that no more capital stock be issued. Flooded with this watered stock, Erie quotations kept falling and falling, and Vanderbilt kept buying and buying, driving the price up only to see it fall an hour or two later. In this struggle even the Vanderbilt fortune, not to mention his platoon of lawyers and any number of compliant judges, were not equal to the power of that printing press. "Give us enough rag paper," gloated Jim Fisk, "and we'll hammer the everlasting tar out of that mariner from Staten Island."

Eight million dollars of the Vanderbilt treasury went gurgling down the Erie drain.

Fisk described the Vanderbilt debacle in colorful terms: "The landslide broke loose; for if we had been able to cut the legal red tape with which Vanderbilt had tried to tie our hands, had found a way to start the printing press to work once more—why, it was good night to the Commodore, because there is no limit to the blank shares a printing press can turn out. White paper is cheap—it is bought by the ream; printer's ink is also dirt cheap; and if we could keep on working that kind of deal—make Vanderbilt pay us fifty or sixty dollars for little pieces of paper that hadn't cost us two cents, we would very soon have all his cash."

By nightfall of March 10, 1868, the Commodore knew that he had been soundly beaten on the Street. His only recourse, once again, was the subservient Judge Barnard. Next morning the judge issued contempt of court citations against Drew, Gould, Fisk and several other Erie directors who were collaborating with them.

On that morning of March 11 there was a jubilant session of the Erie's Executive Committee at the railroad's offices in New York. This self-constituted group consisted of Drew, Gould and Fisk, but it was apparent even then that, though Drew was the nominal head of the raiding operation, the two real executives were Gould and Fisk. The whole printing press scheme bore the stamp of Gould's devious mind and Fisk's bold character. Drew himself was old and timorous, kept looking over his shoulder and waiting for the law to tap him. The shadow of the Ludlow Street jail haunted the old trickster, who really only wanted to enjoy his millions in peace and endow a few more seminaries.

He brightened up only when Fisk, Gould and a few trusted clerks began dumping out satchels of greenbacks—the eight million so cleverly abstracted from Vanderbilt—and tying them up in bundles.

His elation was short-lived, however. Midway in the process of splitting up the loot, the Executive Committee heard that Vanderbilt had had them cited for contempt. The constabulary was on the way. To both Gould and Fisk the solution to avoiding warrants was obvious: get out of town. Drew, however, allowed that sheer homesickness would make the life of a fugitive unendurable. His partners countered that homesickness would be even worse in the Ludlow Street jail, and Drew reluctantly agreed to flee with them. The Executive Committee thereupon took an executive decision to transfer their headquarters across the Hudson to Jersey City, the eastern terminus and operating headquarters of the Erie Railroad. There they'd be close to New York but beyond the reach of the law.

With furious haste they packed their money, stocks and bonds and office records into trunks and told their clerks to head for Jersey City. By 10 A.M. they had cleared the decks. "So complete a clearing out," reported the New York *Herald* the next morning, "has not taken place since the Fenians fled from Dublin on the night of the suspension of the habeas corpus."

Drew and some of their aides departed at once for Jersey City in a hackney coach bearing the trunks of money.

During the rest of that day, while Vanderbilt profanity blued the air over Manhattan, while Wall Street was still in deep shock and Judge Barnard was proclaiming that he would hold the culprits in $500,000 bail apiece if only the constables could lay hands on them, Gould and Fisk prepared for their departure with a leisurely insolence. Gould undoubtedly went home to say good-by to his wife and family. Fisk, who kept his wife in a Boston mansion, far from the scenes of his dalliance, financial and amatory, said his farewells in less respectable circumstances, presumably to the non-acting actress Josie Mansfield, who had captured his fancy above all the other courtesans traipsing through his sybaritic life.

That evening the two financiers met at Delmonico's for dinner. Gould's dyspepsia was acting up, but Fisk dined heartily on steak and champagne. Before they reached the dessert course, a sympathizer bustled up to warn them that the law was closing in.

They jumped into a hack and rode to the Canal Street dock, where they hastily engaged a pair of deckhands on the steamer tied up nearby to row them over to the Jersey shore. An impenetrable fog lay over the Hudson, and it was hours before they reached the legal sanctuary of New Jersey. According to one account, their oarsmen rowed around in circles, lost in the middle of the river, and twice they were almost run down by ferryboats. By midnight they landed on the Jersey shore, soaking wet from the backwash of passing ferries but otherwise unharmed.

At Taylor's Hotel in Jersey City the "triumvirate," as the newspapers called them, took over a whole floor of rooms for themselves and their henchmen. The Executive Committee settled down to a long siege. Rumors drifted across the river that Vanderbilt had organized a force of fifty hoodlums to come over and kidnap them back to New York and the ill-tempered jurisdiction of Judge Barnard. Obviously a strong defense must be arranged.

Here Jim Fisk was in what he fancied to be his element, organizing the defense forces with the hearty cooperation of the New Jersey authorities. Fifteen Jersey City policemen were assigned to guard duty at Taylor's Hotel. The Hudson County Artillery furnished three twelve-pounders to be mounted on the pierheads to crush any amphibious assault from the New York shore. Four lifeboats, manned by Erie clerks mustered in for the duration, patrolled the Jersey shore with rifles at the ready. Units of the state militia were alerted, and rockets were placed on the hotel roof to sound the alarm in case of a night attack. On March 16, when several New York hoodlums were arrested near the wharves, and rumors spread that Vanderbilt had offered a reward of $50,000 to anyone who would bring the triumvirate back to New York, the Jersey City police doubled its contribution in manpower, pulling in patrolmen from outlying beats and providing a quickly-seized opportunity for burglars and stick-up men in the suburbs. And all the while Jim Fisk swaggered around the perimeter of his riverside defenses, puffing on perfectos, slapping backs, looking grim and announcing he would never be taken alive. The triumvirate's brave resistance was, he told reporters, "in the interests of the poorer classes especially."

The other two triumvirs were not quite so noisy. Drew, scared witless by reports of lurking kidnapers, kept muttering he wanted to go home and wondering whether the half-dozen bodyguards in his room were really sufficient.

Gould not only had to buck him up, but plan the counter-moves to Vanderbilt and his busy lawyers.

While Fisk acted as the jovial front man, Gould did battle with the Commodore in courts and legislatures and on the front pages of the newspapers. The object of his campaign, of course, was to force Vanderbilt into some sort of compromise which would permit the triumvirate to return to New York.

Vanderbilt had a receiver appointed for Erie (though its liquid assets were in New Jersey), to which Gould responded by incorporating under the laws of New Jersey and reducing the passenger fare to Buffalo from $7 to $5. By remote control he engineered raids on Vanderbilt's New York Central stock, which slipped from 132 to 109. He took over as operating head of Erie, with all departmental heads reporting to him behind the barricades at Taylor's Hotel. Always appreciative of the pressure that could be exerted through public opinion, he saw to the fabrication of a new public image of the fugitive Erie directorate as a little band of heroes fighting off the Vanderbilt monopoly, an impression dutifully conveyed back to New York by the corps of reporters covering the triumvirates' activities.

Under a propaganda barrage from both sides, the public realized that whichever faction won, it would be the loser, through rising passenger fares and freight rates if Vanderbilt succeeded in obtaining a monopoly, through continued wretched service on the Erie if the triumvirate came out on top. So the public was indifferent, and settled back to enjoy the spectacle. Indifference was just the climate that Gould needed to operate as he must, to carry the fight against Vanderbilt back to New York soil. He had conceived a scheme so bold that Drew almost fainted when he heard it outlined, and Fisk chortled with the true appreciation of one highbinder for another.

Meanwhile, Fisk and Gould had all they could do to prevent Uncle Dan'l from slinking back to New York and making his peace with the Commodore. He missed his Wall Street haunts, his family, and passing the plate Sundays at St. Paul's. There were times when he felt as though he'd fallen in with a pair of desperadoes—Gould with his glittering black eyes, Fisk with his evil habits. That saucepot, Josie Mansfield, had come over from New York and was installed in Fisk's suite. Down the hall a flock of New York newspapermen were swilling down booze paid for by Erie funds. He could only agonize in the midst of revelry.

At their daily council of war, while Fisk and Gould discussed strategy and planned further embarrassments for Vanderbilt, about all that they got out of Drew was the plaintive, quavering plea, "I want to go home." Before a week was out his fellow fugitives were utterly weary of the old man's company, but they couldn't risk letting him out of their sight. The Erie railway detectives called in to augment the police guard at Taylor's Hotel were told to keep a close watch on the venerable treasurer and his trunks full of treasure.

By the closing days of March, Gould knew that he would have to take bold measures immediately, or Erie-in-exile would fall apart. His fellow fugitives, even Fisk, were yearning to return to the lights of Manhattan across the river. Staying holed-up in a Jersey City hotel wasn't *their* idea of how to enjoy their takings.

Gould had already obtained passage of a bill through the New Jersey legislature authorizing the Erie directorate to issue stock at will. Now he decided to obtain the same authority from the New York state legislature, whose members for the most part sold their votes at open bidding in the corridors of the State House. Gould packed a few shirts and $500,000 in two valises and set out for Albany. Erie lawyers and lobbyists, deployed in depth at the New York state capital, assured him that they'd protect him from service of warrants issued earlier that month charging him with contempt of court and other misdeeds.

Hardly had Gould established himself in Parlor 57 of the Delavan House at Albany than the local sheriff arrested him on the New York City warrants. A local judge, under the Vanderbilt influence, set bail at $500,000. Gould needed that particular half million—and much more, as it turned out—to buy up the state legislature, so the bail money had to be forwarded from Jersey City.

This incident and others showed Gould that he had been right in taking personal charge of the legislative operations. The Erie men in Albany were allowing themselves to be outbid and outwitted by Vanderbilt's henchmen, headed by William Marcy Tweed, Boss Tweed of Tammany Hall, who was then faithful to the Commodore. There was the case of State Senator A. C. Mattoon's investigating committee as an instance of how difficult it was to nail down the legislators' votes. Mattoon and his five-man committee had come to Jersey City to investigate the triumvirate's side of the story, and had been persuaded, doubtless with cash contributions from Daniel Drew, that justice was on the side of the fugitives. On returning to Albany, however, Vanderbilt's field workers had immediately contacted them and presented their fiscal arguments. Mattoon himself, according to the New York Tribune's Albany correspondent, had been persuaded to see the light after receiving $20,000 of Vanderbilt money.

Mattoon seemed to Charles F. Adams, Jr. the most contemptible of the whole pack of boodle hounds in Albany. "Here was a senator," he wrote in Chapters of Erie, "rousing gamblers from their beds at early hours of the morning to hold interviews in the faro-bank parlor of the establishment, and to give 'points' on which to operate upon the joint account. Even then the wretched creature could not keep faith with his 'pals;' he wrote them to 'go it heavy' for Drew, and then himself went over to Vanderbilt. . . . A man more shamefacedly contemptible and corrupt, a more perfect specimen of a legislator on sale haggling for his own price, could not well exist."

Albany had never known such delightful madness as those April days during which Gould and Tweed, the latter on behalf of Vanderbilt, flooded the legislature with money and free whisky. "The wealth of Vanderbilt," Adams observed, "seemed pitted against the Erie treasury, and the vultures flocked to Albany from every part of the state. . . . Fabulous stories were told of the amounts which the contending parties were willing to expend; never before had the market quotations of votes and influence stood so high."

Mattoon's investigating committee reported against Erie's bill legalizing the watered stock. Erie was simply being outbid. Its lobbyists had tried to buy the bribable section of the State Assembly, known as the Black Horse Cavalry, at a niggardly $1000 a head. The Black Horsemen pocketed Erie's money but voted against its bill March 27, defeating it by an overwhelming 83 to 32. Obviously with so many millions at stake and so many more in the offing if only this one piece of legislation could be jammed through, the Drew-Fisk-Gould faction had to be prepared to top Vanderbilt's offers no matter what it cost. As Gould later said with the cold contempt of the briber for the bribed, "I made the legislature with my own money," by which he meant, of course, Erie's money.

Both sides knew that they had to continue showering money on the legislators until the issue was decided in the State Senate. Tweed set up six bars in his suite above Gould's to accommodate the lawmakers and impress them with the righteousness of the Commodore's cause. Later he recalled that he doled out $180,000 in hope that the legislators would defeat Erie's bill.

One flight down, in a spacious room filled with cigar smoke, whisky fumes and the delicious scent of fresh greenbacks, Gould passed out thousand-dollar bills with a lavish hand. His lobbyists were equally generous, and the half million in Gould's luggage was soon depleted. When a Vanderbilt lobbyist arrived in town with a fresh supply of cash for the New York Central's cause, Gould, it was reported, presented him with $70,000 simply to disappear with the money.

Five years later a select committee of the legislature, then in a righteous mood because of the depression afflicting the country, investigated the wholesale corruption of the legislative sessions of 1868. To its public horror the committee found that the Drew-Fisk-Gould faction of Erie had spent more than a million dollars that year for "extra and legal services," meaning bribery of the legislature. "What the Erie has done other great corporations are doubtless doing from year to year," the committee's report[1] added. "Combined as they are, the power of the great moneyed corporations of this country is a standing menace to the liberties of the people. The railroad lobby flaunts its ill-gotten gains in the faces of our legislatures, and in all our politics the debasing influence is felt."

Encouraged by his experiences with the pliability of the New York legislature, Gould told this same committee in 1873, he extended his efforts in the political field to buying elections for men running for the Assembly or Senate because "as a rule, such investments paid better than to wait until the men got to Albany." He could no more remember how many legislators he bought this way, he told the investigators, than he could "recall the number of freight cars sent over the Erie Railroad from day to day." With a lordly indifference to the most sacred feelings of the politicians quizzing him, he added, "In a Republican district I was a Republican; in a Democratic district, a Democrat; in a doubtful district I was doubtful; but I was always for Erie."

His single-minded concern for Erie certainly paid off in 1868. The April shower of gold, in the form of greenbacks, swayed both houses of the legislature toward seeing the justice of Erie's cause. When the Erie bill came up for Senate approval, it passed by a vote of 17 to 12. Senator Mattoon had again switched back to Erie. The New York newspapers, making it plain they were referring to Mattoon, reported that one senator had taken another $15,000 from Vanderbilt and $20,000 from Gould.

[1] Report of the Select Committee of the Assembly, Assembly Documents, 1873.

The Senate's passage of the Erie bill on April 18 so disgusted Vanderbilt, who had already decided to make a compromise with Drew, that he pulled out of the bribery contest, leaving the members of the Assembly bereft and enraged. When news reached the Assembly floor that Vanderbilt's agents had cut off their subsidies, wrote Charles Francis Adams, Jr., in *Chapters of Erie*, "the observer was reminded of the dark days of the war when tidings came of some great defeat . . . the lobby was smitten with despair . . . the cheeks of the legislators were blanched." Almost en masse, the assemblymen rushed over to Parlor 57 of the Delavan House to offer their votes for as little as $100. But Gould had snapped shut the catches of his valises. On April 20, the Assembly passed the Erie bill by 101 to 6, though a few weeks earlier they had rejected it (while Vanderbilt money was still circulating) by 83 to 32.

Erie, through its fugitive directorate, was now empowered to issue as much stock as it wanted.

Gould, however, knew they still weren't in the clear. Vanderbilt and his judges barred the way to New York City. And Gould learned from Fisk, back in Jersey City, that Drew had already taken steps to sell out the cause by making a deal with Vanderbilt behind their backs. Gould hurried back to Jersey City to learn the extent of Uncle Dan'l's treachery.

A Vanderbilt agent disguised as a traveling salesman, it seemed, had penetrated the defenses of Erie-in-exile and lodged himself in Taylor's Hotel. The spy bribed a waiter to pass a note to Drew from Vanderbilt which read, "Drew: I'm sick of the whole damned business. Come and see me. Van Derbilt [The Commodore always misspelled his own name]." As Vanderbilt explained to his friends, he had wearied of fighting a crooked printing press, two such slippery customers as Fisk and Gould and dishonest legislators who kept taking his money and switching sides. "This Erie war," he said, "has taught me that it never pays to kick a skunk."

Drew, without telling Fisk, slipped over to Manhattan to

see the Commodore on a Sunday, when no civil summons could be served. He went to the Vanderbilt mansion on Washington Place and practically threw himself into Vanderbilt's arms, bemoaning the fact that a mere railroad had come between two old whist-playing cronies.

"No one knows how my bowels yearn for you, Drew," Vanderbilt sarcastically replied, fending off Drew's embrace, "but let's not get gushy. As I understand it, this is a business talk. So if you'll wipe the tobacco juice off your chin and draw up to the table, we'll talk."

Then and at two other supposedly secret meetings Vanderbilt outlined his peace terms for Drew, who was agreeable. He also reached an agreement with President Eldridge's Boston faction. Fisk and Gould could be dealt with after the weaker members of the "scarlet sisterhood of Erie" had been brought into line.

Fisk learned about Drew's clandestine meetings with their enemy from an Erie railway detective who tailed him over to Manhattan. Investigation also showed that Drew had sneakily removed the Erie treasury back to Manhattan, where it would be available for a settlement with Vanderbilt, presumably without Fisk's and Gould's knowledge or approval. Uncle Dan'l, however, had his personal funds deposited in a Jersey City bank, and Fisk prevailed on a local judge to issue a writ of attachment against them. So Drew had Erie's funds in New York, but Fisk had Drew's personal fortune tied up in Jersey City.

Fisk then braced the old man concerning his underhanded dealings. Drew finally admitted to secret parleys with the Commodore and pleaded that he had taken the Erie treasury back to New York City because it would be "safer" there. He was badly jarred by Fisk's announcement that his own fortune had been attached. The two men then reached an agreement by which Erie's funds were returned to Jersey City and Drew's were unfrozen by another court order.

Gould and Fisk, conferring hurriedly on the former's return from Albany, reached a decision on two matters immediately: (1) they'd have to reach a compromise with Vanderbilt, even on the Commodore's terms, or they'd be frozen out by Drew, Eldridge and other Erie directors who had made their submission to Vanderbilt, and (2) Daniel Drew must have his throat cut from ear to ear, financially speaking, for having broken their solid front.

Under guarantees of safe conduct, they also made the journey to Manhattan and Vanderbilt's mansion. The Commodore studied the two young pirates who had boarded and almost scuttled him with a cold eye and gave them his terms. They'd have to make good on those 100,000 shares of watered stock, somehow, or they'd be arrested the next time they set foot in New York. Several days later the various factions which had been contending for control of Erie got together under Vanderbilt's chairmanship and hammered out a final agreement. Vanderbilt was to be given $4,750,000 for half of the printing press shares he had bought, with the balance to be taken off his hands within the next six months. Eldridge and the Boston plunderbund were to receive $4,000,000 for their practically worthless Boston, Hartford & Erie bonds. Drew had to kick in $540,000 of his winnings, but had all claims against him discharged. A Tweed henchman, Peter B. Sweeny, was paid a $150,000 fee for acting as receiver for the Erie during the three-week exile of its directorate and treasury.

Everybody, on the surface, came out enriched except Fisk and Gould. All they had was Erie's empty till. But that till, as history had proven, was remarkably refillable; and they had control of the railroad, to have, hold, squeeze and manipulate for all it was worth.

"There ain't nothin' left in Erie," was Drew's opinion, but he was wrong—and he was to pay for it.

Back over the river to West Street, in lower Manhattan, went the Erie headquarters. Its financial engineers were getting up steam for another express run, with all switches open.

Shortly after his thirty-second birthday, on July 2, 1868, Jay Gould became the president of a major railroad, having reached that eminence after approximately eighteen months of working and conniving and with the capital investment of probably only a few thousand shares in Erie. Wall Street had never seen such a rocket-like thrust of ambition, the partner in a small brokerage taking over a railroad presidency, over the opposition of a Vanderbilt, in the space of a few hectic months.

On that day the Erie board of directors confirmed the settlement with Vanderbilt, the withdrawal of Eldridge and Drew. Gould was elected president and treasurer, Fisk as comptroller and managing director. Until now Fisk had been the more celebrated of the pair; it was his name that figured in the headlines, since he gave out the interviews and poured the whisky for the press, and his Napoleon III mustaches and corpulent person that delighted the cartoonists. Gould preferred to work without benefit of publicity, and was content for Fisk to continue acting as their mutual flashy front. The air of jovial banditry which overlaid the subsequent operations of the Gould-Fisk syndicate went down well with the public during those postwar boom years, before the economic hangover of '73. In its present mood, the public was more amused than outraged by Fisk's elephantine capers with the demimondes, his high living and free spending. At least he was enjoying himself, a pleasant contrast to the grim parsimony of a Drew, the unabashed grabbiness of a Vanderbilt. Presumably Gould understood that Fisk served as a marvelous smoke screen for the outrages that were to be committed in Erie's name. A financial circus needed a barker in a checked suit. But Wall Street insiders knew that though the voice of Erie was Fisk's, the brain was Gould's.

The really important development of that July board meeting was the election of Boss Tweed, who had run out of money and lost the fight for control of the state legislature on behalf of Vanderbilt, to its membership. Tweed, the Grand Sachem of Tammany Hall, president of the Board of Supervisors and absolute political ruler of New York City, had received a large block of Erie stock from Vanderbilt for his efforts in Albany. Although they had been opponents only a few months before, Fisk and Gould welcomed Tweed into their midst with the utmost joy. The Boss, after all, "owned" three judges, Albert Cardozo, John H. McCunn and George G. Barnard, who would give rubber-stamp approval to anything their master wanted.

In effect, as Charles Francis Adams, Jr. wrote in *Chapters of Erie,* the addition of Tweed to the Erie board gave Gould and Fisk the green light for their wild ride down the tracks. The alliance of the Erie Ring and the Tweed Ring "shot out its feelers far and wide; it wielded the influence of a great corporation with a capital of a hundred millions; it controlled the politics of the first city of the New World; it sent its representatives to the Senate of the state, and numbered among its agents the judges of the courts. Compact, disciplined, and reckless, it knew its own power and would not scruple to use it." Neither the city nor state governments nor the courts could interfere with their plundering. The result was what Adams called "the most extraordinary feat of financial legerdemain which history has yet recorded."

The first move Gould made was a measure of the boldness with which he intended to conduct Erie's affairs. Once again the presses in the basement of the Erie offices on West Street began clattering day and night. Between July and October, Erie's capitalization was increased from $34,000,000 to $54,000,000. This new flood of watered stock enabled Fisk and Gould to conduct a bear raid on Erie stock, one result of which was to trap Drew and even accounts with him for having compromised with Vanderbilt behind their backs. By early November, Erie quotations sank to 35. Then Fisk and Gould decided to reverse the trend, using $12,000,000 they had stowed away as proceeds from selling the watered stock. While Drew continued to sell short, Fisk and Gould suddenly began buying and in a few days had driven Erie up from 35 to 54, later to 62. Driven into a corner, Drew tried to have Gould and Fisk ousted by the courts as unfit to manage Erie's affairs. It was then that the Tweed connection paid off handsomely. Tweed's pet judge, Barnard, circumvented Drew's maneuvers by throwing Erie temporarily into receivership. The receiver: Jay Gould. The receiver's bondsman: Jim Fisk. Wall Street roared with laughter at Drew's discomfiture.

From then on Drew's career as a speculator rapidly declined. In 1875 he went into bankruptcy, sadly admitting, "To speculate in Wall Street when you are no longer an insider is like buying cows by candlelight." Four years later he died broke, his estate consisting of a watch and chain, a sealskin coat, a number of Bibles and hymn books. Before he died, Drew coined an epitaph for Jay Gould: "His touch is death."

Commodore Vanderbilt was also to experience a final bruising encounter with Gould.

He decided to embarrass Erie by waging a rate war while the company was still struggling to overcome the depletion of its treasury following the $10,000,000 settlement. The established rate for carrying cattle from Buffalo to New York was $125 a carload. Vanderbilt cut the New York Central's price to $100. Gould countered with a cut to $75 a carload. Then both roads slashed their price to $25. In his exasperation Vanderbilt finally reduced the Central's rate to $1. Erie suddenly restored its $125 rate and the Commodore gloated, believing Gould had been licked. A few weeks later he learned that he had been celebrating a false victory. Gould had bought every head of cattle his agents could find west of Buffalo and was shipping them via the New York Central at $1 a carload, taking a sizable profit at Vanderbilt's expense. Vanderbilt "nearly lost his reason" at learning how he had been tricked. He called off the rate war.

Henceforth, he publicly announced, he would have nothing to do with Gould "except it be to defend myself."

Shortly before his death, however, he paid Gould the highest compliment one sharper could pay another.

Gould, he said, was "the smartest man in America."

5. BLACK FRIDAY

THE year 1869 was probably one of the blackest in American history. All the nation's resources of patriotism, self-sacrifice and civic morality had been drained dry by the Civil War; the aftermath of the most "idealistic" war in our history was bitterly shameful and squalid, and the worship of money-making, the idolatry of the "smart" man spread outward from the White House to every corner of the country. To the fastidious Henry Adams all the "great active forces of society" were "one dirty cesspool of vulgar corruption." It was the year that General Ulysses S. Grant moved into the White House, with his parasitical relatives and grasping friends; the year that the reconciliation of North and South favored by Lincoln and Johnson was abandoned in favor of a cruelly misnamed Reconstruction.

It was the beginning of what became known as "The Flash Age," a curious reflection of France's second Napoleonic "empire" whose pretensions and vainglory were to be trampled underfoot by the march of Prussian troops through the Arch of Triumph in 1871. The social tone was established by the excesses of the war profiteers, political boodlers and market speculators who were confident that the war boom would go on forever. "In its endeavor to keep pace with the Second Empire the Flash Age took note only of the superficial," wrote the social historians of *Valentine's Manual*, "and like all imitators failed in the matter of good taste, a quality inherent in the French."

A sort of wry and helpless cynicism proliferated among all classes, particularly in New York, where the moneyed people were at the mercy of the Erie Ring and everyone, from the mansions on Fifth Avenue to the slums of Hell's Kitchen, was under the large, inexorable thumb of Boss Tweed, his crooked judges, his demoralized police and other satellites. It could hardly have been otherwise, with Gould and Fisk setting themselves above even the law of the financial jungle, and Tweed and his friends, as the journalist Edward Crapsey wrote,[1] "rioting in suddenly acquired wealth and constantly exhibiting themselves to the public gaze loaded with diamonds and guzzling costly wines, like the vulgar knaves they are. . . . Men who were fit to be ushers at minstrel shows were made State Senators, and the keepers of gin-shops were manufactured into legislators for the great state of New York. Among the police magistrates were the meanest of political tricksters, and a man who had been brought back from a distant state to answer for a felony was made auditor of the public accounts." And people not only acquiesced in this state of affairs but displayed a "general desire to share in the booty."

In the fall elections of 1869, Boss Tweed had succeeded in placing his own man, the fashion plate Oakey Hall, a somewhat less witty forerunner of Jimmy Walker, in the mayor's office, and had installed another creature of his own making, John Hoffman, in the governor's mansion. Politics had become a joke which only a few men like Horace Greeley of the New York *Tribune* failed to appreciate. "The grossest satires on the American Senator and politician never failed to excite the laughter and applause of every audience," observed Henry Adams in his autobiography. "Rich and poor alike joined in throwing contempt on their own representatives. Society

[1] *The Nether Side of New York*, an acrimonious study of Flash Age morality published in 1872.

laughed a vacant and meaningless derision over its own failure."

An amazingly few common scolds rose to attempt to apply correctives or even to warn against the money sickness, the delirium of getting and spending. Horace Greeley was old hat, a specter of prewar morality, an outdated and tiresome reformer; few paid any attention to his complaints that "every dollar taken from the public treasury, in payment for services not required, is so much money wrested from private citizens for the aggrandizement of the wielders of wealth and power." Nor was much attention paid to another scolding voice, that of *The Nation*, when it analyzed the temper of the times: "There is too much truth in the statement that the tendency today in this country is to count up our list of peculiarly American virtues as consisting of audacity, push, unscrupulousness and brazen disregard of others' rights or others' good opinions; that we make no sufficient objection to a display of unmitigated and unmitigable selfishness, if only it be a splendid display—if only it be crowned by success, by the acquisition of wealth or power." The judicial system had become so corrupt, *The Nation* said, that it existed only to "give the strong and the wicked an opportunity to oppress the weak and the honest . . . Many respectable men will nowadays rather bear any loss short of absolute ruin than expose themselves to the disgrace of going into court. To sue has become almost equivalent to levying blackmail. To commense proceedings, for the justest of claims, is becoming disgraceful. It is getting honorable to be charged with the blackest of crimes."

In this delightfully propitious climate, Jay Gould and the stout sybarite whose peculiar abilities dovetailed so neatly with his own naturally flourished. It was made to order for them; they could hardly have prospered so enormously in any more astringent atmosphere. With the huge profits from Erie rolling in, even Gould, conservative as he was in his private

life, expanded somewhat and moved his family to a four-story
house at 579 Fifth Avenue, blandly ignoring the shudders of
his new neighbors. As for Fisk, he positively swelled and
swaggered in the enjoyment of new wealth.

At Fisk's urging, the headquarters of the Erie Railway were
moved uptown from the dingy quarters on West Street to the
baroque splendors of the Grand Opera House at Twenty-third
Street and Eighth Avenue, a corporate Venusberg awash in
champagne, ballet dancers, French opera singers. It was a
measure of Gould's regard for Fisk that he allowed himself to
be transferred to such a place, his own tastes being so Spartan
and his own inclinations being directed toward the family fireside rather than the revelry, on- and off-stage, which formed
a lurid backdrop for the conduct of the Erie Railroad's affairs.
But Gould, who kept all his intricate schemes in his head and
had immense powers of concentration, could work anywhere,
even in these voluptuous surroundings. President Gould could
afford to indulge Managing Director Fisk in his fancy, for the
$820,000 which the opera house cost came out of company
funds, as did Fisk's house next door and his black-haired mistress Josie Mansfield's a few doors down the block. Miss Mansfield was placed on the Erie payroll at $1000 a month for
services rendered the managing director.

In the three floors above the opera house, the offices and
apartments opened on marble corridors with iron statuary
lamps and were decorated in black walnut inlaid with gold,
with silver name plates, crimson draperies, painted ceilings,
and washstands encrusted with nymphs and cupids. "The
carved woodwork, the stained and cut glass of the partitions,
the splendid gas fixtures, and above all the artistic frescoes on
the walls and ceilings," wrote a New York *Herald* reporter,
"create astonishment and admiration at such a blending of
the splendid and practical." Here Jim Fisk played impresario,
bringing to this task the same showmanship that enlivened
his financial endeavors. He engaged two ballet companies,

one blonde and the other brunette, to appear on alternate nights; sometimes he had a different prima donna singing in each act of an opera, and changed the season's programs from heavy German and Italian works to French comic opera.

Any honest old railroadman must have been thoroughly bewildered by a visit to the Erie offices. Through their corridors trooped a procession of Tammany politicians, judges and lawyers being entertained in various bars and salons, ballet masters, singers, dancers, musicians, and men about town. Inside the massive doors on the Twenty-third Street side, or business entrance, which were twelve feet high, twelve inches thick and made of steel, loitered a gang of toughs under the captaincy of a neighborhood hoodlum named Tommy Lynch, whose assignment it was to repel any process servers, maddened stockholders or Erie wreck victims trying to storm "Castle Erie." Printing presses occasionally would rumble in the basement when a new stock issue was ordered by the executives upstairs. The odors of grease paint, perfume, spilled wine, burning Havanas and printer's ink mingled uneasily throughout the building. Occasionally the screech of a soprano reaching for a high note would penetrate upward from the stage.

The unlikeliest sight in this colorful setting was Jay Gould, huddled with his schemes and calculations in a small, barely furnished office, as out of place as a pallid clerk at an imperial orgy. He ignored the unseemly doings in "Fisk's harem." He did not turn a hair when Fisk lost enormous sums at playing impresario, at indulging Josie Mansfield's whims. All the trollops in Christendom could have rioted through the corridors without his raising an eyebrow. According to G. P. Morosini, later his confidential clerk but then an Erie bookkeeper, he kept regular hours, like any employe, and "even on Sundays would spend several hours in the office."

Morosini, an Italian merchant seaman who had migrated to the United States and went to work for Erie in 1855, wrote in an unpublished memoir[2] that "Mr. Gould was the ideal president and such one never existed before. . . . He was affable to every employe from the head of the department to the humblest tracklayer on the road."

His employes, Morosini said, understood that Gould did not approve of "Mr. Fisk's liaisons with notorious women" but ignored them along with "many high-handed acts not at all in keeping with the position he [Fisk] held." Morosini believed this tolerant attitude was induced by that fact that Fisk had opened the door to Erie for him: "Mr. Fisk came across the name of Jay Gould as owner of several thousand shares of the stock. Negotiations were opened and Mr. Gould was asked to become a director of the railroad." Less amiable historians, however, have indicated that Gould's connection with Erie came about through more tortuous preliminaries than that.

But Gould's mind that summer of 1869 was far removed from Erie, Fisk, and his gaudy surroundings. It dwelt not on such amiable pursuits as the boozing and wenching going on around him, but the furtherance of his drive for wealth and power through the boldest operation of his career.

Quietly, without the knowledge of Fisk or anyone else, Gould was conceiving a scheme as grandly operatic as any that Impresario Fisk was presenting on the stage below.

MISE EN SCÈNE: The Gold Room at Broad and Exchange Streets.

THE CHARACTERS: The President of the United States, the Secretary of the Treasury, the Assistant United States Treasurer, the President's wife, sister and brother-in-law, and a cast of thousands.

THE PLOT: To corner all the gold then circulating in the United States.

[2] A grateful document now deposited with the New York Historical Society. Curiously unrevealing, considering how much its author must have known of Gould's dealings, it was addressed to the latter's daughter Helen in the hope that she would be interested in "some of the bright doings of your dear father."

The idea for this extravaganza apparently had been stirring around in his mind for a long time, possibly since wartime, when "General Lee's left wing" had conducted its operations against the Union's financial stability. Until he became president and treasurer of Erie, with the railroad's funds at his disposal, he simply didn't have the cash or credit resources to carry out his plan. About this time, too, he and Fisk acquired a controlling interest in the Tenth National Bank, a Tammany Hall subsidiary, through whose facilities he could issue certified checks to back his gamble, although the money to support such certification was not necessarily in the bank's vaults. In the coming venture, the Tenth National's certified checks would be the equivalent of the watered stock produced by Erie's printing presses during the bear raid of the previous fall.

The scene of his forthcoming campaign had been quiescent ever since wartime, when, as J. K. Medbery[3] wrote, the Gold Room was "a den of wild beasts." Here, when important news arrived from the armies, "the bulls whistled 'Dixie' and the bears sang 'John Brown.'" Since then, as Medbery said, "the star of Erie . . . has dimmed the radiance of the Gold Room." Speculation on the gold market had settled down and become conservative, and "the utmost daily range" of the price fluctuations "had been two percent with occasional fractional additions." As a setting for high drama, the exchange was an unexceptional place, a large, high-ceilinged chamber with a gallery and an alcove for Western Union telegraphers in one corner. On its façade was a gilded indicator registering the price of gold for the benefit of the lesser camp followers operating on the curbstone outside.

Now that an unsuspecting lassitude had settled over the gold market, Gould believed that the time was ripe for stirring up speculation. From early in 1869 onward he had been watching for an opportunity to enter the market and engineer

[3] *Men and Mysteries of Wall Street*, Boston, 1870.

a spectacular rise. It might even be possible to drive up the price to wartime levels.

During the war the government issued so much paper money, contemptuously known as "shinplasters," that the speculators in the Gold Room had been able to drive up the price to $241 for a hundred dollars worth of gold. Representative James A. Garfield pointed to the existence of a double standard, paper and gold, as the main cause of recurring financial crises. "So long as we have two standards of value recognized by law, which may be made to vary in respect to each other by artificial means, so long will speculation in the price of gold offer temptations too great to be resisted."

In the spring of 1869, postwar prosperity having restored confidence in the greenbacks, the price of gold had dropped to 135, then to 131. At the latter point Gould yielded to temptation: he bought $7,000,000 worth of gold in April and sent the price up to 140.

Late that summer he resolved to send gold prices skyrocketing. There was only $15,000,000 worth of gold then actually circulating in the United States, and he owned almost half of it. With Erie's treasury and Tenth National's certified checks behind him, he believed, he could corner the whole gold supply. But there was one possible snag in this plan. The United States Treasury held almost $100,000,000 worth of gold in its vaults, allowing the government to control the price, if and when it chose, by dumping gold on the market whenever it rose too high. Until now the government had been careful to keep enough gold in circulation so that merchants could transact foreign business and pay customs duties, which required specie payments.

Gould's problem was somehow to plug up this governmental safety valve just long enough for him to carry off the swag. He could pull off almost anything in the city or state of New York, thanks to his alliance with the Tweed Ring, but its influence in the federal government was nil. Somehow Gould had to reach into the highest circles of the government to prevent the Treasury from dumping gold during a crucial week or so of his operations; he also had to know whether the Treasury, during August and September, would be hoarding gold or releasing it. To obtain that kind of information and control, he would have to reach into the President's Cabinet, into the White House itself.

And when General Grant assumed the Presidency, still war-weary, always a trifle somnolent, obsessed with enjoying what he fancied were the good things of life, Gould saw his opportunity. He already possessed a human key to the front door of the White House.

For some time he had been cultivating the confidence and friendship of a grizzled old rascal named Abel Rathbone Corbin, at various times a lawyer, editor, and man about Washington. As a lobbyist, he admitted before a Congressional investigating committee in 1857, he had secured the passage of various corrupt bills. In 1868, at the age of sixty-six, he brought off his greatest coup by marrying Miss Jenny Grant, the new President's middle-aged sister. The Corbins were now living in a well-appointed house on West Twenty-seventh Street, where the President frequently visited them on trips to New York. It took money to live up to his position as brother-in-law of the President, so Corbin kept an experienced eye peeled for financial opportunities. Naturally he was hopeful that his growing friendship with Gould, who had thoughtfully bought some New Jersey real estate from him, ostensibly for the Erie's right of way, would lead to more lucrative ventures. In solemn agreement, Corbin listened to Gould's arguments that if the government allowed the price of gold to rise the farmers would benefit through high prices for the expected bumper crop that year, the railroads would profit through hauling the grain to market and the whole economy would be revitalized. Patriotic necessity dictated a bull movement in the gold market. Unequaled prosperity would result. If the government cravenly dumped its gold, on the other hand, a terrible depression would grip the land and, heaven forfend, another civil war might break out.

Late in May the Corbins paid a visit to the White House, a brief sojourn which signalized the beginning of the pressure exerted on the Treasury. Corbin enthusiastically conveyed to his brother-in-law the Gould Program for National Prosperity and the arguments against permitting the government to open the sluice gates on its gold reserve.

Secretary of the Treasury George S. Boutwell, in his autobiography,[4] related that the first signs of pressure from the White House began appearing about this time. It was then customary for the Secretary of the Treasury to announce on the first of the month the amount of gold to be released in the next thirty days. "An attempt was made to induce me to make an announcement for two or three months, which would allow the gold speculators to calculate closely on how much government gold they would have to contend with," Boutwell recalled. "But it was no part of my policy to regulate affairs in Wall Street . . . I refrained from any interference with those who were engaged either in forcing up or forcing down the price of gold." As a key figure in Gould's plans, Boutwell did not offer much initial encouragement, but he could be depended upon not to disturb the general somnolence of the Grant Administration with untoward cries of alarm. The Secretary of the Treasury was a laissez-faire type, one of a totally undistinguished group of men with whom Grant had chosen to surround himself. The President himself was "a very unsophisticated gentleman," wrote Meade Minnigerode, "who never seemed to realize that when birds of a feather are seen together they must be assumed to be working against the common good."

Gould soon realized that there was little reason to fear that Washington would interfere with his plans, at least not until they had matured and the damage was done.

[4] *Reminiscences of Sixty Years in Public Affairs,* Volume II.

When President Grant stopped off in New York to visit the Corbins June 15 on his way to Boston, Gould edged himself closer to the First Family of the Land. He was introduced to the President at the Corbin home and briskly took charge of the Presidential party's entertainment and travel arrangements, seizing an opportunity not only to impress Grant with his views but to show the speculators in the Gold Room how intimate he was with the President . . . an intimacy much exaggerated by Gould and used as a propaganda weapon during his maneuvers that summer. Instead of traveling by train to Boston to attend the Peace Jubilee, Grant might find it more pleasant, Gould suggested, to journey up Long Island Sound on Jim Fisk's newly acquired steamer *Providence*, with Fisk and Gould, naturally, accompanying the party. The President agreed. The exuberant Fisk greeted the Presidential party at the gangplank in his gorgeous uniform as Admiral of the Fall River Line. So off they sailed, an unsuspecting General Nod with a larcenous Winken and Blinken.

Gould and Fisk sat their guest of honor down to a champagne supper followed by brandy and cigars. By the time President Grant had his first cigar drawing properly, Gould turned the subject of the conversation to the gold situation, emphasizing in his gentle insistent voice that (as he later told a Congressional investigating committee[5]) "the government ought to let gold alone, and let it find its commercial level; that, as a fact, it ought to facilitate an upward movement of gold in the fall." Otherwise, he said, a great depression might be expected which would "almost lead to civil war."

Fisk, somewhat presumptuously, asked the President what his opinion was.

Grant's reply must have chilled Gould to the marrow. "There is a certain amount of fictitiousness about the prosperity of the country," the President said, "and the bubble might as well be tapped one way as another."

[5] House Report No. 31, 41st Congress, Second Session, 1870.

Fisk took this statement to mean that Grant was "for returning to a specie basis. . . . He entered into the conversation with a good deal of spirit, and I made up my mind that he was individually paying a good deal of attention to the finances, which he would, to a certain extent, control."

As Fisk recalled, the conversation around the liquor and cigars continued from about 9 P.M. to about 12:30 A.M., but the President apparently was not persuaded by Gould's and Fisk's arguments.

The two partners, along with Corbin and other members of the retinue, entered the Boston Coliseum with the President the next day, with "Admiral" Fisk acknowledging the applause in such a gracious manner that it was obvious "he thought a large share of the plaudits were meant for him." They returned to New York with the party, riding the Presidential coattails for all they were worth. On the night of June 18, Grant, his wife and daughter occupied Fisk's box at the Fifth Avenue Theater with Fisk, Gould and the Corbins, watching a spirited rendition of the cancan number in *La Perichole*.

Grant had punctured Gould's hopes to a considerable extent, had expressed himself so strongly in favor of deflationary measures that even the usually optimistic Fisk was balking at going along with Gould in his raid on the gold market. Perhaps he sensed what was certainly true, that Gould was holding back essential details of his scheme; in any case he was dragging his feet, and Gould decided to proceed without him.

On July 1, through Corbin's connivance, a very important piece in the game fell into place. Major General Dan Butterfield, who could be counted upon to lend his sympathy and a lot more to the conspirators, was appointed Assistant Treasurer at New York. Corbin himself engineered this appointment, which raised his stock considerably with Gould and gave the latter new heart for his enterprise. General Butterfield had served valiantly enough with the Army of the Potomac, but he had a fondness for politics in the high command and overplayed his hand late in the war by intriguing unsuccessfully against General Meade, his army commander. Combined with this weakness for intrigue, for being "on the inside," was an equally ruinous love of luxury. The general was corruptible. With very little effort on Gould's part—almost as little as it took to induce Abel Corbin to join the gold conspiracy—Butterfield was duly corrupted. As Gould later explained the linking together of his creatures in the plot, "Butterfield is all right; Corbin has got Butterfield all right; and Corbin has got Grant fixed all right." Securing the allegiance of these two gentlemen did not, of course, come cheaply. Gould told Congressional investigators the following year that he bought $2,000,000 in gold bonds for Corbin's account, on margin, with the President's brother-in-law to receive the profits accruing from any rise in the price of gold. Butterfield, Gould added, was provided with a similar account for $1,500,000.

The appointment of Butterfield to the subtreasury post in New York apparently convinced Fisk that Gould really had a reliable pipeline to the White House. In the end, Fisk always gave in to Gould. Despite impressions to the contrary, the noisy, hustling Fisk was almost completely dominated by his quiet little partner. Gould, as was soon to be proved, could make him swallow the bitterest kind of medicine without protest.

During July and August Gould, having decided to gamble all the way on Corbin's influence with the President and Butterfield's on the Treasury's gold policy, began buying gold in larger amounts. With spurious "certified" checks issued against the Tenth National's $1,000,000 capitalization, he cornered from thirty to forty million more in gold contracts. Theoretically, by the end of August, Gould owned all the gold then circulating in the United States and held contracts by which he could call upon merchants, bankers, brokers, and other speculators for twice again as much. Price quotations on gold rose to 146 ($100 worth of gold, that is, for $146 in greenbacks). The Gold Room, and all of Wall Street, suddenly was alerted to the fact that an unprecedented raid was being conducted, and the first symptoms of panic began stirring through the narrow streets of the financial district. A resistance movement sprang up, with the Gold Room bears selling short. "I had to buy," Gould later explained, "or else to back down and show the white feather."

Meanwhile he was deviously exerting pressure on the government to keep the Treasury's sluice gates shut tight. By circuitous means he persuaded the New York *Times,* one of the city's two most respected newspapers, to publish his propaganda. He had Abel Corbin, whose pen was as facile as his tongue, write a long and carefully reasoned editorial titled "Grant's Financial Policy," which explained that the President realized it would be necessary to advance the price of gold in order to insure continued prosperity. He then used an Erie stockholder, James McHenry, who was a personal friend of John Bigelow, the *Times* editor, as his messenger boy. McHenry brought the editorial to Bigelow's office and represented it as having been written by "one in the intimate confidence of the President." Bigelow, who had been wartime ambassador to England, apparently suspected that the article was a trifle too insistent on the value of raising the price of gold and had his financial editor tone it down a little. On August 26, the *Times* published the piece, and at least one sentence must have struck terror in the hearts of the bears at the Gold Room: "The President will not send gold into the market and sell it for currency."

But Gould was still not satisfied, for with millions at stake he had to determine the attitude of the Secretary of the Treasury before he plunged deeper. On August 30, he wrote a rather coy letter to Secretary Boutwell: "If the New York *Times* correctly reflects your financial policy during the next three or four months, viz.: to unloose the currency balance at the Treasury, or keep it at the lowest possible figure . . . then

I think the country peculiarly fortunate in having a financial head who can take a broad view of the situation, and who realizes the importance of settling the large balance of trade against us . . . it is only by making gold high and scarce that the difference is equalized, and we are enabled to compete in the London and Liverpool markets. . . . I sincerely believe that when the fruits of your policy come to be practically realized, all classes, the poor as well as the rich, will accord your services a generous appreciation."

Boutwell's reply was cautious and noncommittal. He must have known the kind of game Gould was playing, yet he did not rise up and wrathfully repudiate the *Times'* ghostwritten editorial. Obviously he had decided on a personal policy of see no evil, hear no evil, speak no evil. Let Grant run the Treasury if he pleased. Henry Adams sarcastically called Boutwell "the shrewdest statesman of all" and commented that he "showed how well he understood the situation by turning out of the Treasury everyone who could interfere with his repose."

Gold prices still resisted the artificial trend that Gould was trying to establish, and seasoned gambler though he was by now, his nerves were on edge and he could hardly digest his crackers and milk. Fisk observed that when Gould was sweating out a situation like this he grew even more reticent than usual but would sit by the hour tearing paper into tiny bits. By the end of the day Gould's office at the Grand Opera House would be ankle-deep in this gloomy confetti. Within the next few weeks Gould would have to get the price of gold zooming or his corner would be broken and brokers would be demanding payment on those rubbery certified checks. To get out with a profit he somehow had to reverse the short-selling trend and panic everyone else into buying, then dump all his gold on the market when he judged the price had reached its peak.

On September 2, President Grant paid another visit to New York, which was almost as disastrous as that drunken horseback ride he was supposed to have taken toward the Confederate lines during the strain of the Vicksburg campaign.

The President stopped off at the Corbin home to have breakfast with his sister and brother-in-law on his way to Saratoga.

Hastily tipped off, Gould hurried over to lurk in the hallway while Corbin made his pitch over the breakfast table. It is not difficult to imagine Gould with his ear plastered to the keyhole while Corbin casually renewed his argument for withholding the government's gold supply, no matter what happened in the market.

That morning Grant took the step over which he had been hesitating for ten weeks. He wrote the Secretary of the Treasury immediately suggesting it would not be wise to sell gold in large amounts while the crops were moving to market. The letter was sent to Boutwell's summer home, from which the Secretary of the Treasury telegraphed his assistant in Washington an order not to "sell so large an amount during September" as in previous months.

Corbin, of course, slipped out of the dining room and informed Gould immediately of the letter. A day or two later Gould, as evidence of his gratitude, opened a $500,000 account on the gold market for General Horace Porter, the President's military secretary, and sent him a letter to that effect. Porter, however, bluntly replied by return mail that "I have not authorized any purchase of gold and request that none be made on my account." No matter: Abel Corbin and his wife were making $15,000 every time gold went up a point, which ought to tie in the President's family closely enough. "I did it for the sake of a lady, my wife"—as Corbin gallantly put it before an investigating committee—and his wife was the President's sister.

On September 10, President Grant again passed through New York on his way to Washington, Pennsylvania, where he would continue his vacation. Gould insisted on providing him with the Erie directors' car for the journey, and Grant, who was rarely known to turn down a gift, accepted. His indiscretions had a quality of magnificence, considering that he must have known that Gould at the moment was vitally interested in the wild fluctuations of the gold market. On September 12, Grant wrote Boutwell again, commenting on that situation. "A desperate struggle is now taking place and each party wants the Government to help him out. I write this letter to advise you of what I think you might expect, to put you on your guard. I think, from the lights before me, I would move on without change until the present struggle is over." The President, in other words, would have the Treasury hold onto its gold regardless of its previous policy of selling whenever the price rose too high.

Gold, on the New York market, had been acting erratically ever since the first of the month. More determined bears joined the movement to depress prices, and sometimes the quotations sank as low as 132. On September 13, however, Gould's conspiracy was given a tremendous boost when his partner Fisk decided to jump in with both feet—and $8,000,-000—which began driving the bears to cover. Fisk joined in wholeheartedly on Gould's fraudulent assurance that all the bigwigs were in on the plot "beginning with President Grant and ending with the doorkeepers in Congress." In addition, Fisk was assured by Corbin that the latter was holding $500,000 of his $2,000,000 margin account for the direct benefit of the President's wife. Later Fisk testified that Mrs. Corbin told him, "I know there will be no gold sold by the government; I am quite positive there will be no gold sold, because this is a chance of a lifetime for us; you need not have any uneasiness whatever." Thus Fisk was made the principal victim of the Corbin-Gould confidence game.

This was the decisive stroke in Gould's maneuvers. With Fisk in, the bear movement in the Gold Room was converted into a tremendously bullish upsurge, his "magnetic and infectious enthusiasm" swaying everyone in listening distance. Fisk went up and down the Street telling his tale—the Presi-

dent and his family were members of the conspiracy, financially interested in it, and gold prices would shoot right up
through the ceiling of the Gold Room. No doubt Gould had
counted heavily on the propaganda effect of Fisk's stentorian
voice rallying the bulls, almost as much as on the millions
his partner threw into the gamble.

Perhaps the most bizarre, almost incredible aspect of the
feverish scene was that the report of the President's corruption could be shouted in the market place, and the only reaction was to shift positions in the Gold Room accordingly.
Everyone, apparently, was prepared to believe it and accept
it, none to protest or question or demand an investigation.
This quick and easy acceptance of the rumors about the involvement of the nation's leading military hero, its honest,
plodding conqueror of the Southern Confederacy, all taken
on the word of a knavish clown, was a true and acute measure
of the deadly cynicism which had infected the nation since
Appomattox. Everyone was feathering his own nest, why not
the President?

Now everyone was joining the gold-buying rush, acquiring
the commodity "on call" in amounts totaling ten times the
amount in circulation. Much of Wall Street, even the more
conservative operators, was drawn into the game. On
Wednesday, September 22, gold shot up to 141 and was still
rising when the market closed.

That evening, when everything appeared to be going
splendidly for Gould, he was summoned to the Corbin house
by an urgent message. Several days before, Gould had persuaded Corbin to send a letter to the President at the Summer
White House in Pennsylvania, again urging him to withhold
the Treasury's gold. Somewhat startled by the urgency of its
tone, the sleepwalking President began coming to his senses,
finally began to suspect that he and his family were being
used. He had learned of Corbin's direct participation in
Gould's speculations, and undoubtedly General Porter, his
secretary, had told him of Gould's abortive attempt to engage

his sympathy, for whatever it was worth, by opening a margin account for half a million. At long last Grant began to realize this drift of affairs could not continue.

At his suggestion Mrs. Grant wrote the famous letter signed "Sis" to her sister-in-law, Mrs. Corbin, warning the Corbins that they must "disengage" themselves from the gold speculation. That Grant had his wife write the letter indicated a realization of how potentially scandalous his family's involvement had become. The letter arrived late Wednesday. A few hours later Gould was reading the fatal sentence:

"Tell Mr. Corbin that the President is very much distressed by your speculations and you must close them as quickly as you can."

Gould knew what that meant. The President would order the Treasury Department to dump gold and break his corner. He was warning his brother-in-law that the gold bubble was about to be punctured and he'd better sell out before he was caught in the crash.

Despite Gould's angry objections, Corbin insisted that his margin account be closed out and that he be paid the $100,000 in accrued profits.

Gould managed to wring one very important concession from Corbin, who promised to keep the letter secret. Otherwise, Gould pointed out, "I am a ruined man." That night and the next day only the Corbins and Gould, in New York, knew of Mrs. Grant's warning. Fisk, fat, dumb, and happy as he rallied the bulls to greater exertions, was not informed. At this point Gould had bought $50,000,000 worth of gold on margin and felt he could not risk a leak; nor would the market stand up under selling orders from both him and his partner. Possibly with regret but without any perceptible twinge of conscience, he decided on that gloomy midnight quietly to abandon the sinking ship and pull away in the only available lifeboat, rather than risk swamping it by rescuing his friend and partner. A long time ago Gould had set his course away from such trivial distractions as friendship and toward the polar attraction of great wealth and power. One could not have it both ways, and he had made his choice.

For the next thirty-six hours Gould walked the razor's edge. One whisper of how matters really stood would have blown his scheme and his fortune in paper profits over the rooftops. He had to pretend to be running with the bulls while actually taking over as the biggest bear in the cage.

That Thursday, September 23, he allowed the bellowing Fisk—"I'll bet anyone $50,000 that gold will go over 145!"— and his equally excited brokers to buy all the gold they could lay hands on—"phantom" gold as Fisk later called it. As for Gould, he later admitted before an investigating committee, "my purchases were very light. I was a seller of gold that day. I purchased merely enough to make believe that I was a bull."

While Fisk rampaged around the densely packed and almost hysterical Gold Room, Gould stayed in his office at the Opera House, tearing newspapers into bits and keeping several messengers running between there and General Butterfield's office in the New York subtreasury. The moment the flash came from Washington ordering Butterfield to start selling government gold he was to advise Gould, who would then unload with a crash. Every minute of that day was important, as it allowed Gould to gradually disentangle himself. Every passing hour he had reason to bless the name of Grant. Unaccountably, except for personal reasons, the President was stalling on his executive order. He must then have been thoroughly aware of what was going on in New York, yet he did not act. The only explanation, it seemed, was that he was giving his sister and brother-in-law a day's grace to "disengage," that his familial sense was stronger than his feelings of responsibility as President. And while Grant delayed, hundreds of less fortunately connected speculators were being ruined, in the sly conviction that the President was with them all the way in this glorious uprising in the Gold Room.

When the market closed that day, gold had risen another three points to 144.

That night Gould decided to tighten the screws on those caught in the artificial shortage by publishing a list of 200 merchants who owed him gold through contracts he had negotiated with his so-called certified checks. Every morning paper would carry their names, along with a demand for immediate payment. His lawyers dissuaded him from this excessive ruthlessness by pointing out that he might be charged with engaging in a criminal conspiracy.

Few Wall Streeters slept that night, least of all Gould, who knew that unless Grant had gone back into hibernation the government would have to start selling gold on the morrow.

Friday, September 24, ever afterward Black Friday, was a clear, golden autumn day. Few, except an occasional carefree vagrant, were allowed to appreciate its perfection. The city and most of the nation were caught in the excitement which emanated like shock waves from the Gold Room. People gathered in tense knots outside the big hotels, in saloons and cafes, outside the newspaper offices with their exclamatory bulletin boards; not even Gettysburg had caused so much excitement. Downtown in the febrile financial district the streets were thronged from curb to curb and traffic came to a standstill. "Business of nearly all kinds became suddenly stagnant," a New York *Herald* reporter observed, "and all classes and professions mingled on the sidewalks." A peddler hawking bull and bear emblems, talismans of what became known as the "Bull Run of the stock market," did a rushing business.

That day both Fisk and Gould set up their command posts in the Heath & Company brokerage on Broad Street, Gould slipping in through a back door, Fisk arriving in an open carriage with two expensively gowned actresses who blew kisses to the crowds. A large force of police, deputy sheriffs, and the Erie palace guard captained by Tommy Lynch was stationed inside and outside of the brokerage, undoubtedly on Gould's orders.

Fisk and his entourage occupied one corner of an office; Gould, manufacturing a blizzard of confetti, sat alone in the other. Fisk loudly kept issuing orders to buy through his three principal brokers, William Belden, his former partner; Henry N. Smith, Gould's partner in the all but abandoned brokerage of Smith, Gould & Martin, and the pathetic little Albert Speyers. "Buy all you can," Fisk told them repeatedly. Meanwhile Gould was whispering to a different set of brokers who came to him for orders, "Do nothing but sell—only don't sell to Fisk's brokers." In the early hours of that day Gould dumped most of his gold at prices ranging from 140 to 144, even while it kept zooming upward.

Meanwhile the Gold Room, an amphitheater built around a fountain in which a bronze cupid and a dolphin frolicked, looked like the snakepit of a lunatic asylum. Newspaper reporters wrote of its "wild commotion," "its fearful pitch of excitement," its capacity crowd of brokers and speculators "yelling, screaming, jostling." The New York National Guard was alerted to quell a possible riot on Wall Street. General Butterfield, who had already joined Gould in the underground movement to sell, wired the Secretary of the Treasury: "Gold is 150. Much feeling and accusations of government complicity." Dapper Dan had finally seen his duty, now that his own profits were in pocket, and did it.

Stocks were crashing, commodities were falling, hundreds of business firms were toppling into bankruptcy, the country was paralyzed commercially from coast to coast, yet the strange drowsiness still prevailed at the Summer White House in Pennsylvania, where President Grant strolled out on the lawn after breakfast and played croquet with General Porter.

At 10 A.M. gold reached 150, an hour later 160, and Jim Fisk was offering to bet anyone $50,000 it would hit 200 before the day was over. One broker went home and shot himself. Albert Speyers, one of Fisk's brokers, was shrieking with excitement. In the Gold Room the brokers and speculators were "heaving in masses against and around the iron railing of the fountain."

Shortly after 11 A.M. the price reached its peak of 164.

Gould meanwhile was quietly shoving gold on the market with all due speed, keeping his own counsel and ignoring the confusion around him. "I had made my own plans," he later told a Congressional investigating committee, with his curious primness, "and did not mean that anybody should say that I had opened my mouth that day, and I did not . . . I did not pay any attention to what orders Fisk gave. I sat in one corner of the room reading. I did not want to seem to be listening to their business." He had washed his hands of the whole affair. If other people wanted to behave like lunatics, it was, after all, "their business." People who were reckless with their money deserved what they got.

At 11:25 A.M. a messenger from General Butterfield at the subtreasury secretly brought him the news he had been waiting for.

Secretary of the Treasury Boutwell, having finally got the word from President Grant, ordered Butterfield to sell $5,-000,000 worth of government gold immediately.

It wasn't until a few minutes before noon that Butterfield announced the news to the Gold Room, and every minute of that time lag was probably worth a hundred thousand to Gould.

The scene at the Gold Room was all but indescribable, and taxed even the purplish prose powers of contemporary journalists. *The Nation,* even after a week's cooling-off time, described the "hundreds of howling, desperate men, maddened out of all calculations by frightful alternations of hope and fear, protracted through fifty-six hours, and all this literally in the presence of an astonished, disgusted and alarmed nation."

Gold dropped from 164 to 160, then within half an hour to 133. The spectacle, one reporter said, could have been reproduced only in Dante's inferno. Albert Speyers, "crazy as a loon" and quite unable to comprehend that the golden bubble had burst, was still howling orders to buy at 160 even after the price had dropped twenty-five points. He ran around the

Gold Room shouting, "I am Albert Speyers. Some persons have threatened to shoot me. Well, here I am! Now shoot, shoot!" Hatless and raving, Speyers was finally led away by his friends.

Now the mob turned from the Gold Room to thoughts of vengeance, and burst into the Heath & Company brokerage bent on tearing Fisk and Gould limb from limb. "Who killed Leupp? Jay Gould!" they chanted. But Fisk and Gould had fled the scene.

They departed with more haste than dignity, according to an eyewitness quoted by Henry Clews in *Fifty Years in Wall Street:*

"Jay Gould came creeping out of the back door and looking sharply around to see if he was watched, slunk off through a private rear passage behind the building. Presently came Fisk, steaming hot and shouting. He took the wrong direction at first, nearly ran into Broad Street, but soon discovered his error and followed Gould through the rear passage. Then came Belden [one of Fisk's brokers], with hair disordered and red eyes, as if he had been crying. . . ."

In a hack with drawn blinds they sped from Broad Street to the Grand Opera House, where the thick marble walls, the police and Tommy Lynch's thugs would protect them.

Gould was so haggard with the strain of the past few days and so frightened by the mobs howling for his life that, Fisk said, there was nothing left of him but "a pair of eyes and a suit of clothes."

And $11,000,000 which he had won in selling gold short the past few days, Fisk might have added.

It was a wonder that Fisk didn't simply choke the life out of his little partner when he learned, later that day presumably, that Gould had double-crossed him and come out a heavy winner. Somehow, though, Gould talked him into believing it was all Grant's and Corbin's fault for cutting the ground out from under them. The two men holed up at the opera house, where they were to remain for days until the dust settled, and figured out how to get Fisk out of the debris. It was Gould, of course, who came up with an outrageous scheme to rescue his partner. Fisk simply repudiated his contracts to buy gold, and Gould had two of the Tweed Ring judges, Barnard and Cardozo, issue injunctions by the dozen restraining anyone from trying to collect.

That night the city was boiling with rumors—Gould had lost $30,000,000, Fisk had just been shot to death by a ruined speculator—and toasts were drunk to these false reports. Fisk, as a matter of fact, had been nominated as the villain of the piece, particularly because of his blithe attitude in the face of general disaster. "A fellow can't have a little innocent fun without everybody raising a hullabaloo and going wild," he told a New York *Sun* reporter. Gould said he "regretted" the panic but disclaimed responsibility. General Butterfield was even more self-righteous, proclaiming, "No one has suffered but the gamblers."

Horace Greeley's *Tribune* was hardly mollified by these remarks and complained there was no more honor among gold speculators than among thieves. "They use lawyers' injunctions to prevent the payment of honest debts; obey the rules of the Gold Exchange when they make by it and repudiate when they lose; betray each other's counsels, sell out their confederates and consent to the ruin of their partners. . . ."

Some days after the crash, when Fisk and Gould finally decided it was safe to be seen on the streets surrounded by bodyguards, Henry N. Smith, Gould's brokerage partner who had been thoroughly duped and ruined as one of Fisk's cat's paws, caught up with Gould and told him:

"I'll live to see the day, sir, when you have to earn your living by going around this street with a hand organ and a monkey."

Gould's dark eyes glittered with amusement, and he replied, "Maybe you will, Henry, maybe you will. And when I want a monkey, Henry, I'll send for you."

His fellow speculators were enraged at Gould because he

violated the code of Wall Street, as Gustavus Myers has explained it: "it was like a group of professional card sharps deterring themselves by no scruples in the cheating of the unwary, but who insisted that among their own kind fairness should be scrupulously observed." From then on, Jay Gould would always be an outsider, an outlaw, a rogue male. His fellows would never forgive him for the $11,000,000 he won from them, without saying a word himself but letting Fisk act as his Judas goat, silently encouraging them to destroy themselves through greed, on Black Friday, September 24, 1869.

The following January a Congressional committee chairmanned by a future President, James A. Garfield of Ohio, began what was officially known as the Gold Panic Investigation. Hundreds of pages of testimony were taken from Fisk, Gould, Corbin, Butterfield and many others prominent, either as members or dupes, in the conspiracy. Three rather important figures, President Grant, his wife and sister, were not called, possibly because as Henry Adams wrote "everyone dreaded to press inquiry," they "feared finding out too much." What they feared, of course, was that Grant would be directly involved. "Everyone in public assured everyone else that the President himself was the savior of the situation," wrote Adams, "and in private assured each other that if the President had not been caught this time, he was sure to be trapped the next, for the ways of Wall Street are dark and double." Despite Adams' dark forebodings,[6] however, the investigation actually tended to clear the President and his wife, if not the Corbins.

Gould's testimony, predictably evasive, was interesting in particular when he asserted that it was his short sales, not the

[6] Which undoubtedly were increased by the difficulty he experienced in having his articles on the gold panic published in England. Adams claimed the Edinburgh *Review* refused to publish them "for fear of Jay Gould and Jim Fisk." They were eventually published by the Westminster *Review*, a less conservative periodical.

Treasury order unfreezing gold, which caused the market to break on Black Friday.

Q. "You said a little while ago that an hour before the order came from Washington to sell gold you felt that you almost knew of the order. Tell us how."

A. "A man who is liable to rapid thinking very often arrives at conclusions without being able to tell the process, and yet he is satisfied the conclusions are correct."

Q. "Tell us, as far as it is possible for words to describe, how you knew, or almost knew, this fact an hour beforehand."

A. "I hear of a great deal that happens. I can only say that it is one of those conclusions that a man sometimes arrives at intuitively, that are correct in themselves, and yet, if you undertake to give the evidence by which they are reached, you could not tell how it was done."

That was a fair sample of his nimble skipping around a point, in this case to conceal the fact that General Butterfield had tipped him off to the Treasury order before the news was disclosed at the Gold Room. Butterfield himself had to admit making $35,000 on one transaction and much more on others, when he was called to testify. His resignation as Assistant Treasurer was hastily offered and hastily accepted.

Henry Adams believed that the testimony showed that Grant was guilty of "incredible and inexplicable lapses of intelligence," comparable to similarly mysterious trances which marked his military campaigns, but nothing more suggestive of criminal culpability could be adduced from the evidence on the record.

Jim Fisk made a lively if somewhat unreliable witness who exhibited a strong animosity and contempt for the "tottling" and prevaricating Corbins. He claimed that "Corbin was paid twenty-five thousand dollars for Mrs. Grant in a check." Bank records were introduced to show, however, that Corbin, tricky to the bitter end, had cashed this check himself and used it to pay off a bank loan.

No one was quite satisfied with Fisk's blithely philosophic statement that everyone had to carry out his own corpse when the murderous game was done; there was a general feeling that the investigation had somehow managed to conceal more than it revealed. If the muddy tracks of the conspirators were traced to the White House door but no farther, the President's warmest admirers could not deny that he had been unbelievably torpid, reluctant to act even after he knew what was happening, more determined to succor his kinsmen than to halt the boldest raid yet conceived on the American economy.

As for all the money lost and won that hectic week in September, the investigators had to be satisfied with Fisk's comical assurance that it had "gone where the woodbine twineth."

6. "ALL THE SINS OF ERIE LIE BURIED HERE"

CASTLE ERIE, as the newspapers called the Grand Opera House which Fisk and Gould had made their headquarters, vibrated with excitement night and day. A constant state of siege prevailed, and there were times when a moat and drawbridge would have been most desirable from the viewpoint of its defenders. Flying wedges of process servers, representing stockholders trying to recapture control of the railroad and persons injured in Erie's frequent wrecks, would batter at its twelve-foot gates. Cranks, with or without homemade bombs, and beggars and various persons with real or imaginary grievances were always trying to find a hole in the defenses set up by Tommy Lynch and his Hell's Kitchen boys. Robert Hall, a resident of the formerly dignified Chelsea neighborhood, wrote of "stirring scenes, days of injunctions, mandamuses, seizures with court orders and without them, and battles in the hallways between sheriff's deputies and Fisk's and Gould's henchmen, which gave special interest to the daily papers and were followed by the readers as they did the war news. Every morning the public looked first at the Erie headlines to see what the opposing armies had accomplished the day and night before. . . ."

Jay Gould and Jim Fisk had become the nation's two most famous financiers in a time when the world of finance—cruder, livelier and less inhibited than it is today—was as fascinating to people as spectator sports would be to a later generation. Not even the worst that the newspapers and the moralists could say about them divested them of a scintilla of their glamour. Fisk, spending money like one of the later Roman emperors, was particularly fascinating to his contemporaries, whose appetites were similarly lusty and unrefined. For these men, said Henry Adams, "work, whiskey and cards were life." Jim Fisk, with his sleek carriage horses and his voluptuous Josie Mansfield, was living the kind of fleshly idyll other men could only dream about. To the observant Adams, disapproving though he was of Fisk's profligacy, it seemed that Gould was getting far less out of his trickily acquired millions than his fun-loving partner. "The amusement of the pursuit was all the amusement he got from it; he had no use for wealth. Jim Fisk alone seemed to know what he wanted; Jay Gould never did."

Calm and bland as he appeared on the surface, Gould was inwardly a worrier, a man who could not drown his fear of consequences in the pursuit of pleasure as Fisk did. The turmoil around Castle Erie, much as he strived to ignore it, troubled him. Nor could he shrug off the newspaper attacks as casually as Fisk—the reasoned and dispassionate condemnations of *The Nation* and Greeley's *Tribune*, the hard-hitting editorial campaign of Samuel Bowles' much respected Springfield *Republican*, the pre-tabloid sensationalism of James Gordon Bennett's *Herald*, all of which concerned him sufficiently so that in a few years he would be buying his own newspaper propaganda.

Although he publicly dismissed them as the inevitable hazards of railroading, the "bloody catalogue of disasters" as the New York *Herald* called them, the series of wrecks and derailments on the Erie gave him many sleepless nights. The public could swallow the deliberate mismanagement of Erie's finances but the mounting casualty list caused by ancient equipment and lack of maintenance was another matter. In July of 1869 a passenger express and a freight train collided, killing nine and injuring ten, and in the following March, near Elmira, three cars of a passenger train were derailed, badly injuring fourteen. In between there were almost daily mishaps of a lesser order, most of them preventable had Erie's directors been willing to spend money on better signal equipment, new engines, and replacement of the old iron rails with steel.

But Erie's treasury could not be opened for such trivial purposes as safeguarding its employes and its passengers. Its cash reserves were being used to finance Fisk's ambitions as impresario, and for various operations designed to engorge smaller railroads which could be added to Erie's system.

In these gambling forays, Gould, Fisk, and other Erie insiders, particularly Boss Tweed and his select followers, stood only to gain. If they won, the profits went into their own pockets. If they lost, the stakes being put up by the Erie treasury, the deficit was borne by the railroad's stockholders.

And even Gould and Fisk could lose occasionally. They lost $359,000 in a raid on the Reading Railroad which didn't come off but which was charged to Erie. Hundreds of thousands were also lost in the abortive struggle to seize control of the Albany & Susquehanna, a broad gauge line that ran from Albany to a junction with the Erie at Binghamton, the acquisition of which would have offered serious competition to the New York Central for east–west through freight. This effort was directed by Fisk, with the assistance of two of Erie's otherwise respectable lawyers, David Dudley Field (the brother of Cyrus Field, builder of the Atlantic cable) and Thomas G. Shearman. An attempt was made to have the Albany & Susquehanna thrown into receivership, and thence into Erie's clutches, but the move was thwarted by upstate courts beyond the influence of the Tweed Ring. Joseph H. Ramsey, a stubborn Scot who had spent eighteen years building up the prosperous little feeder line, had no intention of letting it be swallowed up by Erie. His opponents were able to round up only a fifth of the Albany & Susquehanna's 30,000 shares of stock.

Balked in trying to snatch the road by legal and financial means, Fisk and his lieutenants turned to more forceful methods. A small-scale war broke out along the Albany road's right of way, with each side deploying several hundred employes. In a battle over a tunnel, two locomotives charged each other and crashed, and the Erie forces were driven from the field. The war ended when Ramsey leased his line to the Delaware and Hudson Canal Company in perpetuity. Not a whit downcast, Fisk wrote off the venture with a wisecrack, "Nothing is lost save honor."

Another drain on the Erie treasury was the so-called India Rubber Account, through which bribe money was siphoned under the heading of "legal expenses." Boss Tweed, who was a member of the new Erie executive committee along with Fisk, Gould and a lawyer named Frederick Lane, tapped this fund for $650,000 during a three-month period, as he later admitted.

So long as the printing presses were allowed to grind out new stock issues in the basement of the Grand Opera House, however, Treasurer Gould would never find his cupboard bare. During the fifteen months after Gould and Fisk seized control, more than $53,000,000 worth of watered stock was thrown on the market. Little more than a tenth of this was used for improving the road, and no dividends were issued. Wall Streeters predicted hell would be converted into a skat-

ing rink the day Erie issued a dividend. Stockholders who
tried to protest this state of affairs ran into legal roadblocks
in the guise of Tweed Ring judges. One brave fellow who instituted suit to force an accounting from President-Treasurer
Gould not only was restrained from pursuing this course of
action by injunction but was fined $5000 for contempt of
court by Judge Barnard when he persisted.

Perhaps the greatest worry of Erie's insomniac president-
treasurer during the last two years of their association was
Jim Fisk's recklessly complicated personal affairs. In girth,
ego and enterprise, Fisk was expanding in all directions; he
had become a gaudy captive balloon rising higher and higher
over the metropolis, with only his absentee wife and Jay
Gould providing a more and more tenuous mooring to the
earth. He had established himself at a somewhat saturnalian
summer resort at Long Branch, New Jersey, which was attracting the more raffish millionaires. Not content with being
the impresario of the Grand Opera House and admiral of the
Fall River Line, he was purchasing command of a militia
regiment.

Gould woke up every morning wondering what costly gesture his managing director had made overnight.

His deepest concern, however, was Fisk's involvement with
the greedy and capricious Josie Mansfield. Fisk had supplied
his mistress with a four-story residence near the Grand Opera
House, three servants, a carriage and coachman, a private box
at the opera, a collection of Paris gowns, diamonds and other
jewelry, $65,000 worth of furnishings, silverware and other
adornments, but Josie still wasn't satisfied.

Gratitude was not one of Miss Mansfield's weaknesses. Her
protector had discovered her in Annie Woods' high-class
house of assignation with little more than the clothes on her
back. The daughter of a California newspaperman, Josie had
married an actor named Frank Lawlor in her teens and
drifted east with him. A year or two before she wound up in

Annie Woods' establishment, Lawlor said later, the actor learned that "she was going astray" and they separated. Her claim to being an actress was substantiated by only a few walk-ons while she was Lawlor's wife. She was a born courtesan, lazy, demanding, charming when it suited her purpose, with an abundance of sexual attraction in a day when men fancied a well-fleshed woman. "Imagine," suggested a somewhat smitten *Herald* reporter to his readers, "a woman young and vivid, with full, dashing figure, yet not gross, with deep, large, almond-shaped black eyes, luxuriant purple-black hair worn in massive coils, tempting mouth, lips not too pronounced and yet not insipid, magnificent teeth, clear pearl and pink complexion, oval face and nose not *retroussé* and yet not straight, with a quiet ladylike walk and action, sweet soft voice and winning smile. Dress such a woman in a dark silk, flounced with deep Valenciennes, a flowing silk jacket beautifully embroidered with white braid, and a plain gold cross to set off the exquisite contour of her neck, and a dark green Tyrolese hat falling partly over her fair forehead, surmounted by a waving ostrich feather, and you have this Helen Josephine Mansfield. . . ." She claimed to be twenty-four but was close to thirty. Fisk's pet name for her was "Dumpling," and she called him "Lumpsum," which may have been a Freudian slip, considering the demands she was to make on him.

In the fall of 1870 Dumpling and Lumpsum had a falling out over two matters of paramount importance to each: money and sex. Josie was demanding a $25,000 cash settlement from Fisk even while confessing, or boasting, that she had fallen in love with a friend of his named Edward S. Stokes, a handsome man-about-town of her own age, and this was too much for even Fisk's indulgent nature to bear.

He had introduced Stokes, the dashing heir to a Philadelphia fortune, to Josie; not only that but he had helped Stokes financially. The bright-eyed and curly-haired Stokes, who was married but not working at it, had lost much of his inheritance on the horses. About all he had left was a Brooklyn oil refinery,

which would have gone bankrupt had Fisk not given it preferred rates on its shipments over Erie as well as buying Erie's
oil from it.

When he learned that Stokes had captured Josie's affec-
tions, to put it politely, Fisk was thrown into a emotional uproar. He was still in love with Josie, although her demands
for money had grown irksome. Furthermore he could not bear
the thought of the whole town laughing at his discomfiture.
For a time he openly discussed the possibility of hiring a
Lower East Side thug to shoot Stokes. One immediate step
he took was to cancel Erie's agreement with Stokes' refinery,
thereupon ruining his business. Meanwhile he was warning
Josie against her new lover and advising her to "cling to him;
be careful what you do for he will be watchful. How well he
knows you cheated me. He will look for the same." Boss
Tweed and Judge Barnard both tried to reconcile the differences between Fisk, Josie and Stokes, but without success.

About all that Jubilee Jim had to jubilate about then was
his newest acquisition, the Ninth New York National Guard
Regiment.

The militia regiment, commanded by Colonel Charles H.
Braine, had fallen on evil times. Its uniforms were tattered,
its funds were depleted, and its muster roll was at half
strength. The Ninth New York, in effect, was up for sale;
without transfusions of men and money it would have to be
disbanded. The beat of martial drums, to which Fisk had been
deaf during wartime, when a man could get killed playing
soldier, now sounded loud and clear. Therefore an arrangement was made whereby Braine would demote himself to
second in command and Fisk would be elected colonel, in return for enough cash to rehabilitate the regiment. The "Mush-
room Mars," as Bennett's unfriendly New York *Herald* called
him, was duly elevated to command and "declared that there
was a tide in the affairs of the militia which taken at the flood
leads on to glory." From then on, the Ninth New York flourished, what with prizes offered for obtaining new recruits,

more than a hundred Erie employes enrolled, new uniforms and band instruments issued, grand balls and champagne bouts arranged for officers and men alike. Rarely has a colonel acquired so much popularity without fighting a battle. Fisk might have gone on glorying in his gold lace, red epaulets, white kid gloves and gilt sword, except that the worst of fates befell the gorgeous commander and his spoiled regiment—it was called upon to do battle, the last thing it was trained for.

A small civil war had broken out in the streets of New York. On July 12, 1871, the aniversary of the Battle of the Boyne, the Orangemen held their annual parade despite threats by Irishmen of the opposite persuasion, dedicated to overthrowing the British rule in Ireland, to drive them off the streets. The authorities called out five regiments of the National Guard, along with all available police, to protect the Orangemen. Surrounded by militia and police, 160 Orangemen marched down Eighth Avenue until they reached Twenty-fourth Street, where they were showered with bricks from the tenement roofs. The militia, including Colonel Fisk's Ninth New York, began firing into the crowds. Gunfire broke out on all sides, and before the street battle was over fifty-one persons had been killed and 105 wounded.

All his millions, in that horrendous moment, could not buy glory, or even safety, for Colonel Jim Fisk. Only a few feet away Henry C. Page, house manager of the Grand Opera House, was shot through the head. Two other men of the Ninth were also mortally wounded. As soon as he realized that even a rich colonel could get himself killed in this kind of brawling, Fisk threw away his sword and fled from the field, "a bruised and weary pacifist," as one journalist noted. Without pausing even to formally hand over command—it was no longer a time for the delightful formalities of military life—Fisk conducted his one-man retreat. He vaulted over back yard fences until he reached the comparatively peaceful Ninth Avenue. Just at that moment, purely by accident, Jay Gould came along in a carriage. He saw a fat, disheveled, grimy-faced fellow waving frantically at him from the curb, and told his coachman to whip up the horses. Then he recognized Fisk and took him aboard. By nightfall Colonel Fisk had reached his rearmost headquarters in Long Branch, New Jersey. He immediately issued a statement to the newspapers that his ankle had been painfully injured in the riot, which had caused him to withdraw rather than distress his troops with the sight of his wound. Undeceived, the New York *Times* commented that he had run away "in a manner surpassed by few soldiers of any age," and the *Herald* jeered, "Pif! Paf! Pouf! Colonel Fisk led the forlorn hope yesterday and, like General Boum, won his panache."

Next day, with a massive bandage wrapped around his ankle, Fisk held a conference with his senior officers, resulting in a squib published in the New York newspapers reading, "Lt. Col. Braine takes occasion to assert Col. Fisk did his full duty, and there is no dissatisfaction in the regiment with the colonel."

Disbelieving laughter greeted this assertion, and the *Times* proclaimed him "first in peace and first in the pockets of his countrymen."

One of his earlier biographers[1] quoted him as telling his friends with a rueful frankness, "I don't believe I was cut out for the military life. I ain't built for it, for one thing, because I can't run fast enough; and I haven't got the heart for it, for another. We ought to leave all our home fighting to the Irish . . . the more of each other they can kill off, the better they feel about it."

In the public mind, so indulgent until now, he was convicted of excessive nimbleness even for a peacetime militia colonel who bought his regiment. People could laugh at his antics as a lover, financier and impresario, but cowardice was another matter. Nor were they amused when, pleading that his injured ankle demanded that he continue to bask in the

---

[1] Robert H. Fuller's *Jubilee Jim*.

sea air of Long Branch, he absented himself from the funeral for the three men of the Ninth who were killed in the riot.

Even less entertained by all this was Jay Gould, to whom his partner's disgrace was almost the last straw. In October, the reform element finally made its move against Boss Tweed, causing his arrest on charges of fraud. Gould put up most of his $1,000,000 bail. Just as Erie's political protection was crumbling, the railroad's restive stockholders began protesting with new energy against the Gould-Fisk management and the means by which they elected themselves recently to five-year terms on the board of directors.

Fisk was so busy defending himself against the extortionate claims of Josie Mansfield that he neglected to join Gould on this new battlefront, which threatened to drive them both away from Erie's spoils. Now that Stokes was broke, Josie saw that the only way to support herself and her lover was to threaten publication of Fisk's love letters if he didn't pay the "lump sum" she had been demanding. No craven when it came to defending his own pride and wealth, Fisk publicly charged the pair with attempted blackmail. They countered with a libel suit. All of this made splendid copy for the newspapers and miserable reading for Jay Gould.

On the last day of 1871, while Gould nervously tore up strips of newspaper and Fisk blinked away the tears, the two men decided that to "prevent utter annihilation" Fisk should resign from Erie.

A week later, on January 6, 1872, Josie's libel suit against Fisk came up for a hearing in the Yorkville Police Court, at which Fisk's lawyer cut the young woman to pieces under cross-examination. Stokes, his rage mounting, heard himself described as a kept man who had been living off the money his mistress wheedled from his predecessor. Shortly after court adjourned, Stokes, while lunching at Delmonico's, heard a report that he and Josie had been indicted for blackmail on Fisk's charges. (The bearer of the evil tidings was that veteran troublemaker, Judge Barnard, according to Fisk's latest and best biographer, W. A. Swanberg, in *Jim Fisk: The Career of an Improbable Rascal.*)

Shortly after that Stokes headed for his room at the Hoffman House, armed himself with a handy little four-shot Colt and went over to Josie Mansfield's house. What they said to each other in that last private meeting was never revealed, but Stokes left her place with murder on his mind.

About 4 P.M. Fisk, wrapped in his scarlet-lined cloak, gold-headed cane in hand, silk hat on head, arrived at the Grand Central Hotel on Broadway. Some friends of his wife Lucy, who still lived uncomplainingly in Boston, were visiting the city, and Fisk had promised to call on them.

Waiting for him at the top of the staircase was Ned Stokes, still raging that it was his reputation, not Fisk's, which was being damaged in the courts. He fired twice, his aim was good, and both shots found their mark. Round as a barrel, Fisk rolled back down the stairs with bullets in his right arm and belly. Stokes took to his heels.

Too seriously wounded to be removed to a hospital, Fisk was taken to a room upstairs. Seven doctors were summoned to his bedside and decided, after consultation, to probe for the bullet in the victim's abdomen. The probe, delving into so many layers of fat, was unsuccessful. Jubilee Jim would die, the doctors announced, and his friends were summoned for the usual deathbed drama, relieved only by the last flickers of Fisk's durable sense of humor. As Gould, Tweed and his cronies gathered around, Fisk told them he felt just as he had as a schoolboy after gorging himself on stolen green apples.

By that time Stokes had been captured, and Josie was telling reporters that she knew nothing of the shooting and insisting that "I have only my reputation to maintain."

While Fisk cracked jokes with his friends, Gould was observed in a corner of the outer room of the suite with his head buried in his hands and weeping with "deep, audible sobs."

The newspapers recorded that there was more excitement

Jay Gould, a young man of Manhattan, shortly before his marriage.

Jubilee Jim. Fisk at the time he
entered into partnership with Gould.

Colonel of the Ninth. Fisk, in the
uniform of his purchased regiment,
the mustachios courtesy of the
second Napoleon.

Edward S. Stokes, who ended
the Fisk jubilee with a gunshot.

A prayerful scoundrel, Daniel
Drew, not long before
Gould took that frock coat
off his back.

Russell Sage, financial wizard and involuntary philanthropist, with his favorite reading matter in hand.

Mrs. Russell Sage, mother pro-tem to the Gould orphans, who made a career out of giving her husband's
money away.

The Commodore, old Cornelius Vanderbilt, who finally had to concede that Gould was "the smartest man in America."

Cyrus Field, before a Gould squeeze play all but dispossessed him.

Jay Gould in his middle years, the
magnetism of his eyes undimmed.
He was rich enough now to
dispense with the cravat.

The house of Gould, at 47th Street and Fifth Avenue, in
front of which he paced away the night hours of his last years.

George Jay Gould, eldest son and chief heir, who believed a man could play polo and hang onto the family fortune without missing a stroke.

Helen Gould, perhaps the favorite child, busy, as usual, with good works.

Helen Gould with Finley Shepard, whom she married in middle age.

Edwin Gould, second son, an earnest young man, shortly before his father's death.

Howard Gould, third son, uniform either as a yachtsman or conduc on the Missouri Pacific.

in the city that night, while Fisk lay dying, than any since President Lincoln was assassinated. Stokes paced the night away in his cell in the Tombs, occasionally inquiring of the guards whether his victim was still alive. Josie Mansfield stayed home and worried about her reputation.[2]

Shortly after dawn Lucy Fisk arrived at her husband's bedside from Boston. A few hours before he died, Fisk asked her forgiveness for all the humiliation he had caused her. "He was such a good boy," she told the doctors when the life went out of him. Gould's epitaph was almost an echo of Lucy Fisk's. "An excess of youthful spirits," he told reporters, was responsible for Jim's heroic dissipations. Since the break with Josie Mansfield, Gould added, Fisk had reformed and "was in every sense becoming what all who loved him desired he should be."

Faithless though he was in other matters, Gould behaved honorably toward his partner's widow. The Fisk estate, riddled by lawsuits, was not sufficient to carry her through a long widowhood. Gould, she wrote long afterward, "was the only friend of Mr. Fisk who has responded to my actual needs and wants."

A lot of the joy of buccaneering went out of Gould's business life the day Jim Fisk died. Fisk was the only one who would ever be able to appreciate his tricky dealings with a connoisseur's relish even when he was victimized by them. As an artist in trickery, Gould had lost his most perceptive critic and best audience.

But he could not afford any prolonged period of mourning, for his enemies, particularly the long-swindled stockholders of Erie, were closing in for the kill. He may have hoped that the disappearance of Fisk from the Erie directorate would ap-

[2] Stokes, after several trials, was convicted of manslaughter and served four years in Sing Sing. He was operating a restaurant when he died in 1901. Josie Mansfield married a wealthy lawyer, who died in an insane asylum. Through some mysterious source of funds, she lived very comfortably in Paris, a prominent figure in expatriate society, until her death in 1931, when she was about ninety years old.

pease them but actually it had the opposite effect. General
S. L. M. Barlow, soon to be elected an Erie director, noted
that "the feeling against Gould grew in great part since Fisk's
death," because "Fisk was always popular with the people of
the road" and even many of the bilked stockholders. Gould
was now deprived of his best public relations asset.

If he was covertly propagandizing the stockholders that
everything would be all right now that Fisk was gone, as the
newspapers strongly hinted, the maneuver was far from successful. Thomas Nast, the celebrated cartoonist whose shafts
helped bring down the Tweed Ring, published a drawing in
the *Times* which brilliantly mocked this pretension. It was
titled "Dead Men Tell No Tales" and showed Gould and his
fellow looters hypocritically mourning at Fisk's grave, with
Justice on guard nearby. The caption read:

Jay Gould: "All the sins of Erie lie buried here."
Justice: "I am not quite so blind."

Introducing retired generals and military heroes to lend
tone and sanctity to business enterprises was first conceived
in the years following the Civil War, when these qualities
were much needed. A man who had charged up Malvern Hill
was somehow reckoned, often mistakenly, to be the soul of integrity and the guarantor of straight dealing. Thus the list of
those who nominally spearheaded the attack on Gould's control of Erie read like the top echelon of an Order of Battle.

Two months after Fisk's death the anti-Gould forces struck
their heaviest blow. The English stockholders had engaged
General Daniel E. Sickles, one of the noisier claimants to
Gettysburg fame and U.S. Minister to Spain, to come over
and take charge of the effort to depose Gould. On the night of
March 11, 1872, Sickles and his followers invaded the Grand
Opera House and proceeded to elect a new board of directors.
In another room Gould and his cohorts had also congregated.
Forty police had been summoned to oust the Sickles invasion,

but the generals and their friends refused to leave and the cops somehow could not imagine themselves giving the bum's rush to ex-division commanders of the Union Army. As the New York *World* described the scene the next morning, "The doors of both rooms were barred, opening to no one but an avowed friend, each fearful of orders of arrest being served upon them, every spare room in the offices filled with blue-coated officers of the peace, sitting in all the chairs and on the tables, and lying on the floors, and an intense sense of subdued excitement pervading the heavy air of the place."

Among those elected to the new board were General George B. McClellan, former commander of the Army of the Potomac; General John A. Dix, who had served briefly as president of the Union Pacific before the war; General Barlow, General A. S. Diven, Colonel Henry G. Stebbins, and several civilians.

Three days later Sickles went to Gould and suggested that he resign, slyly adding, "If you do, Erie will go up fifteen points. You can make a million dollars."

Gould agreed to resign the presidency in place of General Dix, and also took Sickles' hint, if he needed it, concerning the prospective rise in Erie stock. Sickles, as a matter of fact, underestimated the enthusiasm of speculators on hearing that Gould had quit Erie. The stock went up twenty points, and Gould profited accordingly; by close to a million, the newspapers estimated.

As the *Herald* described the Erie upsurge, "Wall Street yesterday was filled with the ghosts of the ill-omened Black Friday and the resuscitated corpses of 1857. Men whom it was deemed had vanished forever arose again at this last trumpet of wild speculation." There were similar rejoicings overseas, the *Herald* added, and "never has the Atlantic cable been worked as it has been for the last three days in the interest of Erie."

Even with the chief sinner departed, the sins of Erie still were not buried. Without the millions which Gould had abstracted from the treasury, Erie would be crippled for many years; the company was dropsical with $64,000,000 in watered stock issued during Gould's presidency, and the road would have to be provided with new tracks and equipment as quickly as possible. Somehow Gould had to be made to disgorge.

During the next six months an intensive effort was launched by Dix, Barlow and the other new officers of Erie to recover the loot. Gould's evasive tactics were masterful. It was like trying to trap an eel with bare hands, as his new adversaries soon learned.

They thought they had him trapped in November, thanks to the vengeful action of one of his ex-partners. After withdrawing from Erie's administration, Gould had conducted another foray on Wall Street, having learned that Henry N. Smith, his former brokerage partner who had predicted Gould would end his days as an organ grinder, and Daniel Drew, who was making a last sortie in the market, had combined in a short-selling raid on Chicago & Northwestern Railroad stock. Gould had all the money he would ever need to battle the likes of Smith and Drew. They had driven the stock down to 75. Shortly after Gould entered the market and cornered the stock, it shot up to 250, and Smith and Drew were caught short.

By way of revenge, Smith brought the books of the Smith, Gould & Martin brokerage to General Barlow of the Erie board. They showed, among other reprehensible things, that Gould had transferred at least $3,000,000 from Erie's treasury to his own account and that he had charged off the $359,000 loss on his Reading Railroad gamble to Erie.

Finally possessing proof of Gould's defalcations, Erie's new officers proceeded to have him arrested on charges of embezzlement and instituted a civil action for recovery of $9,726,541.

Freed on $1,000,000 bail, Gould told reporters that "the matter is very simple. Drew, Smith and the rest of them were short of stock, and as a desperate resort they watched their time and arranged matters so as to have me arrested just at the moment they expected to be able to create a panic in the Street."

Nevertheless, through intermediaries, he began negotiating secretly with the new regime at Erie. The generals were so elated at having trapped their fox, or so they thought, that they agreed to drop the criminal charges and the civil suit against him in exchange for a parcel of real estate and securities which Gould solemnly assured them was worth $6,-000,000. Gould, they exulted, had finally been punished for his transgressions. But the celebrations on West Street, where Erie had returned to its shabby old offices a short time before from the Byzantine-Barnum splendors of the Grand Opera House, turned out to be most premature. Accountants engaged in 1874 by a London stockholders' committee discovered that the actual worth of the parcel Gould had handed over was approximately $200,000.

Sixty-nine years would pass before Erie recovered sufficiently from the Gould-Fisk management of less than six years to pay its stockholders a dividend.

How much did Gould take out of Erie? Only bits and pieces of the truth ever emerged from the tangle of double entry bookkeeping which covered his tracks.

The only authoritative indication came in the testimony of Augustus Stein, an expert accountant, before the Hepburn Investigating Committee of the New York Assembly.

Q. "Do you think that you could remember the aggregate amount of wrongdoing on the part of Mr. Gould that you have discovered?"

A. "I could give you an estimate throwing off a couple of millions here and there; I could say that it amounted to—that is, what we discovered—amounted to about twelve or thirteen million dollars."

By the most conservative accounting, therefore, it was apparent that between 1866 and 1872, in the gold market speculations and through the drainpipe to the Erie treasury, Gould must have enriched himself by at least twenty-two million and possibly much more. He was only thirty-six years old. For a man of his years, his millions and his proclivities, it was only natural to turn an imperial eye westward.

7. PART OWNER OF THE WEST

IN THE next decade, undeterred by Indian wars, civil insurrection, prairie fires and mountain landslides, and the ruthless competition of the most powerful men in America, Jay Gould was to join wholeheartedly in the exploitation of the West. A great cornucopia of land, minerals, timber, grain, and cattle was spilling forth its bounty, wealth never before conceived in history, and Gould meant to have his share.

The West had engaged his imagination for many years. His sister recalled that as a boy he dreamed of building a railroad to the Pacific "so that California would be closer to us." The boyish vision had changed to something less idealistic but its substance was intact. He would let other men do the building and he was no longer concerned with geographically embracing California; the railroads and the great strips of land granted to them by an indulgent government, however, would be his without the risk and effort of extending them through the trans-Mississippi wilderness, or the fleeting glory of driving golden spikes when they were joined.

Already the possessor of two fortunes acquired through speculation, thievery and thimblerigging, he now moved confidently toward his third. The pattern of conquest was already well defined. He used the arts of publicity and promotion, the twisted genius for corporate accounting, the gambler's facility for bluffing and outmaneuvering his opponents, the confidence man's trick of leverage by which other men's weaknesses became his strengths, and the master financier's device of gambling with other people's money.

As Alexander D. Noyes, the leading financial historian of the nineteenth century, analyzed Gould's operations in western railroading, he "mastered more completely than any other promoter in our history the art of buying worthless railways for a song, selling them at fancy figures to a solvent corporation under his own control, and then so straining the credit and manipulating the books of the amalgamated company as to secure his own safe retreat through the stock market. He was not a builder, he was a destroyer, and the truth of this statement may be easily demonstrated by tracing out the subsequent history of the corporations which he got into his clutches. That Gould had a genius for making combinations is unquestionable; but in almost every instance . . . he obtained this power by tempting other men to join him in a speculation for personal profit acquired through methods which sapped the financial resources of the properties concerned."[1]

Latter-day historians have not been quite so severe, possibly because of the gentling influence of time, possibly also because a clearer view of nineteenth century finance has convinced them that Gould's contemporaries were quite as wicked as he was, but less talented and more sanctimonious. "Again and again," wrote Gustavus Myers in *History of the Great American Fortunes,* "Gould was charged with being a wrecker of property; a financial beachcomber who destroyed that he might profit. These accusations, in the particular exclusive sense in which they were meant, were distortions. In almost every instance the railroads gathered in by Gould

[1] *Forty Years of American Finance,* published in 1898.

were wrecked before he secured control; all that he did was
to revive, continue and elaborate the process of wrecking."

Gould's own attitude toward his motives and accomplish-
ments in this field was almost beguiling in its simplicity.
"I went into it to make money," he told the Pacific Railway
Commission in 1887.

Gould's first tentative moves toward expanding westward
had begun in 1869 while he was still in control of Erie. With
the aim of extending Erie's operations to the Mississippi, he
acquired a large block of stock in the Wabash Railroad,
which handled much of the freight between Chicago and St.
Louis and Kansas City, and tried to link it up with the Lake
Shore line between Buffalo, the Great Lakes and Chicago.
Vanderbilt thwarted this attempt at consolidation by gaining
control of the Lake Shore, but Gould retained his interest in
the Wabash, later gained control of the road and made it the
principal segment of his system east of the Mississippi, carrying the produce of the rich farmlands of Illinois, Indiana and
Missouri.

After his graduated retreat from Erie, Gould's next west-
ering trend attracted him to the possibilities of the Pacific
Mail Steamship Company, which had suffered almost as much
as Erie from scandal and corruption. Originally founded to
carry mail and freight to California via the Isthmus of Panama, the company early in its history had been boarded by
financial pirates, including Commodore Vanderbilt, and had
wasted much of its substance in bribes offered and accepted
for government subsidies. More recently its business had been
decimated by the competition of the first transcontinental
railroads. Late in 1872 its stock was being manipulated by
the Wall Street speculators, and rose to 103 on the exchange.
A bear raid drove it 'way down, upon which Gould bought in
heavily and engineered his election to the board of directors
along with that of Russell Sage, with whom he began a long
and lucrative collaboration, as remarkable for its lack of

treachery and double-crossing as it was for its financial success.

Shrewdly capitalizing on Pacific Mail's fluctuations, Gould and Sage were credited with having realized almost $5,-000,000 in the next year or two. The violent jockeying of its stock, along with huge stock issues floated on behalf of the Northern Pacific and other western railroads, brought on warnings early in the fall of 1873 that a panic was in the making. On September 1, 1873, the New York *World* sternly pointed to Gould as the "money king" whose conscienceless maneuvers would bring on a market crash.

"There is one man in Wall Street today whom men watch, and whose name, built upon ruins, carries with it a certain whisper of ruin," the newspaper said, referring to Gould. "He is the last of the race of kings . . . one whose nature is best described by the record of what he has done, and by the burden of hatred and dread that, loaded upon him for two and one-half years, has not turned him one hair from any place that promised him gain and the most bitter ruin for his chance opponents. They that curse him do not do it blindly, but as cursing one who massacres after victory."

Little wonder that when Gould got around to becoming a newspaper proprietor he selected the New York *World,* and stopped up its scolding voice by stuffing money down its throat.

One of those chance opponents ruined by his machinations was "Commodore" A. B. Stockwell, former president of Pacific Mail, whose naval rank was almost as spurious as the elder Vanderbilt's. Risen from clerking on a Mississippi River steamer, the red-haired Stockwell had married one of the heiresses to the Elias Howe sewing-machine fortune and used his wife's money to buy the presidency of Pacific Mail. When Gould and his fellow raiders got through with him, about all that Stockwell had left was his sense of humor.

Stockwell's description of his rise and fall became a Wall Street classic. "When I came to New York and bought stock by the hundred shares, they called me Stockwell. Then I began buying in larger amounts and they called me Mr. Stockwell. By the time I was trading in thousand-share lots, I was known as Captain Stockwell. They promoted me to Commodore Stockwell when word got around that I had gained control of Pacific Mail. But when Jay Gould got after me and booted me out of the concern all they called me was 'that redheaded son-of-a-bitch from the West.'"

The wild seesawing of the stock market, induced by the activities of Gould and other traders, brought on the panic of late September, which saw the great Philadelphia banking house of Jay Cooke & Company and many lesser financial establishments close their doors. One of the most severe depressions ever suffered by the United States followed, with thousands of bankruptcies, mass unemployment, and great privation among the working classes. It was the inevitable end of the postwar boom, the hangover following a national binge of a dozen years' duration. Midwinter, wrote a contemporary labor historian, "found tens of thousands of people on the verge of starvation, suffering for food, for the need of proper clothing, and for medical attendance." The same writer described a protest meeting of New York City's unemployed at which the authorities allowed Tompkins Square to fill up with men, women and children, then loosed the mounted police "charging upon them without provocation. Screams of women and children rent the air, and the blood of many stained the streets. . . ." On the western frontier, as well as in the eastern cities, the suffering was intense. Thousands of people, most of them innocents lured by the extravagant promises of the railroad builders, had streamed west across the Mississippi and were trying to survive the winter in sod-walled houses on the blizzard-swept plains of Kansas and Nebraska after plagues of grasshoppers and army worms had destroyed their crops. It would be a very long time before any glamour attached itself to the term "pioneer."

But Jay Gould ate well, or as well as a nervous stomach would permit, and slept warmly, and planned greater triumphs. What little thought he could spare to the current depression, as the *World* reported, was centered on blaming "the bad financial managing of the government" and the public's "lack of confidence." Gould had emerged from the crash stronger than ever; far from lacking confidence himself, he saw the slump in stock prices as a marvelous opportunity to get in on the ground floor. For some months he had been buying large blocks of stock in the Union Pacific Railroad, until now he owned 100,000 shares, or about one-third of all its capital stock. Early in 1874 he managed to shoulder his way into the board of directors, much to the dismay of that select and august group.

He had been eyeing Union Pacific covetously for several years, although most speculators considered the road so thoroughly plundered it was hardly worth thinking about. Not even Erie had been so covered with scandal and charges of corruption, smears of which were daubed on the noble brows of some of the nation's leading statesmen. For the building of the Union Pacific had been accompanied by the Crédit Mobilier conspiracy, which until the Teapot Dome scandal of the Harding Administration held the record for being the nastiest mess in which American politicians ever found themselves.

For all the notoriety it acquired, the Crédit Mobilier conspiracy was actually, except for the great names dragged into it, a rather grubby and piddling affair; the bribery involved would hardly have stirred interest in the backrooms of any sizable statehouse. The Crédit Mobilier, based on a similar French company which specialized in financing other corporations, was founded to build the Union Pacific soon after it had been chartered by Congress in 1862 to run from the 100th meridian in Nebraska to the Nevada boundary. Through subcontracts let for exorbitant sums, the Crédit Mobilier siphoned $44,000,000 off the capital raised for construction of the railroad. One of the prime movers of the scheme was Congressman Oakes Ames, a Massachusetts industrialist, who distributed shares in Crédit Mobilier where he thought they would do the most good.

A subsequent, not too deeply probing investigation by Congress itself showed that a number of its members had accepted shares. Among the names blackened in the testimony were former Vice President Schuyler Colfax, the present Vice President Henry Wilson, Senator John A. Logan (the General "Black Jack" Logan of Civil War fame), James G. Blaine, Henry L. Dawes, John A. Bingham, William D. Kelley, William B. Allison, James W. Patterson, James Brooks, and a future President of the United States, James A. Garfield of Ohio. Liberal amounts of whitewash were applied—Congress, after all, was supposed to be a gentlemen's club—and the only direct sufferers were Ames and Brooks, the latter having been one of the greedier shareholders, both of whom were recommended for expulsion from the House of Representatives. Both were allowed to serve out the few remaining months of their terms and died within a year. Colfax retired from public life. The bitter residue of the whole affair was a wisecrack, containing much unpleasant truth, that Ames and Brooks had been punished for turning state's evidence against their fellow Congressmen.

Crédit Mobilier could stand as a model of efficiency and economy in the field of official corruption. Less than a hundred thousand dollars was passed out to Congressional shareholders, it appeared, in exchange for legislation which enabled the financiers—including the firm in which Levi P. Morton, a future Vice President, was a partner—to clear upwards of forty million.

Strictly as a speculative proposition, Union Pacific seemed to promise little after it had been drained white by the Crédit Mobilier operation, having a floating debt of $5,000,000 and another $10,000,000 of income bonds maturing between 1872 and 1874. But its potential was great, both as a railroad monopolizing the central route toward the Pacific and as a government-endowed corporation with 12,000,000 acres of public land which had been handed to it as a gift. The U.P. was the leading cattle carrier from the western ranges. Extensive coal deposits lay close to its right of way. Then, too, in that decade such towns as Omaha, Denver, Fremont, Ogden, Cheyenne, Salt Lake City, and Laramie were doubling and tripling in their population growth. The Union Pacific was the main artery of the richest cattle and grain country in the nation.

With all the artful oversimplification at his command, Gould later explained (before the Senate Committee on Labor and Education) his initial interest in the company and his first moves toward acquiring its control:

"It was in a rather blue condition. The directors were consulting who should be the receiver. I made up my mind that I would carry it through, and I told them that if they would furnish half of the money to pay the debt I would furnish the other half. The stock went down to 15. It was a large loss, but I still kept right on buying so when the turn came there did not seem to be any top to it. It went up to 75 and I immediately went to work to bring the road up. I went over it, started coal mines, and to the surprise of everybody it soon began to pay dividends."

A masterpiece of the disingenuous. This hundred-word history of Gould's acquisition of the Union Pacific did not even begin to tell the story. The truest part of it undoubtedly was the "surprise of everybody" that a Gould-controlled corporation should actually pay dividends, which was striking testimony to the railroad's economic durability.

Actually it took him years of maneuvering—not the least part of which was a masterful specimen of corporate blackmail—to take over the railroad and run it the way he wanted to. First there were rivals to be eliminated. Vanderbilt's New York Central, Thomas Scott's Pennsylvania, with George Pullman and Andrew Carnegie as allies, and a Boston group jockeyed for control but only managed to cancel each other out. In the spring of 1873, the death of Horace Clark, Commodore Vanderbilt's son-in-law and then president of the U.P., opened the way for Gould. The latter bought up 100,000 shares of U.P.'s stock and in the next five years increased his holdings to 200,000 shares. His first move was to install his own man, Sidney Dillon, a veteran railroader, as president.

In these and subsequent operations Gould's chief ally was Russell Sage, another upstate New Yorker, who was twenty years his senior. His business alliance with Sage was one of several examples—Sidney Dillon was another—of a considerable tempering of Gould's attitude toward his associates. Now that he was well on his way, he could afford a measure of loyalty toward them, always provided that they did not seek to oppose or betray him. His relations with Sage and Dillon were long and comparatively harmonious, both men proving they were worthy of whatever trust and confidence Gould could repose in another human being.

Sage also came of Connecticut Yankee stock, and was born in 1816 in Verona township of Oneida County. He rose from small trader to wholesale grocer, alderman and banker in Troy, and in 1852 served a term in Congress. While still an alderman in Troy, he engineered a highly suspect deal whereby the Troy & Schenectady Railroad, of which he was a part owner, was sold to the New York Central, a transaction which enriched him by several millions. The legend was that a chance meeting between Gould and Sage in a railroad station resulted in Sage's interest in railroading but the truth was that Sage was dealing in railroads while Gould was still a boy surveyor. Even before the Civil War, Sage was involved in western railroads, acquiring the line that ran from Milwaukee to LaCrosse, Wisconsin, which was later expanded into the Chicago, Milwaukee & St. Paul. Bribery, corruption, land-grabbing and stock-juggling accompanied most of these transactions, notably the deal by which he and other

Minnesota railroadmen walked off with 14,000,000 acres of public land.

Sage and Gould first became associated as members of the Pacific Mail board, and began what a eulogistic biographer of Sage called "a friendship famous in financial history." Actually their relationship held few of the elements of friendship; it was compounded principally of a wary mutual respect and a recognition of the fact that they could work well together, provided neither yielded to any treacherous inclinations. "A valuable working pair. . . ." as Gustavus Myers put it, "Sage, crafty, somber and reclusive; Gould supplying the public audacity; both equal in inscrutable wiles and stratagems. The one over-cautious, the other over-reckless, each counterbalancing the other. A prodigious respect Gould learned to entertain for Sage; the one associate whom Gould could not overreach or fleece was Sage."

Sage, unlike Gould, was never a plunger. He was a plain, conservative, frugal man, who would bargain over the price of an apple. His penurious nature made him one of the more detested of the self-made tycoons of his era; the public could forgive miserliness when a man was making his way up but he was expected to live sumptuously, as though he actually enjoyed his ill-gotten gains, once he made his fortune. Even among his peers, Sage was detested because when he finally invaded Wall Street he specialized in short-term call loans at usurious interest rates. At one time, it was reported, the non-Semitic Shylock had $27,000,000 loaned out at shark-like rates. If he attained any forgiveness in the public mind it was through his widow Margaret who endowed the Russell Sage Foundation with a good share of his $70,000,000 estate, which he grudgingly yielded up when death claimed him at the age of ninety.

One of the first problems that confronted Gould and Sage as they took over a controlling interest in the Union Pacific was its enormous debt load. If they could not pay the $5,-000,000 floating debt and the $10,000,000 in income bonds maturing in 1874, the U.P. would be thrown into receivership just as Jay Cooke's Northern Pacific venture had ended. First Gould transformed the debt into a long-term bond issue, then he persuaded the holders of income bonds to accept in exchange a new flotation of sinking fund bonds. In thus deferring payment of the obligations, Gould exercised his considerable talent for persuasion and night-blooming publicity, which perfumed the air with optimism and convinced the bondholders and other creditors that they would be wise to ride along with his plans for the railroad.

Meanwhile he kept buying U.P. stock, bolstering its prestige on the securities market, and the road itself began thriving on a bumper California grain crop, which had to be shipped to the eastern markets, and a heavy volume of silver shipments from the western mines. With control of the leading coastal shipping lines (Pacific Mail) and a large segment of the transcontinental rail line, he was able to dictate the freight rates to Union Pacific's advantage. Collis P. Huntington, head of the Central Pacific, conceded that Gould had rate-controlling powers "equal to the control of the whole link" between the Pacific Coast and the eastern railheads on the Mississippi. His domination was so complete, and so injurious to competitors, especially the foundering Kansas Pacific, that Congress passed the Pacific Railroad Acts late in 1874 to halt the Union Pacific's rate discrimination practices.

Behind all this rate-cutting and corporate skirmishing, a purpose was developing that had nothing to do with intercompany rivalry and that would become visible to other men only after the battle smoke cleared years later. Crudely stated, Gould intended to use the Union Pacific to beat down the Kansas Pacific until it became available to him, then use the K.P. as a bludgeon against U.P., or rather its other stockholders. There was no such thing as corporate loyalty in Gould's book, no romance in railroading through the Wild West, no adventure in opening the vast new territories to settlement. If he helped to change the face of the country, it was only inadvertently; his whole attention was focused on a company's books and its fluctuations on the stock market. A railroad to him was a set of books, a safe full of securities, not an engineer pulling down the Johnson bar to outrun an Indian war party while arrows and bullets pierced the cars.

Thus he felt free to use the railroads as pawns, along with millions of acres of former government lands and coal deposits and mountain timber and the life savings of thousands of stock- and bondholders, in a complicated and impersonal chess game.

While still a director of the Union Pacific, he began a four-year campaign to gain control of the competing Kansas Pacific. The two lines ran parallel, with the K.P. to the south. The Union Pacific operated from Omaha to Cheyenne to Ogden, the terminus where traffic interchanged to the Pacific Coast. The Kansas Pacific ran from Kansas City to Denver, where a spur line carried its traffic to Cheyenne. It was therefore dependent on the U.P. for its western outlet. Gould's objective was to capture control of the Kansas Pacific and build it up to the extent that the Union Pacific would be forced to agree to a consolidation, with the bankrupt K.P.'s stock placed on a par with the profitable U.P.'s. The pirate captain, if necessary, was prepared to scuttle his own ship.

During the Pacific Railway Commission hearings ordained by a troubled Congress in 1887, this scheme of Gould's, abetted by his fellow U.P. director Sage and their personally installed president Sidney Dillon, seemed questionable even by the uninhibited business standards of that day. Gould was sharply questioned on the way the Kansas Pacific and Union Pacific were maneuvered against each other, particularly since the Union Pacific had been built with government assistance, had been endowed and subsidized, and was carrying much government (largely military) freight. His frankness on this occasion should have been appalling, except that it was the frankness of man with seventy or eighty million dollars behind him.

Q. "According to the ethics of Wall Street, do you consider it absolutely within the limits of your duty, while a director of the Union Pacific, to purchase another property and to design the extention of the road which would perhaps ruin the Union Pacific?"

A. "I don't think it would have been proper. That's the reason I let it [the Kansas Pacific] go."

Q. "Did you consider your duty to the government?"

A. "I had considered it."

Q. "How would the government claim have been affected by building a parallel line?"

A. "It would have been wiped out."[2]

Forcing his way into control of the Kansas Pacific took a long, hard fight, simple and easy though it may have appeared at the outset. The Kansas Pacific had been thoroughly plundered by its former masters and was now in receivership, and the rate cutting war initiated by the Union Pacific had driven it that much farther toward ruin. It should have fallen like a ripe plum the moment Gould and his cohorts started shaking the tree. Unfortunately for them a determined ex-journalist named Henry Villard had appeared on the scene just in time to oppose them with Teutonic stubbornness.

The Bavarian-born Villard, a year older than Gould, had run away from home and migrated to the United States several years before the Civil War. During the war he served ably as a war correspondent for the New York *Herald* and later the *Tribune* with the Army of the Potomac. His first venture in high and low finance resulted from a trip to Germany in 1873, when the German bondholders in the Oregon & California Railroad appointed him as their representative to straighten out the line's affairs. His success in that undertaking led to his appointment as receiver for the German bondholders, who along with a group of St. Louis stockholders

[2] As reported in the New York *Times*, May 19, 1887.

were holding the bag for the Kansas Pacific. Almost immediately he was confronted by Gould, that "most unscrupulous and most dreaded machinator," who with Sage and Dillon acquired a controlling interest in Kansas Pacific stock at about twelve and one-half cents on the dollar.

Gould at once perceived that Villard was the linchpin holding stock- and bondholders together and decided to test his sticking power. In negotiating for control of the line, Villard wrote, Gould proposed "such a reduction of the principal and interest of the bonds that the offer was rejected," as Gould anticipated. The financier then proceeded to ingratiate himself with Villard, using all his tricks of flattery and cajolery. When that didn't work, Gould offered him "a profitable participation in the syndicate to be formed for the reorganization of the Kansas Pacific." Gould's system of corporate seduction was following a familiar pattern: first ingratiation, then bribery—and finally the bludgeon.

Villard said that Gould appeared to agree to his terms for an equitable plan of reorganization which would protect the interests of the German bondholders, then suddenly reneged by "opening an offensive campaign in which the St. Louis directors, who had at first stood by the bondholders, now joined him." Newspapers influenced by Gould "heaped slander and abuse" on Villard, who found his receivership under fire from all sides.[3] The final blow was the Union Pacific's announcement that it would build the Colorado Central, running from Denver to Cheyenne and paralleling the Kansas Pacific's spur between the two cities. With an outlet to Denver the Union Pacific would drain off much of the Kansas Pacific's mainstay freight traffic.

Villard saw that Gould was "playing for a harvest of millions" but could not persuade his bondholders and the St. Louis stockholders to stand by him. He was removed from the receivership of the Kansas Pacific. He was still the legal rep-

[3] *Memoirs of Henry Villard.*

resentative of the bondholders, however, and Gould returned to his wooing as the great Wall Street boom of 1879, encouraged by the resumption of specie payments, began gathering force. In exerting leverage against the Union Pacific, Gould needed complete control of the Kansas Pacific. One day early in 1879, Villard said, Gould sent for him in New York and said he was "tired of fighting" and wanted to make a settlement. Gould made the concessions, protecting the German bondholders, on which Villard insisted, and the four-year battle was over. Not the least beneficiary of all this was Villard, who won considerable prestige through successfully coping with Gould, and who went on to become publisher of the influential New York *Evening Post* and later one of the chief developers of rail and steamship transportation in the Pacific Northwest. He had demonstrated that Gould could be beaten by an incorruptible man; it was the men flawed by greed and a taste for intrigue that Gould ate up alive.

In the midst of his triumphant maneuvers aimed at control of the transcontinental railroads came the strike violence of 1877 which Gould proclaimed, with artful exaggeration, as the beginning of the end of republican government in the United States. Actually it was the beginning of a determined trade unionism in this country which Gould's successors have been bewailing ever since.[4] Just a modicum of compassion on the part of Gould and his fellow magnates could have averted the strikes which broke out on the American railroads in the summer of 1877, but they had all the cold arrogance of the old French aristocracy. The tone in which they addressed their workers was as a *grand seigneur*. Thus in the spring of 1877, with the country still to emerge from the depression which began in 1873, the heads of the principal railroads announced

[4] The principal Railroad Brotherhoods, destined to become the "aristocrats of the labor world," were formed before the rail strikes of 1877, but at that time they were merely fraternal organizations, not trade unions.

that there would be a general ten percent pay cut. Warnings of a strike, of the bitter despair which had infected the working classes did not give them a moment's pause. Nor did they take note of a certain explosiveness in the national mood, characterized by teenage gangs running wild in many a city's streets, race riots, lynchings, and widespread lawlessness (it was the heyday of the gunman both in the West and in the eastern cities), which would reach the flash point early that summer.

Since Gould's holdings were only indirectly affected by the violent outbreaks, thanks to a certain flexibility which his colleagues lacked, it will not be necessary to provide more than a sketch of the strike's history. William H. Vanderbilt, the Commodore's son and principal heir, had already provided the keynote of the railroad owners, "The public be damned." They had no intention of giving in to their workers because, as one commentator put it, they had already wrung their stock- and bondholders dry and now had "commenced raiding not only the general public but their own employes." Dividends had to be maintained, even if it took every bayonet in the United States to protect them.

The strike broke out at Martinsburg, West Virginia, and then spread like a prairie fire, though without any united leadership, to a dozen railroad centers, particularly Pittsburgh, Baltimore, Chicago, Buffalo, and San Francisco. Governors turned out the militia to protect railroad property and attempted to run in strikebreakers. When the militia was swept aside, the governors wired Washington for federal troops. President Rutherford B. Hayes, setting a critical precedent, ordered the regulars to restore order. Insurrection was finally put down when thousands of regular troops began guarding the terminals, shops and roundhouses and patrolling the tracks, but not before scores had been killed and millions of dollars worth of property destroyed. Racial and religious bigotry also raised its frowzy head in the glare of blazing terminals as Protestant churchmen charged that most of the violence was committed by "Irish Catholic mobs" and that in the looting which followed "the Germans carried the heaviest loads." German and Irish migrants then formed the bulk of the laboring force.

The day after the great Pittsburgh riot of July 21, when the Union Depot was burned to the ground, the Union Pacific was insisting that its wage cut would not be restored, despite the threats of its workers. Its president, Sidney Dillon, telegraphed the War Department, "What protection can the government afford our property against a lawless mob which, judging from actions at Pittsburgh and elsewhere, is likely to follow the strike?" A whole regiment of regulars, the Ninth Infantry, was standing by at Omaha, but the Union Pacific was still uneasy. It need not have been, for Jay Gould, in New York, had already decided it didn't pay to oppose workingmen in a mood to destroy company property. Later that afternoon came telegraphed orders from New York to rescind the pay cut. A few days later Union Pacific employes were holding a mass meeting at which they pledged themselves to the protection of the company's property.

Once again Gould, ignoring the distress of his fellow capitalists and going his own selfish way, played cat in the corner.

The same evening on which he had broken the front against the railroad workers Gould was interviewed by the New York reporters and could not quite suppress a certain smugness. He viewed the whole situation with extreme pessimism but, as the New York *World* reporter observed, "Mr. Gould was in very good spirits, and seemed to contemplate the coming of the general conflagration as serenely as if he had a complete monopoly of the trade in lucifer matches and petroleum."

He told the reporters that the only way to prevent anarchy was to bring General Grant back to the White House. He was quoted as saying he would "gladly give $1,000,000 to see General Grant in the White House today," otherwise it would be the beginning of a "great social revolution" which would lead to "the destruction of the republican form of government in this country and the establishment of a monarchy."

His remarks created such an uproar that one of his leading sympathizers, Ben Butler, the senator from Massachusetts who was almost as notorious politically as Gould was financially, urged him to come along on a yachting trip down the coast of Maine until angry passions subsided. Gould, however, refused, gaining confidence from such long-ranging echoes as General Grant's from London. The General was grateful for Gould's suggestion, since it started a third-term boom in his favor. Wistfully recalling the happy days when Grant was in power, or thought he was, certain politicians began demanding his return to the Presidency as "an invincible barrier against Communism [a Marxist tendency first cropped out in this country among some of the leaders of the railroad strike] and currency inflation." Grant blew his own trumpet in this refrain, writing his friends from London that the strike should have been crushed "so summarily as to prevent a like occurrence for a generation."

Gould's predictions of anarchy and guileful yearnings for Grant's return, either as President Grant or King Ulysses, apparently were pure mischief-making. His probable aim was to drive railroad stocks down further, since he had been selling short that summer. No situation could be so desperate as to suppress his trading instincts. As summer waned, the strikers were suppressed throughout the land and dolefully returned to work, Grant stayed off the throne and out of the White House, and Gould as usual took his profits.

Occasionally, perhaps twice a year, Gould would make a whirlwind tour of inspection. His special car, the Convoy, would be attached to a locomotive, a coal tender and a baggage car, and off he would go, traveling at top speed over the western railroads. He fancied himself an expert railroader—here, for once, he tended to overestimate himself—and liked to harass his general superintendent with suggestions for better maintenance and more economical methods of operation. A "male typewriter," as a stenographer was then called, was installed at his elbow to take down his running comments on technical matters of which he was more ignorant than he assumed.

On his three-week jaunts over the western roads, his own and those of his competitors, he always insisted that top speed, at least fifty miles an hour, be maintained. At that speed, over stretches of rough roadbed, he and the members of his party would be bounced around their car like shuttlecocks. "During such a trip," wrote a New York *Times* correspondent who accompanied him, "he has been known to change seats—from one side of the car to the other—not of his own volition, but without changing countenance." At night when the special train would be drawn up on the siding near some small town, crowds would gather around his darkened car, his saturnine presence "as much a curiosity as a circus."

His mania for speed annoyed at least one engineer, the *Times* man recorded, when Gould kept pulling the bell cord as a signal to pour on the coal. The train was slowed down, finally, for dinner. Just as it was being served, the exasperated engineer opened up the throttle and sent the train bucketing down the tracks while the dinner dishes and their contents were flung all over the special car. Gould's salt-and-pepper beard was decorated with pea soup. At the next stop the engineer was removed from his cab and demoted to service with the slow freights.[5]

It was during one such trip, according to his associates, that Gould conceived his master plan for linking up various smaller roads with the Kansas Pacific and fabricating a through line from St. Louis to Cheyenne which would parallel the Union Pacific almost mile for mile. With the addition of the Wabash system, in fact, it would be longer and would have the ad-

[5] New York *Times*, April 27, 1887. The reporter was recalling a trip he made with Gould some years before.

vantage of operating east of the Mississippi. Then he could play off one railroad against the other, even though he was heavily interested in both. He could not always bend the whole U.P. directorate to his designs, but he was the company's dominating and motivating force and was its operating head through his control of its president. Charles Francis Adams, Jr., president of the road during a subsequent period when Gould's interest in the company temporarily lapsed, said his influence over U.P. operations was comparable to "a captain of a frigate on board his ship." And Sidney Dillon, the figurehead whom Gould installed as president whenever he was in control of the U.P., testified that he "never consulted anyone but Mr. Gould and Mr. Gould was in the custom of giving orders without consulting Mr. Dillon at all."

Hooking together the links of the chain with which he intended to shackle the Union Pacific to his new designs, Gould had captured the Kansas Pacific early in 1879 by settling with Villard and his bondholders. Later that year he moved swiftly to buy up controlling interests in other lines which would comprise a rival system to the Union Pacific—the Denver Pacific, the Missouri Pacific and two feeder lines in Kansas. A short time later he also bought the Texas & Pacific from Thomas Scott of the Pennsylvania Railroad.

The bondholders of the Denver Pacific, which was in receivership, proved harder to deal with than he had expected. He learned of a large block of Denver Pacific bonds held by Dutch investors, and made a quick trip to Amsterdam to buy them up. The haste of this mission was conveyed in Gould's own testimony at a subsequent investigation.[6] To gather up "2,000,000 of Denver Pacific at seventy-four cents," he testified, "I went over and got to Amsterdam in the morning; washed and had my breakfast. I saw them [the Dutch brokers] at eleven; bought them out at twelve, and started back in the afternoon." One can only wonder what worlds Jay

[6] Before the Pacific Railway Commission, April 1887.

Gould might have conquered if jet planes had been available for transportation.

His purchase of the Missouri Pacific was even more critical, since its operating head, Commodore C. K. Garrison, was also threatening to expand westward. The Missouri Pacific's main line ran from St. Louis to Kansas City, and was essential to the system Gould was creating as a bogeyman to frighten the other directors of the Union Pacific. Knowing his need, Garrison and his associates wrung everything they could out of Gould, but, as the latter cheerfully explained to the Pacific Railway Commission's hearing some years hence, "Stock doesn't always depend upon dividends altogether. I paid 750 for my Missouri Pacific—4000 shares at that figure. You pay more for rubies than for diamonds, and more for diamonds than for glass." The Missouri Pacific was to become one of Gould's more permanent possessions, one he intended to leave to his family, and a New York newspaper later described how he ran it by private wire linking its headquarters in St. Louis with his offices in New York, where he "spends some hours each day sitting at a desk that never ought to have cost more than $25."[7]

In his mock-up of a system to rival the Union Pacific, Gould now had the Missouri Pacific (St. Louis to Kansas City), the Kansas Pacific (Kansas City to Denver), and the Denver Pacific (Denver to Cheyenne). In addition he quickly bought up two feeder roads in Kansas, the Kansas Central and the Central Branch, both of which tapped the agricultural regions west of Atchison and threatened further inroads on the Union Pacific's freight business, even though he had to pay $2.39 on the dollar for the Central Branch's stock.

Late that year Gould presented his proposition to his fellow directors of the Union Pacific: the Kansas Pacific and the Union Pacific were to be consolidated and their stock exchanged at par—"notwithstanding the fact that Kansas Pa-

[7] New York *Times*, April 27, 1887.

cific stock was earning nothing while Union Pacific was earning and paying six percent per annum," and Union Pacific
was selling for $60 a share while Kansas Pacific was quoted
at $13 a share. (Gould and his friends, of course, were buying
up Kansas Pacific at this reduced price to make a killing when
and if the consolidation with Union Pacific was announced.)
Gould, the inveterate trader, was in the position of representing both the buyer and the seller. His fellow directors didn't
know whether to laugh, cry, or lynch him. In any case,
they turned him down. Gould thereupon announced that he
planned to extend his new system by connecting the Kansas
Pacific with the Central Pacific at Salt Lake City, giving him
an outlet to the Pacific Coast.

This was probably the boldest steal in railroad history, combining the resources of one weak company with a prosperous
one on equal terms, but the Union Pacific's board seemed
powerless to fend off their relentless colleague. Or perhaps
they were prepared to console themselves by buying Kansas
Pacific stock in time to profit on the market rise when the
merger was announced. Or they had too long been accustomed to bowing tamely before Jay Gould.

The recalcitrant directors, at any rate, lost their nerve and
on January 14, 1880, requested an audience with Gould and
Sage. Clutching each other for moral support, they arrived
in a body at Gould's Fifth Avenue mansion. Gould wasted
little time in preliminaries; he showed them a contract and
advised them to sign. The directors then signed an agreement
"whereby the Union and the Kansas Pacific, with all their
respective assets and liabilities, were put together at par of
their respective capitals . . . to which was added the capital
of the Denver Pacific."

The U.P. directors were so terrified by his threats to run
that railroad into the ground, he claimed before the Pacific
Railway Commission hearings in 1887, that they *insisted* on
the merger. "I offered them a million [to call off the merger],"

he testified, smiling gently at the recollection, "but they would not let me out of the room until I had signed an agreement to carry out the consolidation."

Gould's attack of coyness, as he recalled it, must have afforded the commissioners much sardonic amusement. One of them, after hearing all the testimony, estimated that Gould alone made $40,000,000, give or take a million or two, out of the manipulation of the Union Pacific and Kansas Pacific.

He was ardent in defense of the transaction, claiming that the Union Pacific's indebtedness was "about $80,000 per mile" while the Kansas Pacific's was only "about $40,000 or $45,000 per mile—about one-half."

He also pointed out: "The Kansas Pacific was on hard-pan and could not get any worse than it was. It ran through a better local country than the Union Pacific. Its whole 745 miles was east of the Rocky Mountains. Five hundred miles of the Union Pacific was east of the Rocky Mountains and 500 miles was up on a plateau six or seven thousand feet above tide, unsuited to agriculture." Furthermore, he said, the Kansas Pacific had terminal properties worth $1,000,000 in Denver and $2,000,000 in Kansas City, while the Union Pacific had no such assets.

On even larger details of financing, however, he confessed to slipshod methods hardly in keeping with his reputation, as in this exchange with the commission:

Q. "Do you remember that there was an agreement made between the Union Pacific and the Kansas Pacific dated New York, April 22, 1875 whereby the capital of the Kansas Pacific was to be increased at $20,000,000 and $5,000,000 of bonds were to be issued?"

A. "It seems to me, now that you recall it, there was something of that kind, but never carried out."

Q. "Never consummated?"

A. "Never consummated. I had forgotten all about it."

About other details of the plan to build up a ruinous rivalry between his other lines and the Union Pacific, he could be brutally frank:

Q. "How great an injury to the Union Pacific would the extension of the Missouri Pacific have been?"
A. "Extended through to where?"
Q. "To Denver and San Francisco."
A. "It would have destroyed it."[8]

This testimony, of course, was given during a period when Gould was not financially interested in the Union Pacific.

A year after the completion of his Union Pacific stratagem, when he was forty-five years old, his fortune was estimated at close to a hundred million dollars, but it was subject to violent fluctuations, a paper empire based on the imponderables of stock market speculation, as flimsy as a kite fluttering up and down in a spring breeze. And there were so many people eager to see that kite come crashing down to earth and entangling its owner in the wreckage.

[8] *United States Pacific Railway Commission*, Vol. I.

8. ANOTHER VANDERBILT BITES THE DUST

"For Vanderbilt and Company 'tis indeed a gilded age
But poverty increases, 'tis thus that tramps are made.
Shall it be continued when the people's votes are weighed
As we go marching on?

No! We'll hang Jay Gould on a sour apple tree,
And bring grief to the plotters of a base monopoly;
From the ghouls of booty we shall go free,
As we go marching on."

—Antimonopoly song of the 1880s.

WILLIAM HENRY VANDERBILT should have been forewarned. In addition to the $90,000,000 he inherited from the Commodore as his chief heir, he was bequeathed the soundest advice the elder Vanderbilt had winnowed out of his years of experience: never become involved, either as a friend or an enemy, with Jay Gould. His own searing experience with Gould in the fight for Erie convinced the Commodore that Gould should be belled and isolated like a leper. Several years before his death the patriarch of the Vanderbilt clan caused to be published in the New York *Times* a statement that he would never have anything to do with Gould and "I have, besides, always advised all my friends to have nothing to do with him in any business transaction. I came to this conclusion after taking particular notice of his countenance. The almost constant parade, therefore, of my name in association with his, seems very much like an attempt to mislead the public, to my injury, and after the publication of this, ignorance or misinformation can no longer be urged as an excuse for continuing this course."

William Henry, fourteen years older than Gould, did his best to follow his father's advice. He took particular care to avoid antagonizing Gould, even while the Vanderbilt interests were taking over the Chicago & Northwestern. Gould had established a corner in that railroad's stock shortly after being ousted from Erie, and as late as 1878 still owned 29,000 shares. It was a majority interest, though Gould satisfied himself with sitting on the board of directors rather than assuming control of the management. Three years passed before the Vanderbilt group acquired financial control, quietly buying up various blocks of stock and taking care not to offend Gould by flourishing its power. Gould, in fact, was allowed to remain on the board after his holdings declined to a mere rooting interest in the company.

Gently did it—or so William Henry Vanderbilt and his advisers hoped. If they spoke softly and carried a small stick, perhaps the monster would not take notice of them. Perhaps his appetite would not be aroused by the near-monopoly of the telegraph system which Western Union, dominated by Vanderbilt, had gradually built up.

William Henry, in truth, was ill-equipped to take on any struggle with Gould, whom even his domineering father could not handle. Almost from his birth in 1821 he had been pushed around, harangued, and ridiculed by his father, who probably hoped that he was toughening the boy up. His nature, as the Vanderbilt biographer Wayne Andrews wrote in *The Vanderbilt Legend*, was "plodding, patient and unadventurous." The old Commodore customarily referred to him as a "sucker"— and the epithet meant the same then as it does today. He kept his son working as a nineteen-dollar-a-week clerk long after the young man was married. Later, his health broken, William Henry took up farming on Staten Island and did well enough, in his small way, to win his father's reluctant approval. The Commodore had no choice but to designate his eldest son as the prime inheritor of his fortune. His second son, Cornelius Jeremiah, was an epileptic, the victim of a disorder which Victorians regarded with shame and horror, with whispers of "tainted blood"—unless and until it struck someone close to them. His third son, George Washington, entered West Point, contracted tuberculosis while serving with the Union army, and died in 1864. The Commodore also had sired nine daughters, but they counted no more with him than with some worthy mandarin on the other side of the world.

He died in January of 1877, mourned at length in the newspapers but little elsewhere. In its editorial on the elder Vanderbilt's death, the New York *Sun* of January 9 took the occasion to predict that the late Commodore would never be succeeded in his late eminence by anyone so ill-favored as Jay Gould. To the *Sun's* editor, Charles A. Dana, Gould "is too sly and tricky to win substantial success. He is undoubtedly the master of great blocks of stock, but he can't get people to buy them. His Union Pacific no one will touch. . . . He is the weakest point in any company of which he can get control. . . . Jay Gould is no such man as Vanderbilt but stands in comparison with him somewhat as Iago with Othello."

Perhaps the phlegmatic William Henry was encouraged by this downgrading of the family bogeyman when he succeeded to the management of the Vanderbilt fortune and fell heir to heavy holdings in Western Union. Aside from the New York Central, Western Union then was the family's chief investment. The company's board of directors was a miniature social directory, with the names of Astor and Vanderbilt leading all the rest.

During the panicky summer of 1877, to their dismay, Gould began buying into Western Union, and suggested that a place be made for him on its august board. He had already been blackballed by the New York Yacht Club, and the Western Union board considered it sheer impertinence for him to seek entry to its even more exclusive precincts. For Gould, to the Vanderbilts and Astors, was an out-and-out bounder, a cad, a villainous outsider. Worse yet, it was whispered, a Jew—which may or may not have been infinitesmally correct—and in that day the self-constituted upper class did not attempt to conceal or mute its anti-Semitism. Western Union's directorate was a gentleman's club, composed of those whose wealth was sanctified by slightly longer possession than Gould's, and it did not choose to admit Gould, whatever his financial interest in the company. Socially, by their lights, this may have been an impeccable position to take; but in the business sense it was calamitous. William Henry, heedless of his father's antemortem advice, probably thought he was safe enough in such an impregnable position, with such imposing allies.

Gould, however, would not tolerate such a snub, and he was already equipped with the means to torment Western Union and place it on a rack such as even Erie and Union Pacific had not been forced to endure.

He had been interested in the possibilities of the telegraph business since the Civil War, and even while conjuring with the Union Pacific's assets, telegraphy had been an overlapping if not overriding interest. It will be recalled that during the Civil War he had rigged up a telegraphic system by which he learned in advance of Union victories and defeats, enabling him to speculate accordingly. The source of his information may have been the Military Telegraph Bureau, which received the reports from the Union armies in the field and was headed by Major Thomas T. Eckert, who subsequently became a principal ally, along with Russell Sage and a select group of speculators, in the assault on Western Union. After the war Eckert, brevetted a brigadier general, became superintendent of Western Union's eastern division, with three former cipher clerks, Albert B. Chandler, Homer Bates and Charles A. Tinker, as his chief aides. General Eckert, an imposing figure with his white walrus mustache and the face of a Norse sea rover, never hesitated to circumvent his superiors whenever he chose. In the closing phases of the war, General Grant had ordered that General George H. Thomas be relieved of his command at Nashville when he refused to attack the Confederates until his army was ready. On his own responsibility Eckert held up the telegram ordering Thomas' relief, and next day the "Rock of Chickamauga" annihilated the enemy. The happy outcome of this venture in disobedience doubtless confirmed Eckert in his opinion that it did not always pay to slavishly follow the dictates of those above him.

Early in 1875, when Western Union refused to follow his advice, Eckert went over to Gould. The latter, as part of his dealings in Union Pacific, had acquired control of his own telegraph company, the Atlantic & Pacific, whose wires ran from San Francisco, along the Union Pacific right of way to Omaha, and then on to New York. Two years later it had 17,759 miles of line and was a serious rival to the Western Union. General Eckert not only assumed the presidency of Gould's company but brought along Chandler, Bates, and Tinker.

A matter of days before Eckert quit Western Union he saw to it that his new master acquired Thomas A. Edison's quadruplex sending system, an automatic device by which 1500 words could be transmitted from New York to Philadelphia in fifty-seven seconds. This was accomplished through a complicated double cross to which Gould, Eckert, and Edison all were parties. Edison had developed the quadruplex system under an agreement with Western Union, whose president, William Orton, provided him with the necessary funds and laboratory facilities. The company's chief electrician, George B. Prescott, helped Edison work out a means of sending four messages simultaneously in the same direction. As Orton later testified in one of the ensuing court actions over the quadruplex patents, he offered Edison $25,000, plus a royalty for each circuit installed, late in December 1874. A few days after that, Orton said, Edison disappeared and could not be located. A cloak-and-dagger atmosphere pervaded the whole affair, as was customary when Jay Gould embarked upon corporate skulduggery.

Edison, not yet a national hero as the "wizard of Menlo Park," took up the story from there:

"One day Eckert [still superintendent of the eastern division of Western Union] called me into his office and made inquiries about money matters. I told him Mr. Orton had gone off and left me without means, and I was in straits. He told me I would never get another cent, but that he knew a man who would buy it [the quadruplex system]. I told him of my arrangement with the electrician, and said I could not sell it as a whole to anybody; but if I could get enough for it I would sell all my interest in any share I might have. He seemed to think his party would agree to this."

Eckert's party, it developed, was Jay Gould, the owner of the Atlantic & Pacific. Eckert took Edison to Gould's house on Fifth Avenue, glancing nervously around for any Western Union spies that might be lurking in the vicinity.

"It was in the evening," as Edison recalled, "and we went in by the servants' entrance, as Eckert probably feared that he was watched."

Gould doubtless had been informed by Eckert that Orton had offered Edison a down payment of $25,000 for his patents, and after a little preliminary bargaining proposed paying Edison $30,000. Edison accepted, and somewhere along the way chief electrician Prescott was abandoned, though Edison admitted that his assistance had been a material value in developing the quadruplex.

During the next few weeks Western Union learned that Gould had not only lured Superintendent Eckert, plus Chandler, Bates, and Tinker, over to the Atlantic & Pacific but had also snatched away Edison's patents, which were obviously essential to increasing telegraphic efficiency. The Western Union went to court over this hijacking of an invention it had sponsored, but Gould fought a delaying action until subsequent events precluded pressing the suit.

In the next two years Atlantic & Pacific expanded by swallowing up the Franklin Telegraph Company and became

Western Union's leading competitor. The latter tried rate-cutting, but Gould weathered the storm. There was nothing to do, the Western Union directorate decided, but to absorb his company. Late in 1877 it bought 72,000 shares of A. & P. stock, mostly from Gould, for $912,550 plus 12,500 shares of Western Union stock. The income of the two companies was to be pooled, with Western Union receiving 87½ percent and Atlantic & Pacific 12½.

It was then that Gould politely requested admission to the Western Union board, and William Henry Vanderbilt and his colleagues turned up their newly aristocratic noses. Rarely has snobbery been so painfully rewarded. Less than eighteen months later Gould was forming yet another telegraph company which he designed as a second force-feeding experiment, with Western Union as the reluctant laboratory specimen. Western Union, like a Strasbourg goose, was being stuffed to death.

Gould's new telegraph company was the American Union, whose organization was announced on May 15, 1879 with a capitalization of $10,000,000. A familiar cast of characters, somewhat like baseball's Tinker-to-Evers-to-Chance, was introduced. General Eckert was president, Bates and Tinker were co-incorporators. Regarding the capitalization, Bates later testified that he and Gould and Tinker "subscribed $10,-000,000; I subscribed $2,500,000, and paid for my subscription in the shape of Jay Gould's check." Bates and Tinker, in other words, were dummies—but it was no dummy corporation, as Western Union may have suspected. The treasurer was also a familiar face in Gould's entourage, Giovanni P. Morosini, who had served as his bodyguard and confidential clerk since the Erie days. Morosini, it seems, was also a dummy treasurer; he later testified that he had never seen a set of books, drawn a check or kept a bank account for American Union. The whole operation was conducted in Gould's amazingly complex brain, preoccupied as it then was with rigging the Kansas Pacific—Union Pacific merger.

American Union, built from scratch, began growing at an amazing rate. Gould organized the Central Construction Company to build new lines and leased the wires of the Dominion Telegraph of Canada. President Robert Garrett of the Baltimore & Ohio Railroad was named a director of American Union, and a short time later his telegraph system, which had been leased to the Atlantic & Pacific, was turned over to the new company. The wires along the Union Pacific and Kansas Pacific right of ways were seized by force, and Western Union held onto the telegraph systems of two other Gould-dominated roads, the Missouri Pacific and the Central Branch, only by obtaining temporary injunctions. American Union then succeeded in grabbing the Wabash Railroad's wires, and a battle of injunctions, contempt citations, subpoenas and bench warrants erupted in courts from New York to San Francisco. At the end of the first year, American Union had established 2000 branch offices and had strung up or acquired 50,000 miles of wire.

Meanwhile, Gould organized a pool of bear operators to drive Western Union's stock down. Until now it had been a blue-chip item on the market, and its downward trend in April 1880 mystified Wall Street, unaware of Gould's short-selling tactics.

The Western Union's directorate probably had a good idea what was causing the stock to bobble so erratically, but swore mighty oaths to each other that this time, by gad, Gould wouldn't force them to ingest another unwanted company. They proclaimed themselves undismayed by the fact that Western Union's business had dropped off by $2,000,000 in the year since American Union was organized. By the end of 1880 its receipts were cut by an average of $5000 a day, and its stock fell below 90 for the first time in three decades.

In all these maneuvers Gould was aided by a new instrument which had come into his hands, a New York newspaper, whose suborned and artificial thunders were to help mold public opinion in his favor to some extent (allowing for the in-

tense suspicion with which he was viewed in many quarters).
It was not that Gould had suddenly decided that journalism
was an evangelical calling; he had long been interested in the
newspaper business as a propaganda arm of his various business interests. As a boy promoter in Roxbury, he had bought
the favorable attention of his hometown newspaper. He had
taken note of how the Tweed Ring, and to a lesser extent Erie
itself, had been allowed to flourish a decade ago through the
complaisance of the New York newspapers (excepting Greeley's *Tribune*). Some years before he had loaned Whitelaw
Reid, publisher of the New York *Tribune* since Greeley's
death, enough money to keep the paper afloat. The loan was
secured by controlling stock owned by Reid. The *Tribune*,
therefore, had been a fairly faithful echo of Gould's opinions.
But Gould wanted his own mouthpiece in New York, and
through a "mere accident" as he claimed much too protest-
ingly, the New York *World* fell into his hands. Until then the
World, a Democratic newspaper, had been very harsh with
and critical of Jay Gould.

Gould took over the *World* as part of a package deal with
Thomas Scott, in which he also acquired the Texas & Pacific
Railroad. As Gould later told the story,[1] he met Scott in Berne,
Switzerland, during one of his quick trips to Europe. "Mr.
Scott was very much depressed and broken up . . . I felt a
profound sympathy for him. He asked me as a favor to take
his Texas & Pacific Railroad off his hands and I concluded to
do so. In arranging the details Mr. Scott appealed to me to
include the *World* in the transaction. . . . I cared nothing
about it but finally yielded. . . . It was really a mere accident.
I never cared anything about the *World* while I had it."

Perhaps not; perhaps he allowed Scott to press the *World*
into his small white hands as an act of charity, but somehow
the *World* was made to serve a Gouldian purpose during the
three years of his ownership. Then known as the white ele-

[1] Quoted in Don C. Seitz's *Joseph Pulitzer: His Life and Letters.*

phant of Park Row, it was published in the same triangular block, between Park Row, Beekman and Nassau Streets, as the more prosperous New York *Times*. Gould thought enough of it to move it to new and better quarters at 31–32 Park Row and equip it with modern Hoe presses.

And in the months during which Gould was building up the American Union and tearing down the Western Union in market raids, the *World*, in slanted news stories and stentorian editorials, was its new master's voice. Gould, ignoring his recent grab for the western railroads, publicly aligned himself with the growing and vociferous antimonopoly movement. To his ostensible horror, he discovered that Western Union was the most vicious of all the monopolies, trying to oppress its smaller competitors. He conveniently ignored the fact that less than two years before he had built up the Western Union monopoly by foisting the Atlantic & Pacific on it. Day after day the *World* denounced Western Union as a "blood-sucking, un-American, criminally mismanaged monopoly."

As the year ended, Western Union stock dropped to 78 and rumors began circulating that it would be forced to make a deal with American Union.

Reporters who questioned Norvin Green, who succeeded Orton as president of Western Union three years before, were told that such an outcome of the struggle was unthinkable. "Impossible!" snorted Green, whose portraits bear a striking resemblance to the silent-film comedian Ben Turpin, with the addition of a constabulary mustache, and whose antics in the crisis might have served as a model for that dashing member of the Keystone Kops. "It would bankrupt Gould and all his connections to parallel our lines, and to talk of harmony between him and us is the wildest kind of speculation." A reporter noted that the "genial Norvin" viewed himself as master of the situation and "regarded with contempt the efforts of Gould and his colleagues to bring the company to terms."

The New York legislature took the reports of a Western Union–American Union merger much more seriously and tried to pass a bill preventing it, but Gould money was always plentiful in Albany and the measure failed. A telegraph company employes' journal, *The Operator,* also took alarm and predicted what would happen if the consolidation was effected: "Mr. Gould will make $5,000,000 by the transaction, some hundreds of clerks will be thrown out of employment, and hundreds more retained at a point just above starvation wages. But that is the usual 'divvy' in such cases."

Meanwhile, William Henry Vanderbilt and his fellow directors of Western Union were strangely silent, as befitted men who were thinking hard and preparing themselves to swallow a very bitter dose of medicine.

It was the saddest day in the business history of the Vanderbilts. On the Sunday morning of January 9, 1881, William Henry, his bushy side whiskers drooping in defeat, sat in the ornate but almost bookless library of his palace at 640 Fifth Avenue and faced the fact that, once again, the Vanderbilts must knuckle under to the upstart Gould. Western Union's stock continued to nose under, its earnings were shrinking at an alarming rate, and the directors had no heart for a fight to the finish. It was up to him, as the majority stockholder, to make the decision whether to defy American Union, its rate-cutting threats, Gould's short-selling (abetted by Sage, Dillon, and others), the *World's* denunciations and all the psychological pressures his opponents were exerting, or to sue for peace. His father was fond of saying it didn't pay to kick a skunk; the old Commodore always knew when to conduct a strategic retreat, and to hell with pride. People said he was the richest man in the world, and William Henry would solemnly agree with this statement, but it was his duty to conserve that wealth, not squander it in Wall Street guerrilla campaigns.

William Henry sighed, reached across the richly carved

desk and took up pen and note paper. Words did not come easily to him on any occasion, but he finally managed to compose a message from which any possible hint of emotion had been wrung. The note read:

"Dear Sir: I would like to see you a few moments, at 9 o'clock, if convenient to you, at my house. Very truly yours, W. H. Vanderbilt."

That evening Vanderbilt and the diminutive terrorist of the financial canyons downtown sat down and arranged a truce in Vanderbilt's library. Gould, as he said frankly to the rather slow-witted man who was suing for peace, was willing to "listen to reason." From then on, negotiations proceeded rapidly and secretly. The ticker, most accurate of seismographs, recorded the effects of those unpublicized meetings, from which the insiders, of course, were reaping benefits. Western Union had suddenly stopped quaking. On the Tuesday following that first meeting of Vanderbilt and Gould, Western Union jumped from 78 to 103½. The next day it rose to 114½.

By February 15, 1881, when the Western Union board of directors ratified the settlement arranged between Vanderbilt and Gould, the capitulation was no longer a surprise. But its terms must have startled the more conservative financiers: solid old Western Union's capitalization was being raised to $80,000,000, one-fourth of it watered stock, and enormously juicy melons were carved up for the various beneficiaries of the deal. Western Union's subsidiary, Atlantic & Pacific, was formally taken into the fold, with 140,000 shares of its stock at $60, a total of $8,400,000; $5,000,000 was bestowed on American Union on bonds pledged to the Central Construction Company, which had been originally capitalized at $5000; another $10,000,000 went to American Union for its capital stock; $41,073,410 represented the capital stock of Western Union, and finally a whopping 38½ percent dividend, representing "increase of property by purchase and construction since 1866," was decreed. The dividend amounted to $15,526,590. Gould, Sage, Dillon, and Eckert were elected to the board of directors. Norvin Green was allowed to remain as president but General Eckert became vice president and general manager—Eckert the faithless employe, now bountifully rewarded for having walked off with the most valuable invention developed in the company's laboratories. William Henry's cup of hemlock truly ran over the following November when it was disclosed that Gould held a controlling interest in the company, $30,000,000 worth of Western Union stock. Meanwhile, determined on physical possession of his prize, Gould transferred his headquarters to the massive new Western Union Building at 195 Broadway, and *The Operator* mourned on behalf of the victimized employes of the merged companies, "The cormorant of the past has been swallowed and the Western Union of today is only the Western Union in name, and the American Union in fact."

Some years hence, before the Senate Committee on Labor and Education, Gould was urged to reveal his methods and motives in taking over Western Union, as though they shouldn't have been strikingly apparent to the most obtuse legislator. With studied impudence, he declared that the whole plot had been concocted in the sacred name of friendship; he had done it all for dear old General Eckert. Since it was inconceivable that Gould expected any of his auditors to believe him, knowing his record, his testimony can logically be read only as a prime specimen of counting room comedy.

"I am interested in the telegraph," he told the committee, "for the railroad and telegraph systems go hand in hand, as it were integral parts of a great civilization. I naturally became acquainted with the telegraph and gradually became interested in it. I thought well of it as an investment and kept increasing my interests. When the Union Pacific was built, I had an interest in a company called the Atlantic & Pacific, and endeavored to make that a rival to the Western Union. We extended it considerably, but found it rather uphill work.

We saw that our interests lay more with the Western Union. Through that we could reach every part of the country and through a small company we could not; so we made an offer to sell to Western Union the control of the Atlantic & Pacific.

"At that time a very dear friend of mine was the manager [of Atlantic & Pacific], and I supposed that he would be made the manager of the Western Union, but after the consolidation was perfected it was not done, and I made up my mind that he should be at the head of as good a company as I had taken him from. The friend was General Eckert, and for him I started another company, the American Union, and we carried it forward until a proposition was made to merge it also into the Western Union.

"As the stock of the latter went down, I bought a large interest in it, and found that the only way out was to put the two companies together. General Eckert became general manager of the whole system. Meantime I bought so much of its property and its earning power that I have kept increasing my interest. I thought it better to have my income go into the things that I was in myself, and have never sold any of my interests, but have devoted my income to increasing them. This is the whole history of it."

The transcript of that testimony, published in the New York papers, must have made many a Wall Streeter's breakfast table rock with disbelieving laughter.

Considerably greater insight into Gould's cool and masterly manipulation of Western Union stock, the erratic behavior of which was one of the principal reasons Vanderbilt and his colleagues decided to give up the struggle, was provided by a young stenographer in Gould's employ. The young man was Edward Bok who, after turning his back on the manifest evils of Wall Street, became a leading magazine editor and the author of a celebrated autobiography, *The Americanization of Edward Bok*. Impressed with the youth's speed in taking dictation, Gould had made him something of a protégé and dictated all his orders to his brokers to young Mr. Bok.

Referring to himself in the third person throughout, Bok, in his autobiography, told how he became involved in his employer's maneuvers in the market. "Edward watched the effects on the stock market of these little notes which he wrote out and then shot through a pneumatic tube to Mr. Gould's brokers. Naturally, the results enthralled the boy. . . . Having a little money saved up [he] concluded to follow in the wake of Gould's orders. One day, he naively mentioned his desire to Gould when the financier seemed in a particularly favorable frame of mind, but Edward did not succeed in drawing out the advice he hoped for. . . .

"Construing the financier's silence to mean at least not a prohibition, Edward went to his Sunday-School teacher, who was a member of a Wall Street brokerage firm, laid the facts before him, and asked him if he would buy for him some Western Union stock. Edward explained, however, that somehow he did not like the gambling idea of buying 'on margin' and preferred to purchase the stock outright. . . . So, prudently, under the brokerage of his Sunday-School teacher, and guided by the tips of no less a man than the controlling factor of stock-market finance, Edward Bok took his first plunge in Wall Street.

"Of course, the boy's buying and selling tallied precisely with the rise and fall of Western Union stock. It could scarcely have been otherwise. Jay Gould had the cards all in his hands, and as he bought and sold, so Edward bought and sold. The trouble was, the combination did not end there, as Edward might have foreseen had he been older and thus wiser; for as Edward bought and sold, so did his Sunday-School teacher, and all his customers who had seen the wonderful acumen of their broker in choosing exactly the right time to buy and sell Western Union. But Edward did not know this.

"One day a rumor became current in the Street that an agreement had been reached by the Western Union Company and its bitter rival, the American Union Telegraph Company, whereby the former was to absorb the latter. Naturally the report affected Western Union stock. But Mr. Gould denied it *in toto;* said the report was not true, no such consolidation was in view or had even been considered. Down tumbled the stock, of course.

"But it so happened that Edward knew the rumor was true, because Mr. Gould some time before had personally given him the contract of consolidation to copy. The next day a rumor to the effect that the American Union was to absorb the Western Union appeared on the first page of every New York newspaper. Edward knew exactly whence this rumor emanated. He had heard it talked over. Again, Western Union stock dropped several points. Then he noticed that Gould became a heavy buyer. So became Edward, as heavy as he could. Gould poohpoohed the latest rumor. The boy awaited developments."

A day or two later, Bok recalled, his Sunday-school teacher-broker inquired very anxiously whether he was certain that Western Union was going to resume its rise. "Edward thought his teacher looked worried, and after a little while came the revelation that he, seeing that Edward was buying to his limit, had likewise done so. But the broker had bought on margin, and had his margin wiped out by the decline in the stock caused by the rumors. He explained to Edward that he could recoup his losses, heavy though they were —in fact, he explained that nearly everything he possessed was involved—if Edward's basis was sure and the stock would recover.

"Edward felt keenly the responsibility placed upon him. He could never diagnose clearly his feelings when he saw his teacher in this new light. The broker's 'customers' had been hinted at, and the boy of eighteen wondered how far his responsibility went, and how many persons were involved. But the deal came out all right, for when, three days afterward, the contract was made public, Western Union, of course, skyrocketed, Jay Gould sold out, Edward sold out, the teacher-broker sold out, and all the customers sold out!"

Bok also saw his revered employer in a new light as he observed with the priggishness of self-made youth how, inadvertently or not, the influence of that self-contained little man could corrupt even a Sunday-school teacher. He soon decided that his soul would not be safe in Jay Gould's domain. . . .

Lawyers always fattened on the aftermath of a Gould takeover. After the capture of Western Union, as with Erie, Union Pacific, and all his other coups, the court calendars were crowded with lawsuits against Gould and his associates, most of them reflecting outrage at the way Gould had used two small companies to seize control of a gigantic monopoly. One William S. Williams, a Western Union stockholder, battled Gould in the courts for years, forcing revelations that much of the profit deriving from American Union's merger with Western Union was siphoned off through the Central Construction Company, which charged American Union enormous prices for stringing its lines and was capitalized for only $5000—a small-scale model of the Crédit Mobilier. Its president was Washington E. Connor, in whose brokerage Gould was a silent partner, and its treasurer, almost inevitably, was his confidential clerk, Giovanni P. Morosini.

None of the stockholders' suits succeeded in nullifying the consolidation. Whenever he was summoned as a witness, Gould was a barrister's dream of a witness, always calm, polite, modest, bland, and endlessly evasive. He was always ready to answer a question, but never to give a straight answer. To the opposition lawyers, who had no more success at pinning him down than a man trying to harpoon a jellyfish, he was the picture of insolence cloaked in humility, Uriah Heep brought to life. One of his opponents was the forensic genius Colonel Robert G. Ingersoll, the notorious agnostic, who proclaimed after a bout of cross-examination with Gould, "I do not believe that since man was in the habit of living on this planet anyone has ever lived possessed of the impudence of Jay Gould."

Even more vociferous and potentially more menacing than the stockholders' suits was the rise of the antimonopoly movement throughout the United States. Gould's maneuvers with Union Pacific and Western Union in the past year, of course, gave the movement a new urgency. Monopoly had become a synonym for all the ills and evils of capitalism. The Greenback Party had adopted an antimonopoly plank in its platform. A somewhat giddier spirit animated the National Anti-Monopoly Cheap Freight Railway League, which solemnly proposed toll-supported public railways.

Shortly after the American Union–Western Union merger, the Anti-Monopoly League of New York held a clamorous meeting at the Cooper Union. The antimonopoly marching song, with its forthright pledge to hang Jay Gould to a sour apple tree (a fate once reserved for Confederate President Jefferson Davis), was sung by a glee club. A parade of speakers denounced the Republican Party for succoring the monopolists; boos and hisses greeted every mention of President-elect James A. Garfield's name.

But when a speaker first brought up the name of Jay Gould the rafters of the old meeting house shook with yells of "Hang him!" and "Cut his throat!"

All this caterwauling barely penetrated the thick walls of Gould's library in the Fifth Avenue home where he secluded himself, after the last tap of the ticker, with his beloved books. He had some sense of history, personal and general, and could remember how his father had contemptuously stood up to the antirent mobsters during his boyhood. And if the mob turned violent, as it would a few years hence, he could always make a run for it. A boat was always waiting a few blocks crosstown at its Hudson River dock to spirit him away from the displeasure of his fellow citizens.

Perhaps the definitive word on Gould and his associates was uttered, however unlikely the setting, on the floor of a Congress which numbered more than a few of their beneficiaries.

Senator Vest of Missouri, whose epigrams sparkled in the general murk of his chamber's standard oratory, was speaking of the monopolists when he delivered himself of this succinct indictment:

"When they speak they lie; when they are silent they are stealing."

9. A MASTERPIECE OF THIMBLERIGGING

"thimblerig—a gambler's sleight-of-hand game played with three small cups and a small ball or pea . . . to cheat by any trick."

—*Webster's Dictionary.*

DURING the seventies, the population of New York was growing so fast that rapid transit facilities became necessary. Steam-driven elevated street railways seemed to be the solution and soon the island of Manhattan, already raucous with the noise of surface traffic, was filled with the pounding of the "Els" overhead. Up and down Second and Third, Sixth and Ninth Avenues ran the roaring El trains on their steel platforms, their engines scattering soot, smoke, and sparks on the thronged streets below, their structures blotting out the sunlight for six or seven whole decades, until finally they were torn down and people felt strange in the sunlight and open air of the denuded avenues.

If the Els constituted a public nuisance with their smoke and noise, the methods by which they were financed and enfranchised were no less noisome.

Manipulation of the resources of the elevated railways was

controlled through three separate companies, the Manhattan, the Metropolitan, and the New York Elevated Railway. The first was simply a holding company, the other two were the operating forces. Franchises for the two operating lines were obtained in the usual way—legislative bribery. It was testified before the Hepburn Committee's Railroad Investigation of the State of New York that the charter for the Metropolitan was secured through a considerable outlay of cash and favors in New York and Albany. José de Navarro, one of Metropolitan's officials, told the investigators that a "corruption fund" of $650,000 was expended before the franchise was granted.

Both the Metropolitan and the New York Elevated's lines were built by the New York Loan and Improvement Company, which was organized mainly by the directors and leading investors of the two companies and thus enabled them to let contracts to themselves and profit from both ends. (The inventive ghost of the Crédit Mobilier walked again.) The Manhattan Elevated Railway Company had been organized in 1875 with a capitalization of $2,000,000. Its promoters hoped to build two rapid transit lines, but the depression of the mid-seventies and the unexpected imposition of real-estate taxes, upheld by the State Court of Appeals, made them decide to siphon off a quick profit and abandon the project without building a foot of line. Instead the Manhattan was designated as the holding company for the Metropolitan and the New York and, without legal authority, its capitalization was raised to $13,000,000. Manhattan then used this illicit stock issue to lease the two operating lines.

It would have taken a squad of Philadelphia lawyers to untangle the three companies and rescue them from the morass of inefficiency into which they had sunk through years of mismanagement. Stockholders in all three companies were at odds. No dividends were being paid. The three companies had combined tax arrears of almost a million dollars.

Yet, to the discerning eye, the elevated railways also had their inviting aspects. The growing metropolis obviously needed rapid transit lines, whose proceeds could be increased simply by boosting the five-cent fares then charged. With the companies' investors at odds, control could be achieved that much easier. Stock in Manhattan, the controlling company, was selling at a steady 55 to 57 throughout 1880 before it was subject to the panicky fluctuations induced the following year. Its stock was waterlogged but if control of all three companies could be obtained and their affairs placed on a sounder operating basis, the elevated railways would be an excellent long-term investment.

The discerning eye which penetrated the corporate gloom enveloping the transit companies was, of course, Jay Gould's.

He had hardly finished encompassing Western Union before he proceeded with plans to take over the elevated railways.

Again, with his Napoleonic grasp of all aspects of the financial battlefield, he began marshaling the forces which enabled him to conquer. Not only the money, which was as expendable as ammunition, not only the men who would be his lieutenants and secret agents, but the psychological elements which would panic his opponents and bewilder the public at large until his blitzkrieg was completed. No field marshal disposed a wider selection of forces. He had Russell Sage as his chief lieutenant, his elite guard of brokers and speculators through whom he would make his moves, his propaganda arm (the *World*), his lawyers and judges who would clear the way for his assaults on the financial position of the three companies, and his fifth column of collaborators within the companies themselves.

In the forthcoming campaign the New York *World* was to prove itself an admirable weapon. Rarely had an investment of several hundred thousand dollars returned so much, indirectly, as Gould's purchase of the *World*. It did not rank high journalistically, being as dull and stodgy a sheet as could be found in Manhattan, but its editors were so wonderfully amenable to the owner's suggestions. Ethics and editorial re-

sponsibility were cast to the winds the moment Gould mur-
mured an idea for an editorial or an item in its "Wall Street
Gossip" column.

The ultrasuggestible editor of the *World* was William
Henry Hurlbert, whose trickiness, overlaid with a sanctimonious air, was so notorious that James Gordon Bennett's
Herald referred to him as "The Reverend Mephistopheles."
His personal conduct, it appears, was as impeachable as
his editorial. George Templeton Strong, the sturdy moralist
whose diary was a catalogue of the Gilded Age's vulgarity
and mischief-making ("I wish I could flee into the wilderness
as Lot fled Sodom and take refuge in some dull but decent
New England village"), had only the deepest contempt for
Hurlbert, concerning whom he wrote:

"He is among the very few human creatures whom I loathe,
as a gaudily-colored and fetid bug. My correspondence with
him in August 1857, of which I retain certified copies, proves
him to be among the basest of mankind. I never read such a
combination of profligacy and insolence. First, he tried to
seduce his friend's wife and nearly succeeded. Then he demanded to be made a party to any settlement between her
and her husband and threatened to make the affair public
('to appeal from the narrow circle of private prejudice to the
wide horizon of the public heart') unless his modest demands
were granted. Then he long refused to give up her letters,
and at last had the infamous audacity to name certain ladies
as his backers, as cognizant of the intrigue and as his advisers
and endorsers!"[1]

Strictly a cad, Mr. William Henry Hurlbert, but Gould was
willing to overlook all that in view of his editor's quickness
to seize upon a suggestion and translate it into cold type. In
May of 1881, like the rumbling of a preliminary artillery
bombardment, the *World* began demanding that something
be done about the elevated railway companies, charging that

[1] *The Diary of George Templeton Strong*, Vol. IV.

they were insolvent, that their directors were engaged in an
unstated conspiracy, that the public and the stockholders
were suffering from their mismanagement. The implication
was that some unnamed but public-spirited citizen should replace them. Murky and insinuating though their tone, the editorials should have alerted Wall Street, at least, that Jay
Gould was on the march again. But Wall Street apparently
had its nose buried in the *Times* or the *Herald*, neither of
which saw any crying need for a reform of the elevated railway system.

By this time Gould had his agents planted in all three companies. Sage had bought a large block of Manhattan stock,
doubtless at Gould's suggestion, and was thus enabled to have
a voice in the company's management. José de Navarro, of
Metropolitan, had allied himself with Gould. Another Gould
collaborator was to be Cyrus W. Field, the eminent indus-
trialist, philanthropist and all-around public benefactor . . .
a whited sepulchre, in the phrase beloved of contemporary
pulpits, whose whiteness was soon to be discolored. At first
Field, relying on his nobler instincts, had opposed the entry
of Gould into the traction field—he was then heavily interested in both the Manhattan and the New York Elevated—
and was reported "breathing out threatenings and slaughter
against all enemies, his eye being evidently most steadily fixed
on Mr. Gould." The induction of Cyrus Field, one of the nation's most distinguished and socially impeccable figures, into
Gould's charmed circle is still something of a mystery, but
apparently it was based on the well-tested commandment, "If
you can't beat 'em, join 'em." Field had been associated with
Gould in the Wabash operation; his brother, David Dudley
Field, had been Gould's legal brain during the Erie wars, so
he must surely have known what he was getting into and what
he was avoiding, in the way of reprisal, through knuckling
under to Gould. Possibly, too, he was persuaded that joining
in Gould's schemes would result in better transportation for

the city's masses, although that would presume that Field's naïveté was all but inexhaustible.

Cyrus Field was a divided man in the best nineteenth century tradition. He wanted wealth and social position, but he also yearned to be known for his good works. An offshoot of Puritan stock, he was born in Stockbridge, Massachusetts, in 1819, one of four brothers who made their mark in the world. In addition to David Dudley, the former Gould mouthpiece, they were Stephen, a justice of the United States Supreme Court, and Henry, a noted clergyman and author. Cyrus left home in his middle teens and became a paper manufacturer by the time he was twenty. Thirteen years later, having piled up a quarter of a million dollars, he decided to retire from business. In 1854, after returning from a trip to South America and bringing back a live jaguar and an Indian boy as trophies, he was urged to end his retirement and confer a boon on mankind by building the first Atlantic cable, then regarded as a near-Utopian project which would join the Old and the New Worlds together in an everlasting feast of amity. The man who kindled his imagination, and inadvertently depleted his fortune, was Lieutenant Matthew D. Maury, the celebrated hydrographer.

Thus began a twelve-year struggle against the winds and currents of the North Atlantic. With the financial cooperation of Peter Cooper, his Gramercy Park neighbor, and other New York businessmen, he spent four years laying the first fragile line across the ocean floor from Newfoundland to England. On August 16, 1858, the first message was cabled from Queen Victoria to President Buchanan. The newspapers referred to him as "Cyrus the Great"; even headier was one journal's opinion that "the old Cyrus conquered the world for himself and the new one conquered the ocean for the world." The praise was premature, however, as it developed that the cable wasn't sufficiently insulated to permit efficient transmission. The next year Field and his fellow promoters hired the *Great Eastern,* a monstrous white elephant among steamships, to lay a new cable with heavier insulation, but the line snapped in mid-ocean. It wasn't until 1866 that an efficient cable was finally laid.

Later Field became a newspaper proprietor (the New York *Mail and Express*), and in 1877 was persuaded that he should interest himself in the tangled rapid transit situation. He offered to buy a majority of the stock in the New York Elevated if the company's creditors would accept bonds at sixty cents on the dollar for the money owed by the company. Later he also invested in the Manhattan. For a man of his age and experience, it appears that he was rather easily gulled; his vanity about being Public Benefactor No. 1 was a chord upon which shrewder men could strike with advantage to themselves. The perfect proposition, to Cyrus Field, was one which would simultaneously yield him hosannas in the newspapers and a neat little profit on the side. As a kindly biographer wrote, Field "possibly overestimated the value of his enthusiasm and frankness in overcoming the selfishness and ingratitude of others." Pollyanna in a beard and frock coat, he was beyond his depth dealing with Gould, Sage, de Navarro and their confederates in thimblerigging and El-raising.

The group made their first move on May 18, 1881, when New York Attorney General Hamilton Ward, "acting on information he possessed," appeared before Justice Donahue of the New York State Supreme Court and applied for permission on behalf of the people to sue for nullification of Manhattan's charter. The complaint was drawn up by the law firm of Lawrence & Waehner, which by no coincidence whatsoever was also the legal representative of Washington Connor, Gould's principal broker. Just why Attorney General Ward was playing Gould's game was never determined, since he did not profit from any of the transactions; perhaps, unlikely as it seems, he was persuaded that he was acting in the public interest. Permission to seek the charter nullification, in any case, was granted, but it was never pressed. Gould's purpose in the legal move was simply to frighten Manhattan's stock-holders and drive the price of Manhattan stock down.

With this and each succeeding move, there was an ominous counterpoint sounded in the columns of the New York *World*. In an editorial appearing the morning after the Attorney General's appearance in court, Gould's organ noted that "Attorney General Ward, in an interview which appears this morning in our stock columns, sustains every position the *World* has taken against the solvency and good faith of the Manhattan Elevated Railway Company." More menacingly, Editor Hurlbert pointed out that "his views seem to go far toward making its original directors amenable to the statutes against conspiracy."

A day later the *World's* financial editor was writing that "there were rumors that papers in new suits were preparing today against the members of the Manhattan board of directors individually. The men who are fighting the directors are very strong."

All this cannonading from the *World* and the rumors and threats being circulated by various other Gould agents naturally had a violent effect on Manhattan stock prices. The stock had been selling as high as 57 at the end of 1881, but on May 20 it slid to 25. Gould was creating a bearish atmosphere in which the elevated stocks would sink to a fraction of their value, and control of the transit companies could be secured at bargain basement prices.

On June 2, the financial page of the *World* carried this depressing item: "The governing committee of the Stock Exchange, which professes to be very particular as to the class of securities admitted on the list for dealing, would do well to order an investigation at once into the condition of the Manhattan Company . . . the elevated railroad properties may be very valuable, but the business of these roads is not valuable enough to warrant the present prices of the stock."

By mid-June, Wall Street was humming with reports that Gould and his cohorts were secretly buying into the three elevated companies. Since he was then busily hammering prices down, Gould took alarm at the reports, which might encourage any number of speculators to jump on his band wagon and ruin his bear campaign. His faithful tuning fork on Park Row reverberated indignantly. On June 15, the *World* asserted that "the rumor, industriously circulated, that Mr. Gould's party is largely interested in the Manhattan and Metropolitan Companies has been put forward merely to make a market on which to sell the stocks of these companies . . . Most people agree in conceding that the longer the Manhattan Company exists the greater its indebtedness will become."

Four days later, June 19, when the rumor would not die a decent death, the financial editor of the *World* reported:

"Mr. Gould and those connected with him express themselves very clearly to the effect that they will not allow their names to be used as directors of either the Manhattan or the Metropolitan Company."

It took Gould just nineteen days to make a liar out of his own newspaper.

Meanwhile, Manhattan and the two operating companies were assailed on all sides by injunctions, petitions for receivership and derogatory rumors. Financial journalists other than the *World's* liegemen helped the Gould cause by reporting that the traction companies were on the rocks. The Philadelphia *North American* warned that Manhattan's stock soon would be "worth fully the ragman's price for the paper on which it is printed, but hardly more." Enthusiastic echo from the *World:* "Complete wiping out of the Manhattan Company and its stock would be a great blessing to Wall Street." Attorneys for Gould's broker, Washington Connor, obtained an injunction restraining Manhattan from paying dividends to Metropolitan shareholders. A few days later, on July 1, George S. Lespinasse, acting through the same law firm of Lawrence & Waehner, obtained a similar injunction aimed at

New York Elevated's stockholders. Mr. Lespinasse, it developed, was an associate of José de Navarro, who was a confederate of Gould's. Still later Cyrus Field, as majority stockholder in the New York, began court action to cancel Manhattan's leasehold on its lines. To the outsider it would appear that all three companies and their chief stockholders were embroiled with each other; only above the artificial fog of battle were visible the terroristic tactics of Jay Gould and his friends, aimed at depressing the companies' fortunes to just the point where they could be retrieved by a new management. By July 9, Manhattan's stock was down to 23; by the end of the month, to 15½.

Gould's next step was to throw Manhattan into a receivership managed, through the art of financial puppetry, by himself.

The obliging Attorney General, Hamilton Ward, not only instituted State Supreme Court proceedings to this effect but obtained a change of venue to Albany, where Judge Theodore R. Westbrook was sitting. The judge was certified to be equally amenable to Gould's bidding: many years ago he had served as Gould's first legal counsel. Now he appointed as Manhattan's receivers two men eminently suitable to Gould's designs, A. L. Hopkins and John F. Dillon. Hopkins was an official of the Wabash Railroad. Dillon (no relation to Sidney Dillon, the Union Pacific president) was a Gould lawyer.

That same day, July 8, Gould emerged as a director of Metropolitan Elevated, notwithstanding the *World's* assertion of June 19 that he would never, never serve on the board of any of the elevated companies.

During August, Manhattan stock fluctuated between 16 and 20 as certain parties began buying heavily, despite the fact that the company had been declared legally insolvent. Early in September the extraordinarily amiable Judge Westbrook came down from Albany and installed himself in an office next to Jay Gould's in the Western Union Building, where he would be handy for signature of writs, injunctions and any other papers Gould thrust before him.[2]

Judge Westbrook undoubtedly earned his keep while occupying Gould office space. He prepared a petition in bankruptcy for the Manhattan company, the mere report of which served to further depress its stock prices. He also signed an order enabling the Manhattan receivers to issue certificates which ostensibly would allow them to raise the money to pay off its indebtedness. The certificates, however, were a "financial absurdity," as Julius Grodinsky has written; instead of being secured by a lien on the Metropolitan and New York companies, the Manhattan's only sources of income, they were backed only by the nonexistent net earnings of the holding company. Having engineered their issuance, Gould now proceeded to attack them through an affidavit which read: "The Manhattan Railway Company is hopelessly and irretrievably insolvent, and the borrowing of money by its receiver will be a most desperate expedient which can at most afford to said company only a temporary relief from its fatal embarrassments. I verily believe that the certificates of said receiver, should any be issued, will be utterly worthless and that no person will advance money thereupon with the expectation that such certificates will ever be paid."

Similarly worded affidavits, similarly designed to create the impression that Manhattan's position was hopeless, were signed by Field and Sage.

Speaking of the receiver's certificates in a salty aside to the New York *Tribune*, Field commented that he wouldn't "give a dollar for as many as a jackass could draw downhill."

Everyone concerned in the elaborately staged farce publicly joined in writing off Manhattan as a corporate monstrosity, a punctured balloon, which should be carted off the premises as soon as possible. The public-spirited Mr. Gould and his associates, including "Cyrus the Great," would not

[2] Westbrook later was impeached by the State Assembly but was cleared by the State Senate.

be able to sleep nights, it was implied, until all the Manhattan's benighted stockholders unburdened themselves of their worthless securities. Equally conscientious, the *World* joined in the good work and reported every bleat of alarm. The paper's financial editor wrote on September 23, "We are informed on very good authority this afternoon that the New York and Metropolitan Elevated Companies have decided to unite their forces in an attack upon the Manhattan Company, with a view to getting their roads into their own hands. Should they succeed—and we see no reason why they should not—Manhattan will be wiped out as a thing of the past."

With this bear campaign in full swing, Gould was able to buy up 48,000 shares of Manhattan, enough of the 128,000 issued to obtain control of the company. Manhattan's board of directors was reorganized to include him along with Field, Sage, and Sidney Dillon. For his part in bringing about this happy event, the *Wall Street News* reported, Field had been rewarded by a Gould tip to buy Western Union stock just before it jumped in value; he was also elected to the Western Union's board of directors . . . and perhaps even then he did not realize that he had acted as the Judas goat for the slaughtered sheep who had owned stock in the elevated companies.

And now the *World's* financial editor was able to discern a ray of hope for the Manhattan company. On October 9, he wrote, "The event of the day has been the development of the fact that Mr. Gould and his associates appear at the closing of the Manhattan Railway Company's stock books as the owners of quite one-half of the stock. . . . The change, it is thought, means that the Manhattan Company will rise the victor out of the troubles with which it has been overwhelmed." Gould did not control "quite" one-half of Manhattan's stock, of course, but the journalist's enthusiasm was pardonable in view of the miraculous recovery made by the company, which only two weeks before had been adjudged a "thing of the past."

It was really marvelous the way Manhattan's prospects re-

vived under the ministrations of Gould & Co. Again there was
much paper work for the diligent Judge Westbrook, who decided that Manhattan was now being operated in the best
interests of the public and should not be interfered with. He
denied the appeal of the New York Elevated for recovery of
its lines. Manhattan's receivership was abruptly terminated.
On October 25, Manhattan resumed its stewardship of the
Metropolitan and New York companies. All injunctions and
stockholders' suits were withdrawn. In clearing up the Manhattan's artificially created difficulties, Judge Westbrook announced at one point that "I am willing to go to the very verge
of judicial discretion"—a precipice which the dauntless jurist
actually had plunged over many times that busy summer.

Late in October Manhattan's stock, reflecting all this new-
found enthusiasm, rose to 45, causing the *World's* financial
editor, disregarding his summer-long forebodings, to crow
that "As I said long ago, the elevated railway franchise is too
big a thing to give away, and I never believed but that Manhattan would be rescued by the men who have the brains and
means to make the most of it."

By November 9, Manhattan was selling at 55, virtually the
same price it commanded one year ago, before Gould and his
colleagues began their raid. It had taken just six months for
Gould to undermine the city's elevated railway companies,
terrorize and drive out their stockholders and obtain effective
control of their managements. There was a certain amount of
backfiring and legal wrangling in the aftermath, particularly
from Sylvester H. Kneeland, a major stockholder in Manhattan and Metropolitan who did not propose to be bluffed out
of his holdings or his influence in their management, but
Gould prevailed through his domination of the judicial system and his freezing-out tactics on the stock exchange. There
were outcries from the press, particularly the New York
Times, but these could be safely ignored, even the remark of
Bennett's *Herald* that Gould should not be called the "Wolf
of Wall Street," a title to which so many briefly held claim,

but the "Skunk of Wall Street," in honor of his perseverance if nothing else.

With Cyrus Field as its titular head and Gould as its actual presiding genius, the elevated railway system inevitably proved to be a bonanza for the insiders who now controlled it. Eventually an issue of $26,000,000 worth of new Manhattan stock was authorized, all of it going to Manhattan, Metropolitan and New York Elevated stockholders. When this gigantic melon was sliced, with Gould, one may be sure, presiding over the division, $11,000,000 of the new issue went to Manhattan's shareholders, $7,800,000 to New York's and $7,200,000 to Metropolitan's.

A system so beneficial to the companies' investors required that their revenues be greatly increased; in other words, that fares be doubled. Accordingly, the price of riding an elevated train was raised from five to ten cents, which in those days of the $8 weekly pay check was a considerable burden on the lines' users. The fare increase aroused the crusading instincts of the New York *Times* to the point that it devoted several pages of its December 27, 1881 issue to detailing just how Gould, Sage, Field and their associates had seized control of the rapid transit facilities. The exposé was headed:

PUBLIC TRUSTS BETRAYED
The Stock Jobbing Scandal of
the Elevated Roads
How the Gould Clique Gained
Their Present Control

The *Times* outlined the labyrinthine conspiracy in all its essentials, not the least of which was the "daily sheet belonging to Jay Gould and making pretensions to influence as a newspaper [which] was persistently used to hammer down Manhattan stock and depreciate the value of the elevated railways generally."

On its editorial page, the *Times* charged that "There is no more disgraceful chapter in the history of stock jobbing than that which records the operations of Jay Gould, Russell Sage, Cyrus W. Field and their associates in securing control of the system of elevated railroads in New York City. . . .

"There is nothing specially surprising in the fact that Mr. Gould and his accomplices should resort to any means in their reach to gain control of other people's property by stock jobbing devices which should frighten or force its possessors to yield it up at a sacrifice. We have never been led to expect that they would have a fastidious regard either for the rights of other men or the interests of the public where an opportunity was presented for putting millions of dollars into their own pockets. . . . But what is both surprising and disgraceful is the facility with which they succeeded in using the Attorney General's office and the Supreme Court of this state to further their object. . . ."

This crackling of journalistic thunder was, if not music to their ears, an old refrain to Gould and Sage. Park Row could roar its head off for all they cared.

But Cyrus Field, mindful of his reputation as a Public Benefactor and fearful of his family's social standing in the quiet elegance of Gramercy Park, was appalled at being placed by the respectable New York *Times* in this financial rogues' gallery. He felt pricklings of conscience which, to his fellow traction magnates, was a worse disease than leprosy. He alone protested his innocence of the *Times'* charges and declared that the El system would always be operated in the best interests of the people it served. Worse yet, he whipped up such a feeling of remorse among other stockholders—or at least an equally efficacious fear of public opinion—that the El fare was cut back to five cents.

Gould's outrage may be imagined. Through his carefully plotted maneuvers, Field was made richer by millions, along with the other Manhattan–Metropolitan–New York Elevated insiders. The only price he had to pay, aside from any possible tribute to his conscience, was to keep a stiff upper lip when their critics and opponents yowled at a little perfectly legal (before public utilities commissions governed such matters) fare boosting. Hadn't W. H. Vanderbilt ("The public be damned") laid down the law for all time? No Bowery gang leader hearing that one of his abler lieutenants had succumbed to the ravings of a street-corner evangelist could have been more indignant at this defection.

One of Wall Street's more sinister legends—unfortunately not very well documented—concerns how Gould, aided by Russell Sage, ate his revenge cold and waited almost six years to teach Cyrus Field a lesson in loyalty among thimbleriggers.

According to Henry Clews and other annalists of the financial district, as well as the anti-Gould press at the time, Gould and Sage heard, in the fall of 1886, that Field was buying up large blocks of Manhattan stock. His plan obviously was to gain control of the elevated railways and squeeze out his old comrades. If Gould and Sage were outraged by his squeamishness over raising the El fare, they were quietly amused at the report of old Cyrus pussyfooting about the task of freezing them out of Manhattan. A trap thereupon was laid for the trapper.

Field's heavy buying had driven the price of Manhattan up to 175, three times its value when the Gould plunderbund seized control in 1881, and he was bullishly predicting it would rise to 200. Field was determined to corner Manhattan at any price. He borrowed heavily from the banks as more and more Manhattan appeared on the market, Gould and Sage dumping their holdings to increase the strain on Field's resources. At the same time Field's elder son, Edward, whose brokerage was conducting the buying campaign, was also heavily involved in speculation. Suddenly, and possibly at the suggestion of Gould and Sage, the banks began calling in their loans, and Field was trapped, "overloaded," caught between his collapsing credit and a fluctuating market. The bubble burst on June 24, when Manhattan began plummeting toward 125 and Field was forced to sue for peace. He had no alternative but to sell his 75,000 shares of Manhattan, bought mostly at the inflated price of 175, to Gould at the latter's price of 120. Cyrus the Great was a ruined man. Wall Street was convinced that Gould had planned it that way, lured Field into overextending himself, and then smashed him, deliberately and vengefully.

It is only fair to add that the Gould family, its apologists and even some of the less biased observers claimed that Gould bought out Field only to save him from bankruptcy and the market from a large-scale panic.

John T. Terry, a broker who acted as Field's intermediary, told the New York *Tribune* (pro-Gould, thanks to his loans to its publisher) a few days after Gould's death that the financier played a completely heroic role in the Field debacle:

"Mr. Gould was applied to for aid, and he generously loaned $1,000,000 of bonds, taking therefor no security whatever. This not being sufficient he purchased most reluctantly and at much personal inconvenience $5,000,000 of the stock of the Manhattan Elevated, at 120. A few days later he stated to me that he feared this was not sufficient to afford all the relief needed, and he thought he would be obliged to take the remaining $2,800,000, which he did at the same price, and distributed all or the greater portion of it among his friends. But this was not the end. A few days later I was again asked to his office, when he said to me, 'More assistance is needed, but I have declined to go any further. Won't you please look at their papers [Field and his son Edward] and see if you can suggest any way for them to obtain the money.'

"After looking into the matter, I said, 'Mr. Gould, you have already done more than could be reasonably asked of any man, but I am assured that $300,000 more will be sufficient, and I think you can loan it safely, although the securities are not otherwise available.' He replied, 'Very well, I will draw the check.' Here was assistance rendered of over $9,000,000 and although the stocks were purchased upon thirty days' time, the necessities of the case required immediate payment, which Mr. Gould made at much personal inconvenience. . . .

"This transaction not only saved the parties, but beyond question saved a panic in New York."

Gould's niece, Alice Northrop Snow, in *The Story of Helen Gould: Daughter of Jay Gould, Great American,* wrote that she was present at her uncle's summer home at Irvington-on-Hudson when Cyrus Field appeared to beg for help, looking "physically sick . . . a drowning man beseeching a rope from shore . . . a picture of abject despair." The "entire impression" was that of "a man in great extremities come to ask, to implore, the assistance of a friend." She quoted her mother, Gould's sister Sally, as saying that "Jay appreciated fully that the failure of Mr. Field would have brought down several stock exchange houses and one National Bank, involving large losses to Wall Street, possibly producing a panic; and it was largely that knowledge which caused him to render the assistance which he did. It was a matter of great mortification to him, and of disappointment also, that he should be allowed to rest under the imputation that Mr. Field had been unjustly treated by his hands."

Gould's motives in the latter phases of Field's comeuppance may have been tinged with altruism and compassion; it is not beyond all possibility that, rather late in life, he acquired a concern for his fellows. Yet it is also true that he profited immensely from Cyrus Field's failure. He acquired complete control of the rapid transit companies through Field's forced withdrawal, and he thought enough of their potential to make them a permanent part of his holdings, never to be relinquished in any speculative enterprise. He also installed his eldest son, George, as vice president of Manhattan, further stamping the property as the exclusive domain of what he believed, most passionately, would be a long and successful dynasty.

As for the much-diminished Cyrus Field, he was to live out his remaining several years in anguish and comparative poverty. He managed to maintain his household, according to one of his daughters, only through money raised by his

friends. His daughter said that on his seventy-second birthday, in 1891, he found that he owned only 1000 shares of
Anglo-American stock. J. Pierpont Morgan advanced enough
money to save his country home, near Gould's at Irvington-
on-Hudson, and paid the premium on his life insurance policies. He died in 1892. It may be a matter of satisfaction to
those who believe that money can't buy everything that Jay
Gould, sixteen years younger than Field, lived only a few
months longer.

As overlord of the Els, Gould deserved at least one footnote
to the social history of New York and a heartfelt curse from
his feminine passengers. His engineers tried to persuade him
to switch the trains from soft coal to electric power, which was
cleaner and more efficient. He was talked into attending a
demonstration of one of the electric-powered trains. Unfortunately a fuse blew out near where he was standing, and
Gould leaped several feet off the ground in fright. He came
down swearing he'd never trust electricity again. As a result,
wrote one of the city's social historians, for twenty years "the
faces of lady passengers were stenciled with smoky replicas
of the patterns of their veils," and coal smoke and soot continued to shower the streets below.

After his successful operations of 1881, in which the New
York *World* had served most usefully as his propaganda
organ, Gould decided that he had no further use for the newspaper. During his ownership and Hurlbert's editorship, the
paper had steadily declined both in merit and in financial
standing. A few more years of that and the *World* undoubtedly would have expired instead of becoming, for half a
century, one of the two or three greatest newspapers in American journalistic history. Its diminishing readers not only lost
faith in its integrity, knowing that it served principally as a
weapon in Wall Street forays, but it was a damnably

dreary sheet "about as exciting as Gray's *Elegy in a Country Churchyard*."

Casting an eye on its equally dismal balance sheet, Gould determined to sell it early in 1883 and began looking around for a buyer. First he tried to interest his broker, Washington Connor, who learned that the *World* was losing $40,000 annually and decided it was a luxury he could not afford.

By May, the circulation was down to 12,000, but one day a gentleman from St. Louis with a thick German accent came to his office at 195 Broadway and announced that he was interested in buying the *World*. The prospective purchaser was Joseph Pulitzer, who had migrated from Budapest before the Civil War and made a great success of the St. Louis *Post-Dispatch*. Now he was looking for a publishing foothold in New York. There was little haggling; Gould was too eager to sell, Pulitzer too eager to buy.

How much did Gould want for the property? Pulitzer wanted to know.

Exactly $346,000, Gould quickly replied, for the plant, equipment, advertising contracts, and . . . even Gould must have hesitated at mentioning this dubious asset . . . its "good will."

Pulitzer must have suspected he was being taken for a sucker, for in later years he remarked that "any man could capitalize a property upon earnings of ten percent, but Gould was the only man in the world who could capitalize upon a *loss* of twenty percent."

After a sleepless night, Pulitzer returned to Gould's office the next morning and announced he would accept the financier's terms.

Gould had the contracts already drawn up and wasted no time in shoving them in front of him.

Pulitzer signed, Gould smiled with satisfaction, and then, elaborately casual, he remarked, "By the way, Mr. Pulitzer, I had quite forgotten that some time ago I gave a small block of this newspaper stock to my son George. I would like to have him retain his interest. I assume you will have no objections to the boy's keeping this little holding."

"Not," replied Pulitzer sharply, "if you do not object to seeing it stated each morning in the year that the Gould family has no control or influence in the property."

Gould seemed "a trifle hurt," Pulitzer said later.

"Oh, well," the financier said, "if you view it in that light, never mind. I only thought you might like to have the young man in with you."[3]

With five great coups behind him, and five fortunes, from the gold corner, Erie, Union Pacific, Western Union, and Manhattan Elevated in pocket, Gould still could not resist the temptation of hornswoggling a few extra thousands in a deal he had been seeking for months. He would never be rich enough, cosmopolitan enough, or Fifth Avenueish enough to shuffle off the instincts of the sharp little back-country trader.

[3] According to Pulitzer's official biographer, Don C. Seitz, *Joseph Pulitzer: His Life and Letters.*

PART THREE

PARVENU'S PROGRESS

Some reflections of Jay Gould's contemporaries, mostly of an uncomplimentary nature:

James Keene, an embittered ex-confederate: "Jay Gould is the worst man on earth since the beginning of the Christian era. He is treacherous, false, cowardly and a despicable worm incapable of a generous motive."

Daniel Drew, ditto: "His touch is death."

Col. Robert G. Ingersoll, a noted advocate: "I do not believe that since man was in the habit of living on this planet anyone has ever . . . possessed . . . the impudence of Jay Gould."

Major Selover, an assailant: "He is notoriously treacherous."

An anonymous editorial writer of the New York *Herald:* "He should be called the Skunk of Wall Street, not one of its ubiquitous Wolves and Wizards."

Joseph Pulitzer in the New York *World:* ". . . one of the most sinister figures that have ever flitted bat-like across the vision of the American people."

Judge John F. Dillon, a business associate: "He was a superb executive officer. He applied the military rule to his subordinates. 'I do not want processes, but results,' was his doctrine. His great genius consisted in a knowledge of the value of corporate properties."

Song composed by a wag (quoted in the New York *Times,* November 10, 1869) supposedly sung by Jay Gould:

"O Jimmy Fisk, my Jo, Jim,
We'll never, never weary
Of squeezing every penny from
The stockholders of Erie.

And if by chance, Jim,
We to the gallows go,
We'll sleep together at the foot,
O Jimmy Fisk, my Jo."

Collis P. Huntington: "I know there are many people who do not like him. . . . I will say that I always found that he would do just as he agreed to do."

10. MONEY BAGS, VULGARIANS, AND PARVENUS

"The newcomers to New York society are vulgarians and parvenus . . . money bags of indiscreet speculation."
—N.Y. *Dramatic Mirror*, Oct. 23, 1883.

IN THE several fogged and forgetful years before she died in 1908, Mrs. William Astor—*the* Mrs. Astor—lived among the shades and phantoms of society's most opulent era between the Civil War and the end of the more or less gay nineties. Frequently, donning her celebrated diamond stomacher and tiara, whose regal glitter had all but blinded her contemporaries on state occasions, she would station herself under her life-size portrait by Carolus Duran in her drawing room, inclining her head in the old queenly fashion, greeting imaginary guests long since dead and "exchanging pleasantries with ghosts of the utmost social distinction."

Once she had been "Queen of the Four Hundred," and such names as Goelet, Livingston, Beekman, Schuyler, Whitney—even, after a slight, frowning hesitation, Vanderbilt—fell from her withered lips. But never Gould; she never slipped so far into dotage as to mention *that* name.

She was the last of the Old Guard, and she had protected the portals of her world with the devotion of a janissary. It may have been stuffy, snobbish, airless, and humorless, and given to overelaborate display that could be accomplished only by corps of servants, social secretaries, caterers, dress-makers, interior decorators, King Lehrs, Ward McAllisters, and all sorts of obsequious lackeys. But it had its standards; it kept out the upstarts, the climbers, the unworthy, and saw to it, thanks to Queen Caroline, that if a Gould could sit with an Astor on a board of directors, that same scoundrel and his family would never dance at one of its cotillions.

Her ascendancy, unfortunately for whatever hopes Gould had for his children's social progress, closely paralleled his rise to fortune. A descendant of the unassuming ship chandler Peter Schermerhorn, she married William Astor, who in-herited one-third of the Astor estate with its vast holdings of Manhattan slum property, in 1853. Eventually her husband showed a much greater interest in his yacht *Nourmahal* and other extramarital pleasures than in the proud and self-contained Caroline. In her frustration she turned to making herself the absolute ruler of New York society. In this task she was immensely aided by Ward McAllister, her court chamberlain and *"arbiter elegantiarum,"* whose cousin Sam Ward was married to William Astor's sister. McAllister took his duties very seriously. "Knowing that his decision was re-garded as the verdict of the Supreme Court of Appeal where matters of etiquette were under discussion, he devoted his whole life to compiling his famous set of rules for the guidance of social New York. He read books on heraldry and preced-ence, studied the customs of every Court in Europe. He rev-elled in forms and ceremonies, his cult of snobbishness was so ardent, so sincere, that it acquired dignity; it became almost a religion."[1] His most frequent advice to those jealous of their position was, "You can never be absolutely certain whether people are in society or not until you see them at four or five of the best houses. Then you can make advances to them with-out the danger of making a mistake." It was McAllister who observed that Mrs. Astor's ballroom held approximately four

[1] *King Lehr and the Gilded Age,* by Elizabeth Drexel Lehr.

hundred persons and decided that the totally eligible in New York society must never rise above that figure.

"Despotic and self-willed," Mrs. Astor played the role of *grande dame* to the hilt. As Elizabeth Drexel Lehr, whose husband succeeded McAllister as her cotillion-leader, wrote in her memoir,[1] she held her head high even while the society she dominated was twittering with gossip about her roving husband and his antics. "She had so cultivated the art of never looking at the things she did not want to see, never listening to words she did not wish to hear, that it had become second nature to her. New York would ring with gossip concerning the latest doings of William Astor; stories would be circulated of wild parties on board his yacht. . . . The rumors grew more and more exaggerated as they flew from mouth to mouth. Everyone wondered what Mrs. Astor, giving her stately dinners and musicales at her Fifth Avenue house, thought of it all, but their curiosity was never satisfied. When someone would ask tentatively after her husband she would reply placidly: 'Oh, he is having a delightful cruise. The sea air is so good for him. It is a great pity I am such a bad sailor, for I should so much enjoy accompanying him. As it is I have never even set foot on the yacht; dreadful confession for a wife, isn't it?' And her smile would hold nothing but pleasant amusement over her inability to share her husband's pleasures. . . . She always spoke of him in terms of the greatest affection and admiration. . . ." Obviously the old girl had a touch of class, even aside from the diamonds and ermines she wore, as the New York *Times* observed, "with the utmost prodigality."

The Astor Ball, of course, was the premier event of the social season, an "occasion for much heartburning . . . weeping and gnashing of teeth on the part of those who did not receive the coveted slip of cardboard, 'Mrs. Astor requests the pleasure. . . .'" And the epitome of social acceptance was to be invited to sit on the enormous divan with red silk cushions which was accurately described as "The Throne," on which Mrs. Astor placed herself and her current favorites.

Even Mrs. Astor finally was forced to recognize that a social revolution was occurring in the early eighties with so many new multimillionaires clamoring at the gates and so many of the older families losing their substance. Ward McAllister, as her grand vizier, took note of their claims when he wrote (in *Society As I have Found it*):

"Up to this time, for one to be worth a million of dollars was to be rated as a man of fortune, but now, bygones must be bygones. New York's ideas as to values, when fortune was named, leaped boldly up to ten millions, fifty millions, one hundred millions, and the necessities and luxuries followed suit. One was no longer content with a dinner of a dozen or more, to be served by a couple of servants. Fashion demanded that you be received in the hall of the house where you were to dine, by from five to six servants. . . . Soft strains of music were introduced between the courses, and in some houses gold replaced silver in the way of plate, and everything that skill and art could suggest was added to make the dinners not a vulgar display, but a great gastronomic effort, evidencing the possession by the host of both money and taste." But McAllister warned the newcomers that "the best quality for them to possess is modesty in asserting their claims; letting people seek them rather than attempting to rush too quickly to the front."

As McAllister said, *hereditary wealth* was the criterion for social acceptance. On this basis, the Vanderbilts, for instance, could be admitted because their money had been passed down by the old Commodore and had lost some of the taint of the methods by which it had been acquired. If the Astor fortune came out of a butcher shop, in part, and continued to flow from slum rentals, the passage of several generations had sanctified it. Other fortunes in the new multimillion dollar class had been acquired through methods no less reprehensible than Jay Gould's but with much less notoriety. It

was Gould who was being held up in the headlines as
the archmonopolist, the most flagrant manipulator of stocks
and corporations, the most predatory of the new capitalists.
Worse yet, in business, he had made monkeys out of his social
betters.

Queen Caroline would devote all her energies to excluding
the Goulds and seeing to it that her friends snubbed them as
the grossest of upstarts.

In truth, whatever else he deserved, Jay Gould did not
merit the label of parvenu. He was no gate-crasher; he had
too much pride, too great a sense of proportion to truckle to
anyone, however much he secretly desired social acceptance
for his children. Then, too, he must have been quietly amused
at the fact that a man of his lineage should be regarded as
an upstart by the descendants of German butchers and Dutch
ferrymen. Who of his Fifth Avenue neighbors could boast of
the equal of his forebear, Colonel Abraham Gold of the Fifth
Connecticut Militia, son of the colony's lieutenant governor,
who died at the head of his untrained regiment as it sought
to drive the British out of Ridgefield? Intellectually and cul-
turally, Jay Gould was the superior of most of the men who
costumed themselves for Mrs. Astor's ballroom. He spent his
nights in his library while his fellow nabobs enjoyed lustier
pursuits, caressed the leather of a first edition with the ardor
others reserved for the flesh of accessible actresses. His morals,
aside from money-making, were unimpeachable, never questioned even by his worst enemies; and *his* yacht was reserved
for family outings as William Astor's was maintained for more
scandalous pursuits. It wasn't Jay Gould against whom the
Rev. Thomas De Witt Talmage thundered when he listed the
Lepers of High Life, "stockbrokers from Wall Street, large im-
porters from Broadway, representatives of all the commercial
and wealthy classes. . . . I prefer that kind of heathenism
which wallows in filth and disgusts the beholder rather than
that heathenism which covers up its putrefaction with camel's
hair shawl and point lace, and rides in turnouts worth three

thousand dollars, liveried driver ahead and rosetted flunky behind." The "haunts of iniquity," reported the Rev. Dr. Talmage, were thronged with "men in high places smoking cigarettes, with their feet on Turkish divans." Jay Gould not only kept his slippered feet off Turkish upholstery and solidly planted before his own fireside but abstained from tobacco, liquor and all the other ordinary vices. His only mistress was the Stock Exchange. But he would never daintily point a toe in any fashionable cotillion, or find himself encased in the satin breeches of a French courtier, or come within salaaming distance of Mrs. Astor's imperial divan.

The Goulds were still being rejected when the Vanderbilts, hitherto among the excluded, achieved their skillfully managed breakthrough in March of 1883, a coup comparable in the social sense to one of the late Commodore's corners in the stock market.

Mrs. William K. Vanderbilt, who married one of his grandsons, served notice that her tribe meant to storm the Astorian ramparts when she installed herself as chatelaine of Fifth Avenue's most imposing new residence—the new $3,000,000 château at No. 660 with its delicate spires, limestone exterior, entrance hall and staircase of Caen stone, two-storied paneled dining room and Moorish billiard room. It put the older châteaux along the Loire to shame, for extravagance at least (New York Central was then selling at 125 and paying eight percent dividends). On March 26, 1883, Mrs. Vanderbilt announced, she would reign over the most magnificent ball in the history of the metropolis.

Advance publicity on the ball flooded the society columns of the New York papers and whipped up so much interest that even Mrs. Astor was intrigued and let it be known that she and her daughter Carrie would deign to attend if an invitation was tendered. But Mrs. V. demanded complete submission from Mrs. A. after years of being ignored when invitations to the Astor Ball went out. Just as circuitously, she let it be known that she could hardly invite Mrs. Astor since the latter had never paid a formal call. A few days later a footman in the blue Astor livery deposited Mrs. Astor's calling card on a silver salver held by a footman in the Vanderbilt maroon. The invitation was forthcoming.

Mrs. Vanderbilt's Fancy Dress Ball, according to all the press accounts, lived up to its billing. The second-story supper room was transformed into a tropical forest, with potted palms festooned with thousands of orchids, and the disapproving New York *World* estimated that the affair cost at least $250,000, including $155,000 for costumes and $65,000 for champagne and catering. Henry Clews, who attended, wrote that "That ball seemed to have the effect of levelling up among the social ranks of uppertendom, and placing the Vanderbilts at the top of the heap in what is recognized as good society in New York." In sheer splurging, Mr. Clews thought, it would rival the feast of Alexander the Great at Babylon. Twelve hundred persons had finally received invitations, fretting over which, the New York *Times* said, "disturbed the sleep and occupied the waking hours of social butterflies, both male and female, for over six weeks."

Among those who waited, and possibly fretted, in vain were the occupants of 579 Fifth Avenue, the comparatively modest brownstone into which the Jay Gould family had moved the year before. None of the family chronicles detail, or even admit to, any anguish over being ignored by the Vanderbilts on the splendid occasion. Yet it must have been a blow to the family pride. It was bad enough to being excluded from the Astor Four Hundred, but to be similarly debarred from the Vanderbilt Twelve Hundred was three times as humiliating.

Society reporters wrote the day after the Vanderbilt ball that the No. 1 topic of conversation over supper under the orchidaceous palms was the absence of any member of the Gould family on the guest list. "Thus the House of Vanderbilt avenged Erie."

At the next Astor Ball, on January 21, 1884, Queen Caroline

received the William K. Vanderbilts, formally recognizing what she and her set called "the new people."

It would be a good ten years before any Gould broke bread or broached a bottle of champagne with the topmost layer of society—and that only after Jay the First had vanished from the scene. Henceforth, the society gossips observed, Gould would take his family on a cruise to Florida whenever a great social event was in the offing, in a rather pathetic attempt to ameliorate whatever pangs they may have felt at being snubbed.

There was a measure of consolation for the Gould family when they were included in the plans for the new Metropolitan Opera House, principally, perhaps, because they were able to contribute a considerable sum toward its construction. Until 1883, the Academy of Music on Irving Place had been the operatic center of New York, but the Old Guard held sway there and the Livingstons, the Schuylers, the Bayards, and the Beekmans wouldn't permit the "new people" to join them in the dress circle, even when they offered $30,000 for boxes. The banker August Belmont offered a compromise, by which twenty-six new boxes would be added to the dress circle, but the newcomers wanted seats in the *old* boxes, on the worn red plush imprinted with stately old bottoms. If they had to put up with something new, they decided, they'd build it themselves. Under Vanderbilt leadership, therefore, the Metropolitan Opera House was financed and constructed uptown, where the path of empire lay. On the opening night, October 22, 1883, the tone-deaf Jay Gould, who could barely distinguish between *The Star-Spangled Banner* and the sextet from *Lucia*, his wife and older children sat in one of the boxes, along with a splendid array of Vanderbilts, Goelets, Whitneys, Drexels, Rockefellers, Morgans, Millses, Huntingtons and Bakers. In the two rows of boxes designated the Diamond Horseshoe, reporters estimated, was represented wealth totaling more than half a billion dollars—an exceedingly conservative estimate. The newspapers, recognizing the monetary as well as the cultural aspect of the occasion, assigned their financial reporters in addition to society editors and music critics.

"All the *nouveaux riches* were there," reported the *Dramatic Mirror* in hoity-toity accents. "The Goulds and Vanderbilts and people of that ilk perfumed the air with the odor of crisp greenbacks. The tiers of boxes looked like cages in a menagerie of monopolists. When somebody remarked that the house looked *as bright as a new dollar,* the appropriate character of the assemblage became apparent. To the refined eye, the decorations of the edifice seemed in particularly bad taste."

For himself, Jay Gould was as disinterested in Society as he was deaf to music. Social pretensions could hardly have been anything but ridiculous to a man who could buy out any dozen husbands of the snootier hostesses who prided themselves on barring the door to him and all his connections. Besides he had no taste or aptitude for the kind of elaborate romps and routs organized by the social leaders of the time; no stomach for rich foods and lashings of champagne; no fund of small talk and flattery; no ability to dissemble his contempt for the mincing dandies who led cotillions and flitted sexlessly through the boudoirs of the lionesses who ruled Fifth Avenue. He was, in every sense of the word, antisocial. Out West they would have called him a loner.

He did his best, however, to enjoy his wealth without giving up very much time to the project. Unlike Russell Sage and a few other magnates, he was no miser; it was simply that his capacity for enjoyment was so limited. The pleasures of wealth, so far as he was concerned, consisted of getting the money, outwitting others for it (big beefy men who towered over him, but could be humbled amazingly across a desk), and using it to bend other men to his will. When it came to spending, Gould did so lavishly, if not wildly. His family, of course, was thoroughly spoiled, lacking his intimate knowl-

edge of the reality of money and how bitterly it must be acquired in large amounts.

The Goulds lived in all the luxury, all the servant-borne
ease, that could be arranged in the overstuffed and over-
privileged Gilded Age. The solidity of the magnificence with
which a few people lived then can be glimpsed even today
in the heavy and ornate possessions they have handed down,
in a study of the servants' quarters which honeycombed the
great houses of Fifth Avenue, Louisburg Square, Newport,
Bar Harbor and other enclaves of the super-rich, in the menus
drawn up with all the gravity of a state council every day, in
the surviving carriage houses, conservatories, and formal
gardens—all resting, as their fortunes did, on the backs of immigrant labor. It was a good time to be rich, provided your
conscience was well insulated.

Gould was sensible about his style of living, striking an intelligent balance between comfort and sheer ostentation. The
massive, four-story brownstone at the corner of Fifth Avenue
and Forty-seventh Street into which the family moved in
1882 and which served as Gould's town house until his death
may have been dingy compared to the Vanderbilt château
farther up the avenue, but it held every comfort and conven-
ience and was spacious enough to accomodate any number
of visiting relations. He really splurged when he built his
country house, Lyndhurst, at Irvington-on-Hudson, on 500
acres of riverside property. Lyndhurst was a Gothic masterpiece of the time—overblown and pretentious as it appears
to the modern eye, crowning its slope like a medieval castle with transatlantic excrescences—a sprawling affair of
huge, square towers, tall, mullioned windows, massive porte-
cocheres, haphazard wings, steeply pitched roofs, and façades
crawling with ivy.

Once past the stoutly guarded gatehouses—there were two
of them—the visitor was swept up driveways bordered with
great elms and graceful lindens until suddenly one was confronted by its massive ramparts and lordly bell tower. The

house itself had forty rooms, but there was a separate building for servants' quarters, another for the laundry. Elsewhere among its groves and immaculately tailored lawns and formal gardens were the conservatory and flanking greenhouses where Gould kept the largest collection of orchids and other tropical flowers in the world; here, in a quiet ecstasy, he tended 8000 orchids, some of them imported "from beyond Trebizond," 2000 azaleas and other rare blooms. Even his taste in flowers, it was observed, ran to the jungle and (to the imaginative) its somewhat sinister growths. Down on the riverfront there was a separate structure housing a bowling alley. Nearby there was an enclosed swimming pool with Doric columns, where a lifeguard was always on duty (in a rowboat, so expansive was the pool). A network of telephone lines connected all these buildings, with extensions from the main house to the gatehouses, the carriage houses, the conservatory and greenhouses, the superintendent's house, the butler's pantry, the bowling alley, the swimming pool, the yacht landing, and the laundry. Through this network, help could be summoned quickly, for life at Lyndhurst was often enlivened by alarms that prowlers, cranks, burglars, and plain nosy tourists had been sighted lurking in the shrubbery. The grounds were patrolled around the clock, particularly at night, with a small private army always standing under arms to repel invaders. One of the hazards of that time, it must be remembered, was the bomb-throwing or otherwise lethally equipped anarchist who sought merit in the eyes of his activist comrades by eliminating some notable. Between the Civil War and the early 1900s three Presidents were assassinated and a considerable number of capitalists menaced or murdered. No rich man of the Gilded Age could turn down the gaslight at night without wondering whether some whiskered anarchist would pounce on him before dawn.

The third of the pleasures with which Gould distracted himself from such fears and recuperated from the stress of his Wall Street maneuvers, in addition to his books and tropical flowers, was yachting. His first boat was a steam launch named *Rosamond* in which he commuted, often with Cyrus Field and John Terry, before Field eliminated himself from the Manhattan Elevated picture, between Lyndhurst and his downtown Manhattan offices in the summer. Later he acquired the steam yacht *Atalanta,* which became his proudest possession. The yacht cost him almost $1000 a week to maintain and was one of the most luxurious craft afloat, 250 feet long, ranking with William K. Vanderbilt's *Alva* (285 feet), William Astor's floating seraglio *Nourmahal* (233 feet) and James Gordon Bennett's *Namouna* (226 feet). To his niece, Alice Northrop Snow, it seemed like "a fairy palace," and as she described it:

"The dining-saloon alone fairly stopped my breath. The portholes were curtained with plush, strawberry edged with dull gold. A marvelous oriental rug, one of the largest I had ever seen, covered almost the entire floor. The whole room was furnished in a wood of light color, with paneling on which were carved groupings of fruit, so wonderfully done that I could easily imagine myself in the act of picking a pomegranate, perhaps, or luscious-looking peach. In another place, a built-in upright piano took my eye, and of course I couldn't keep myself from sitting down to try it. I sat down delightedly, too, in every luxuriously upholstered chair. I opened drawers and bookcases. The berth in Aunt Helen's [Mrs. Jay Gould's] stateroom had a plush cover, deep red with her monogram in gold, and curtains to match. Walking on to the galley, I was received by the head steward who showed me through. . . ." Guests aboard the *Atalanta* were conveyed from the private landing at Lyndhurst in a rowboat manned by "eight or ten of the *Atalanta's* uniformed seamen." Captain Shackford maintained "navy-like discipline" among crewmen wearing the blue and white Gould colors.

Her Uncle Jay, Miss Snow recalled, liked to stand beside the man at the wheel, and "for a fleeting time," when he forgot his cares, would "look almost boyish."

No yachtsman on the eastern seaboard cast anchor in more style, but Gould was refused membership in both the Eastern and New York Yacht Clubs. Undaunted, he founded his own, the American Yacht Club, which attracted a number of his fellows who likewise had been blackballed by the older and swanker organizations.

On land as well as on sea, Gould traveled in luxurious privacy aboard his railroad car, also named the *Atalanta*. Servants from Lyndhurst staffed its galley and served its passengers. He rode from one end of the country to another, over his own and rival systems, in the *Atalanta* with its observation platform, staterooms, parlor, dining area, galley and servants' quarters. Often he took one of his older sons, George or Edwin, along on his tours of inspection to give them a grounding in how his western rail empire operated, but his favorite traveling companion was his daughter Helen, who greatly resembled her mother in looks and temperament as well as in name. Helen became a railroad buff and would often ride up in the locomotive, dressed in a linen duster with hat and veil, white silk gloves and a pair of goggles. Once the train halted at a whistle stop and a male passenger caught a glimpse of her in the cab of the locomotive. "What's this country coming to?" he complained. "Now they've got wimmen running the railroads." Helen learned telegraphy aboard the *Atalanta*, clicking away at her key in the parlor of the car while her instructor tapped out messages at the other end of the wire in the dining area. Undoubtedly there were times when her father regretted that she would not succeed him as ruler of the Gould interests instead of his older sons, who early displayed more interest in spending money than in acquiring or conserving it.

Ironically, the man who was depicted as a "wolf," "shark," "skunk" and other predatory beasts in his business life, was the gentlest and most domesticated of creatures the moment the door closed behind him at 579 Fifth Avenue. Home was his sanctuary from the stress and turmoil of an unusually

volatile career, of juggling millions, making fortunes and un-
making men, and he wanted no discord there. There is little
reason to doubt the testimony of his niece, Alice Northrop
Snow, the daughter of his sister Sarah, in her memoir *The
Story of Helen Gould,* that he was "a devoted father, a
thoughtful and considerate husband. Almost without exception, Aunt Helen said, he could be counted upon to arrive
home on the expected train. The coachman never drove back
from the station without him, never was forced to 'wait over
another train.' There were no telephones at the time I am
speaking of, but Aunt Helen seldom received telegrams that
he was 'detained at the office' or 'would not be home for dinner.' Though he dealt at times in millions, even the most
trivial details concerning his family were to him of paramount
importance."

His wife Helen—whom he called "Ellie," while his eldest
daughter was always "Nellie" to her father—having descended from an old New York family of conservative merchants and having been raised in the sedate Murray Hill
tradition, was "quiet, dignified, unostentatious." Her portraits, showing a serene and steady-eyed woman of no great
beauty but considerable quiet charm, bear witness to her
niece's description. She devoted herself, also in the best Murray Hill tradition, to providing a sanctuary for her husband
when he came home from the battles of the market place.
"Aunt Helen," wrote her niece, "managed the household with
an adroit and also an exceedingly firm hand. Uncle Jay's home
. . . was his solace. And when he returned, weary, seeking
quiet and repose, Aunt Helen made sure that he had it. Servants melted from view as though through mysterious trap-
doors when their functions had been performed. Often, at the
table, Uncle Jay was too exhausted or preoccupied to speak.
Sometimes he would not give utterance to a word during
the entire meal. . . . I used to wonder if he knew what he
was eating. At such times, Aunt Helen, with a look, enforced
the strictest silence.

"No detail of Aunt Helen's domain was allowed to disturb her husband. She managed everything connected with the running of the household, from the smallest to the most important matter. She decided upon the dessert for dinner, or 'did over' the house, if necessary, even at a cost of thousands of dollars, without consulting Uncle Jay—that is, unless he expressed the wish to be consulted, which he rarely did. . . . She appreciated quality unerringly, but detested show, no matter in what guise. Her costumes, though beautiful and always the best obtainable, were tastefully inconspicuous. In fact, as a girl, I was secretly disappointed that she did not look more the part of the *grande dame*."

Mrs. Gould kept formal social life to a minimum because "Uncle Jay never attended such functions from choice." He referred to the small dinner parties she occasionally gave as "the inescapables."

For himself, Gould was content with the company of his wife and children, her parents (who had taken a house a few doors down Fifth Avenue from the Goulds'), and his sisters and their children. He never really felt at ease outside the family circle, partly, perhaps, because the world outside his door was so thronged with enemies. His domestic routine rarely varied: dinner with his family, then a long evening in his library reading Mark Twain, Sir Walter Scott, Charles Dickens—especially Dickens. One wonders what he made of Scrooge, Uriah Heep, and other Dickensian villains. Only rarely, during a market crisis, would he confer with associates in his library. He preferred to shut out the world he knew and escape into a more manageable one created by writers who, each and every one of them, would have found him detestable (but fascinating). Sometimes he would leave the library for a few minutes to inspect a very respectable collection of paintings, among them the works of Corot, Rousseau, Bouguereau, Rosa Bonheur. His taste in painting was not only selective by any standard but was his own; he chose the works adorning his walls himself, without advice from the art dealers catering to the newly rich and their new-found passion for culture.

Later in the evening his six children would troop into the library to kiss him good night. Even when they were grown men his older sons paid him this nightly tribute of affection. As a father, he displayed only what was gentle in his nature; none of his children ever saw him angry or even indignant— merely saddened, on occasion, by their missteps. Whatever discipline they knew—and it must have been inconsiderable— was applied by their mother. It must have been a continuing mystery to his children that, outside the home, their father was considered the most ruthless and hateful man of his time; a mystery around which they had to grow their own psychological callouses out of self-preservation, at a cost to the spirit which was reflected in their generally (with the notable exception of Helen) disordered and futile lives. Not only his victims but those he loved best paid for the Gould fortune, for the fierce joy he received in the battles for its acquisition.

To an adoring niece, Gould was also a perplexing contrast to the cruel, vulpine creature limned by newspaper cartoonists, usually with dollar signs flecking his silk hat and vest. "His hair and beard were dark, as were his eyes, which were large and soft, yet, paradoxically, capable of going straight through you. His clothes were invariably the same; of good quality and cut, they were either black or, on occasion, deep blue. His ties were usually black, though now and then a subdued shade of blue or some other color was worn. A conventional felt hat, his preference for the greater part of the year, in summer was replaced by a Panama. He never wore jewelry of any description, unless that term could be applied to his modest watch and chain. When you looked at him your impression was that of a small, dark, yet somehow strikingly powerful man, who, unlike many commanding men of slight stature, had neither need nor taste for display.

"Uncle Jay was exceedingly quiet. His words were both few and carefully chosen. He was perfectly poised, always. In my many months of residence as one of his family I never once

saw him give way to anger. Self-control, I should say, was one
of his most pronounced attributes. In matters connected with
running the household, he was both fair and considerate, and
no suggestion or complaints were ever made to members of
the staff except in private. As a result, there was not a man
or maid on the place but held it an honor to wait on him,
genuinely wished to please him. . . . Stories that Jay Gould
was a petty tyrant in his domain were as untrue as many
other things which have been said of him. . . . It has often
been repeated that Jay Gould was a man who took little pleasure in life; that the very magnitude and uniformity of his
success robbed existence of flavor. . . . The truth was that he
derived unlimited pleasure, satisfaction, from many things,
but that his enjoyment was deep, contemplative, appreciative
in quality. . . ."

The only time his niece saw his habitual composure shaken,
she said, was on a July day at Lyndhurst, when a servant
brought a telegram to the bench in a grove of birches over-
looking the Hudson where he liked to sit and read. "Alice,"
he said in a shocked whisper, "Garfield has been shot, President Garfield has been shot." Her uncle "turned very white
. . . he put his head back to rest, and rally that iron will. . . .
At dinner no one could have told how that telegram had
shaken him." Someone less adoring might have suspected that
Gould feared that what happened to the President was just
as likely to happen to him, what with the increasing number
of Knights of Labor, anarchists, syndicalists and other violent
types loose in the land, but his niece was certain that he was
so deeply affected because he had always "entertained a profound admiration" for the President. Somehow the suspicion
lingers that his concern was more self-centered, considering
his well-founded and long-demonstrated contempt for the
politicians of his time whose favors he bought through lobbyists as casually as he would buy any other commodity through
his brokers.

Alice Northrop's affection for her uncle was perfectly understandable, likewise her trust in the purity of his motives. When her mother was widowed and left with eight children to rear, her husband having been an unsuccessful storekeeper, Gould telegraphed her immediately: "Don't worry Sarah stop I will help you." From then on his eldest sister never had a moment's worry about finances; every year she received four quarterly checks and another on Christmas, and all her children were educated in the best schools.

Most wealthy men had "poor relations" to care for, usually with the utmost reluctance and condescension—the impoverished cousin or aunt, half drudge and half scapegoat, was a stock character in sentimental fiction of the time. On the testimony of his sister's children, however, Jay Gould performed his duty with the utmost grace and sensitivity. There is style in benevolence, and Gould had it.

"Uncle Jay," his niece Alice testified, "came into the lives of my brothers and sisters and myself as infinitely more than an uncle. He kept the family together in our great emergency, helped financially as one by one we got on our feet. His help came quite unsought. He took, moreover, in many ways, during his remaining years, the place vacated by father. Though his own family was a large one, and his responsibilities were almost superhuman, he never relaxed his watchful interest in everything concerning us." With their uncle's assistance, Alice and her sister Ida later founded Raymond Academy, which subsequently was accredited as a Vassar preparatory school.

Christmas at 579 Fifth Avenue was always a highly sentimental occasion, with Uncle Jay displaying a smile "much wider than any I had ever seen before," as his niece wrote. So many presents were waiting in the library that there wasn't room under the Christmas tree and they were scattered around on the chairs and tables. Her mother had warned her "not to expect too much," but the first package she opened contained a monogrammed gold watch and the girl couldn't help exclaiming, "Oh, this is Christmas enough for me!" But there was also a star-shaped brooch set in pearls, among other gifts, and a sizable check from Uncle Jay. Her uncle's presents were always in the form of a check. "I felt that he trusted me because he didn't say a word about how I ought to spend it. Uncle Jay was like that. If he only spoke to us, he thought of our childish feelings." On another Christmas, Miss Northrop and the older Gould children were taken to the Metropolitan Opera and sat in the family box in the Diamond Horseshoe, where a "number of glasses . . . continued to be leveled our way." One of the attractions in the Gould box may have been the pearls and pendant worn by Mrs. Gould, which had once adorned the Empress Josephine. The Goulds were somewhat shocked at the ballet which opened the program, and her cousin Helen whispered to Miss Northrop, "I do not approve of the ballet, and I never look at it. Why do you?" Miss Northrop obediently averted her eyes from the sinful spectacle on the stage below.

Miss Northrop, in later years, could recall only a few occasions, during her visits, when the Gould home was filled with guests from the outside world. The few intruders on what Gould always referred to as "inescapable" occasions, however, seemed to have been a picturesque lot. One guest of honor was the bloody-handed dictator of Mexico, "President" Porfirio Díaz, who had been ruling his country with an iron fist for nearly a dozen years. The company dined on plates originally ordered by the Khedive of Egypt, Miss Northrop noted, but what Gould and Díaz had to say to each other was not recorded. Gould may have been interested, just then, in extending his railway system through northern Mexico to circumvent the Southern Pacific.

The only frequent callers at the Gould home, outside the family, were the Russell Sages, who lived nearby on the insistence of Mrs. Sage and over the protests of Mr. Sage that "high rents are a lot of poppycock."

Sage's mind, to the embarrassment of his wife, was always on "good value." He had the distressing habit of clutching a man's lapel, rubbing the fabric between thumb and forefinger, and demanding how much had been paid for the suit.

The first thing he would say to his host on entering the Gould home was, "Gould, see this hat!"

Mrs. Sage, who was to compensate for her husband's parsimony by giving most of his fortune away after his death, would beg him not to keep harping on money, but he was undeterred.

"One dollar," Sage would boast, flourishing his hat at Gould. "Never pay more for a hat. Not worth it. Wear mine as long as yours."

Gould was inclined to agree with Mrs. Sage that two eminent capitalists, two of the richest men in the country, should have something more elevating to discuss than the price of a dollar hat, but he "always examined the bargain closely, politely, though with only perfunctory interest."

Another who observed that Gould in his "domestic mood" was "quite different from his Wall Street aspect" was Edward Bok, the young stenographer who quit his employ to become, eventually, the editor of the *Ladies' Home Journal* and a leading crusader for women's rights (culminating, several generations later, in that magazine's overweening advice to the male population against underestimating the power of womanhood). In his autobiography, Bok recalled that when he announced his resignation Gould tried to dissuade him from leaving and offered him a raise in pay. Bok, however, was determined to quit Wall Street in favor of the book publishing business. "You are making a mistake," Gould said gravely. "Books are a luxury. The public spends its largest money on necessities, on what it can't do without. It must telegraph; it need not read. It can read in libraries. A promising boy such as you are, with his life before him, should choose the right sort of business. . . ."

Some years later Bok was cruising up the Hudson with a yachting party when Lyndhurst was sighted, and several of the women on board expressed the desire to see Gould's celebrated collection of orchids.

Bok sent a note ashore to Gould, asking whether he and his friends would be welcome. The lord of Lyndhurst immediately replied by note that they would be, and Gould himself greeted them on his private landing. Bok's companions were turned over to the gardener with instructions that they be shown around the conservatory and greenhouses, but the young editor was taken aside by his host for a private conversation. Gould said he had been following Bok's career and was pleased that he was "making his way."

When Bok expressed surprise that Gould had taken the trouble to follow the fortunes of an ex-employe, the latter said, "I have because I always felt you had it in you to become a successful man. But not in that business. You were born for the Street. You would have made a great success there, and that is what I had in mind for you. In the publishing business you will go just so far; in the Street you could have gone as far as you liked. There is room there . . . none in the publishing business." Gould paused and added significantly, "It's not too late now, for that matter. . . ."

Bok, however, felt—though he kept the thought to himself —that "his path lay far apart from that of Jay Gould—and the farther the better!"

Gould was then within a few years of the end of his life, with almost three decades of strife, accumulated bitterness and hatreds behind him, but he still could not imagine any finer career for a young man than the cannibalistic frenzies of the Stock Exchange.

11. BELSHAZZAR'S FEAST AND
OTHER ACTIVITIES

LITTLE wonder that Gould's home was a sanctuary dedicated to mending his mind and spirit, that his offices in the Western Union Building were a heavily guarded and "bombproof"— so the newspapers said—citadel. Outside those refuges his enemies were always lying in wait. In those days decorum was at a premium in Wall Street, and enraged speculators would often set upon each other with canes, umbrellas or fists. Gentlemen still settled their differences through physical violence, and while dueling had gone out of fashion, it was still socially correct to horsewhip a newspaper editor or someone who tried to seduce one's wife, daughter, or sister.

Gould sensibly shrank from displays of violence, since he was smaller and frailer than most men, but a mere unwillingness to fight proved to be insufficient protection, particularly against large unruly Californians. Two such Californians were James Keene, "the Silver Fox of Wall Street," and Major A. A. Selover, both of whom were worsted in market operations with Gould.

The English-born Keene had invaded Wall Street in the middle seventies with a fearsome reputation as a bear operator. In San Francisco, to which he had migrated at the age of seventeen, he worked his way up through various menial jobs to speculating bearishly in the California and Nevada mining stocks, bucking the "bonanza kings" and the Bank of California in his spectacular forays. Strictly a gambler, a plunger, he came east with $4,000,000 and a determination to repeat his western successes in Wall Street; it was said that he would bet on anything from race horses to railroad stocks, and in

the commodity markets dealt in everything from lard to
opium. Gossipy Henry Clews said Keene was highly regarded,
personally, in the financial district. "The archives of Wall
Street since the days of the first meetings of the brokers in the
Tontine Coffee House early in the century," Clews reported,
"can furnish no such parallel of princely generosity."

Keene and his friend Selover joined Gould in an early bear
raid on Western Union stock, but soon found that operating
in a pool with him was a tricky business. As Henry Clews
was informed, "Keene and Selover sold the stock in large
blocks but it was absorbed by some party or parties unknown
as fast as it was thrown out. It was gravely suspected that
Mr. Gould was the wicked partner who was playing this absorbing game behind the scenes."

At a showdown in Russell Sage's office one day, it was reported, the enraged Keene brandished a pistol in Gould's face.

By now Keene should have learned that participating in
pools playing the eternal Wall Street game of bulls vs. bears
was a highly risky procedure, in which the known proclivities
of one's partners should be taken into account. A man might
join in a pool of bears dedicated to raiding the stock of a
designated company, or to a group of bulls in driving a certain issue's price up, but there was no guarantee that his partners might not seize an advantage to change from bearish
to bullish or vice versa. The "sellout" had become a fairly common practice. Very often a situation created by a buying or
selling pool would offer a cagey and uninhibited operator the
opportunity to turn a large and quick profit at the expense
of his former collaborators . . . larger and quicker, that is,
than remaining loyal to his associates, one of whom might be
meditating the same kind of trickery.

The Californian, however, saw Gould's maneuver only as a
piece of treachery rather than as an essential part of his education as a speculator.

Keene and his partner apparently decided it wouldn't be

worth risking the gallows to put Gould out of business but he must be taught a lesson.

One day in August 1877, the two men met by prearrangement on New Street, at the rear entrance of the Stock Exchange, on the route Gould walked every morning from his office to the floor of the exchange.

They "interchanged intelligent glances on the subject," Clews reported in his elliptical style, "after the fashion of those passed between Bill Bye and his companion at the card table with the Heathen Chinee."

Then Selover "walked down the street with blood in his eye," and at Exchange Place, near New Street, caught sight of Jay Gould. The husky Selover walked up to Gould and struck him in the face. Gould stumbled backwards against the wall of a building but stayed on his feet. When he refused to tangle with his assailant, Selover picked him up by the collar of his coat and the seat of his pants, carried him bodily to the steps of a down-a-flight barber shop, and dropped him like a sack of rubbish. The areaway was seven or eight feet below the surface of the sidewalk and Gould could have been seriously injured in the fall, but according to the newspaper accounts the next day he survived with only a few bruises and a bad shaking up. George Crouch, a newspaperman specializing in Wall Street coverage, came to his rescue, hauled him back up to the sidewalk and helped him back to his offices.

Although Selover was a muscular six-footer, years younger, pounds heavier, and six inches taller than his victim, the newspapers generally quoted with approval the major's statement that Gould was "notoriously treacherous" and deserved a worse beating. And James Keene gloated in print, to his future sorrow, over the punishment meted out by his fellow Californian. "Jay Gould," the Silver Fox told reporters, "is the worst man on earth since the beginning of the Christian era. He is treacherous, false, cowardly and a despicable worm incapable of a generous motive."

Gould refused to have Selover arrested for the assault but

Anna Gould, youngest daughter, who inherited her father's dark eyes and deep-seated pride.

Anna Gould at her second marriage, bride of the Duke of Talleyrand.

Jay Gould at the summit of success.

dith Kingdon, when her "barbaric beauty" made her one of the most promising ingénues on Broadway.

Edith Kingdon Gould, profile and figure intact, displaying the pearl necklace valued by Tiffany at $500,000.

George Gould and his family returning from Europe. He is carrying his wife's jewel case.

Carriage drive winding through George Gould's Georgian Court estate.

Merely one of the outbuildings of the Georgian Court
—the stables, in fact.

rivate hippodrome on the Gould estate, with a circus giving a special
erformance for the George Goulds and their guests.

Beauty under a picture hat. Marjorie Gould, daughter of George and granddaughter of Jay.

Marjorie Gould and her bridegroom from the Phila-delphia Drexels.

Vivien Gould, daughter of George, wistful in white satin.

Vivien Gould and her bridegroom, Lord Decies, in his Hussar's froggings, gold braid, cordons, and stripes.

The Gould line: Jay, on the left, and his lively descendants, as irreverently captured in a tabloid's "composograph" of the twenties.

avenged the pain and humiliation of the affair, according to Clews, by soon afterward arranging "a transaction by which Selover lost $15,000 more."

Trapping the Silver Fox for having encouraged Selover in his corporal punishment took more time, but Gould was always patient in such matters. If Keene was lulled into a false sense of security, so much the better. Finally one day Addison Cammack, a broker who switched sides as nimbly as Gould or Keene, came to Gould's office with a tip. Keene reportedly was engaged in a grandiose plan to corner the country's wheat supply, a scheme equaled in boldness only by Gould's gold operations of 1869. The rumor was that Keene was overextended. Gould and Cammack thereupon conducted a bear raid, causing wheat prices to tumble, brokers to call for more margin, banks to call in short-term loans. Not only was Keene's corner broken, but he was technically ruined and lost seven million dollars in the space of a few days. Clews wrote that Keene was a hairbreadth away from bringing off his coup as "chief of a syndicate which had purchased twenty-five million bushels of wheat, which would soon have netted many millions of profit," until Gould intervened and "the syndicate went to pieces, and both profits and capital vanished." Keene was bankrupt, but would make a comeback and cause Gould deep embarrassment on at least one more occasion. The bitterness between the two men was intensified when Keene was forced to sell a much-prized painting, Rosa Bonheur's canvas of a cattle-fair scene, for which he had paid $24,000. Acting through an intermediary, Gould bought the painting for $16,000. It hung in the Gould dining room, possibly serving as a non-alcoholic *apéritif* for his uncertain appetite.

There was one other consequence of the Selover assault: Gould never again walked the streets without one or more protectors at his elbow. G. P. Morosini, his confidential clerk and the man he trusted more than any other, accompanied him whenever he left his offices on Broadway. Subsequently Police Captain Byrnes, whose solicitude for wealthy men was legendary in Wall Street and who ordered his subordinates to arrest on sight any known criminal venturing into the financial district, assigned two plainclothes men to act as Gould's bodyguard during the business day; another detail guarded the Gould home around the clock. Gould henceforth moved around the city like a wealthy Londoner of the Middle Ages with his linkboys and armed retainers. The family was so apprehensive of kidnapers that they wouldn't permit publication of photographs of their children until they were grown. A relative wrote of the constant "secrecy and precautions which surrounded, pervaded, the family's doings, accepted, inevitable, a part of everyday living." So nerve-wracking was the unending watchfulness of the household that she concluded that "even poverty could have very genuine compensations."

Even at his well-guarded retreat up the Hudson, the household and its scores of retainers were constantly on the alert. Alice Northrop recalled one day on which she drove up to the gatehouse with her cousin, Helen Gould, to find Lyndhurst in a state of alarm. The guards at the gatehouse told the two girls to go directly to the main house, where they were greeted by a "deathly pale" Mr. and Mrs. Gould. Her uncle's hands, Miss Northrop said, were "perceptibly shaking" as he led the two girls into the house. A prowler had somehow got past the defenses and a search was in progress. Some time later Gould returned to the house and reported that the intruder had been caught hiding in a clump of shrubbery near the house. All that her Uncle Jay would say was that "The crank and his arsenal are being well taken care of." During such alerts everyone was herded into the main house and stayed there until the estate guards searched every foot of the property. "With all its beauty and luxury," Miss Northrop learned, there was another, less pleasant side to Lyndhurst, "the burglar alarms and armed auxiliaries, the postman bringing letters you destroyed or gave to the police, then tried to forget."

Cranks, crackpots, and desperadoes of all kinds were lurking on the periphery of Gould's daily life.

On October 15, 1881—just as one of many instances—he received a note signed "Victim" which warned him that within six days he would be shot through the heart and "I therefore entreat you to make your peace with God." On the advice of the police, Gould offered financial assistance to "Victim" in a series of personal-column advertisements. "Victim" promptly snapped at the bait and continued the anonymous correspondence. Chief Inspector Thomas Byrnes (he'd recently been promoted for his services to apprehensive Wall Streeters) noted that the threatening letters were mailed in the midtown district served by Post Office Station E, and posted detectives at all the mailboxes in that section until the extortionist was arrested November 13 as he mailed another letter to Gould. "Victim" was identified as Colonel J. Howard Wells, a ruined speculator, who said that he was only trying to force Gould to pass along "market tips."

A more ambitious operator in the same field was a fellow who signed himself "Vice President No. 71" and who announced that his aim was to achieve a more equitable distribution of the wealth. As the first leg on the journey to his private Utopia, he proposed that Gould hand over five million. Gould's family physician, Dr. Munn, acted as intermediary and helped police throw a net over the rampant idealist.

Another addlepate, styling himself Prince Von Michael of Brooklyn, came to the door at 579 Fifth Avenue and announced that he was going to kidnap and elope with Gould's daughter Helen. He was still trying to explain himself as the police detail at the house led him away to Bellevue.

Neither the hawk-eyed Chief Inspector Byrnes nor his private constabulary, however, could protect Gould from the predators who skulked in the Wall Street jungle, many of them personal enemies eager to turn his own tactics against him. "In the ceaselessly troubled precincts of Wall Street," as Matthew Josephson has written in *The Robber Barons*, "these mercenary soldiers, who could seldom trust each other with their backs turned, were all united against him. Their repeated conspiracies against Gould formed some of the most romantic legends of the Street." Romantic or not, one such conspiracy was that engineered by Addison Cammack, whom a contemporary described as an "uncouth Southerner," the same double-dealer who helped Gould trap James Keene in the frustrated wheat corner, and a broker named Travers. During a spring storm in 1881, the wires of the telegraph companies were blown down and Gould was forced to rely on messengers to carry his orders. Cammack and Travers kidnaped one of his messengers and replaced him with a youth in their own pay. The pair established a secret headquarters at the Windsor Hotel—just across the street from Gould's town house—where they intercepted Gould's orders before sending them on their way. Thus they were able to inflict "grievous" losses on Gould before he discovered the plot.

At the close of 1881—the year in which he engulfed both Western Union and the Manhattan elevated railroads—Gould may have appeared to be sitting on top of the financial world. Actually, the foundation under his throne was cracking, and largely because of overextension his hold on the western railroads was being threatened. Competition from rival rail systems began endangering his position, and for once an excess of optimism, a vice in which he seldom indulged, promised to be his undoing as a railroad magnate. At the end of 1881 he controlled 15,854 miles of railroad, including not only the Union Pacific, the Missouri Pacific, the Texas & Pacific and the Wabash, but newer holdings in the Denver & Rio Grande and the Missouri, Kansas & Texas; but instead of freezing his rivals out, his constant expansion only encouraged them to extend their own lines in self-defense and increase the pace of competition.

The Union Pacific, gigantic plum among railroads though it was, had always been running over financial quicksands.

Built before the traffic was large enough to make it pay, its artificially inflated construction costs burdened the company with an indebtedness that was all but impossible to meet, no matter how much wizardry was performed by the management. The most onerous obligation was the government's $65,000,000 bond issue, with interest at 6 percent, which was due thirty years after the road's completion. Uncle Sam was becoming an impatient creditor.

Under the Thurman Act of 1878, Union Pacific was required to establish a sinking fund and put aside 25 percent of its net earnings for the retirement of its debt. Thanks to intensive lobbying in Washington, however, an escape clause had been inserted in the legislation. Through this loophole, Union Pacific could tap the sinking fund if the remaining 75 percent of the net was insufficient to pay the interest on the company's bonds. The Union Pacific thus continued to expand even while it proclaimed itself unable to discharge its indebtedness to the government, building 1249 miles of new trackage between 1879 and the end of 1881. (During the same period, other Gould-controlled lines added almost 3000 miles of track.) The U.P.'s expansion was dictated by stepped-up competition from the Atchison, Topeka and Santa Fe, the Southern Pacific, and the Northern Pacific.

Meanwhile, on the approaches to his trans-Mississippi system, Gould was meeting with difficulties only too enthusiastically compounded by the Pennsylvania Railroad and the Vanderbilt interests.

He had aroused the ill will of the Pennsylvania by seeking to extend his Wabash system to the Atlantic Coast through an alliance with the Baltimore & Ohio and several smaller roads. The key to his plan was the Philadelphia, Wilmington & Baltimore line, which he and a syndicate including Sage, Dillon, and Garrett of the B. & O. intended to buy. One of the larger stockholders in the Wilmington was Nathaniel Thayer of Boston, who agreed to sell what Gould and his colleagues mistakenly believed was a majority interest. Two weeks after the

Gould group announced it was in control, Pennsylvania upset
its calculations by buying up the stock of a group of shareholders who had organized themselves to resist the Gould
takeover. Once again the Pennsylvania had demonstrated its
considerable capacity for dealing with rival monopolists.

Undismayed by this setback, Gould now proposed to the
Pennsylvania that it help him build a new route between New
York City and Toledo, where it would link up with his Wabash
system. Although they did not immediately turn Gould down,
the Pennsylvania's executives were not enthusiastic about a
plan which would divert some of the east-west traffic from
their road to a new line. Gould then applied pressure, inform-
ing Pennsylvania that if it didn't cooperate he would combine a number of broad-gauge short lines in Ohio and Pennsylvania. Overruling its president, the Pennsylvania board of
directors agreed to give Gould the trackage rights he wanted,
undoubtedly impressed by his argument that such a combine
would take business away from Vanderbilt's New York Central, Pennsylvania's leading competitor. Gould also bought
into the Delaware, Lackawanna & Western, and moved to
secure control of the New York & New England to compete
with the New York, New Haven & Hartford, in which Vanderbilt was heavily interested. W. H. Vanderbilt thus found
some of his most valuable properties threatened by jerry-built
competition rigged up by Gould.

A long and costly rate war then broke out between the
Gould-controlled roads and those of the Vanderbilt system
. . . a struggle which Vanderbilt, operating from a firmer
base, was destined to win. Throwing his weight first in one
direction, then in another, Gould hoped to cause one of the
leading eastern trunks to show weakness, make a fatal mistake, which would allow the supreme opportunist to shoulder
his way into control of a major through-line between the Mid-
west and the Atlantic Coast. Somehow he could never find
firm footing east of Toledo. Yet even his death did not prevent
the Gould system from pursuing a post-mortem attempt to

fulfill his dream, or nightmare, as it turned out to be for successors who lacked his strategic genius. In fairness to the inheritors of this ambition, however, it must be noted that Gould himself never managed to break the Pennsylvania and New York Central grip on eastern rail traffic. . . .

While maneuvering against those two systems, Gould was simultaneously jousting with an equally powerful adversary in the West, the Southern Pacific and its subsidiary, the Central Pacific, whose operating (and conniving) genius was Collis P. Huntington. In Huntington, who was sometimes referred to as the "Jay Gould of the Pacific Coast," he found an adversary worthy of his talents. It was Huntington who blocked his ambition to extend the Gould system to the Pacific as the Pennsylvania and the Vanderbilt interests prevented him from reaching the Atlantic. The long-nosed and long-headed Huntington, with the face of a Holbein portrait, was a native of Connecticut who joined the California gold rush in 1849 with a pack of trade goods. Prospering as a merchant in Sacramento, he joined Leland Stanford, Mark Hopkins and Charles Crockett in building the Central Pacific Railroad across the Sierra Nevada to Ogden, Utah, the western terminus of the Union Pacific. In 1884 Huntington and his partners organized the Southern Pacific, with its extension down the coast to Los Angeles. The Central Pacific was then leased to the Southern Pacific, which became the kingpin of Pacific Coast railroading.

A shrewd, relentless and vindictive man, Huntington early recognized the fact that, as the chief guardian of the Southern Pacific's interests, he would always have to stand on the alert against Jay Gould's encroachments. Operating most of the time in New York and Washington to make sure that Southern Pacific wasn't nudged away from the congressional pork barrel, he opposed government aid to the Texas & Pacific before and after Gould acquired control of it, suspecting that Gould would try to push that line through to the coast. He knew that his road would have to act swiftly and aggressively on its southern flank to block the Gould expansion, but he was confident that his abilities as a "practical railroad man" were superior to Gould's. "I wouldn't go into the stock market against Gould," he once told his secretary, George Miles, "for he would whip me at that game. That is his business. When it comes to building and operating railroads in the most efficient and economical way, I can beat him, for that is my business."

Like Gould, he keenly appreciated the importance of possessing legislative backing for his schemes. During the Seventies he wrote a series of letters to David D. Colton, financial director of the Central Pacific, detailing his operations as a lobbyist in Washington. The letters were published in the New York *Sun* (December 29–30, 1883) after Huntington and his partners tried to swindle Colton's widow out of her interests in the company. Publication of the letters, in all their cynical venality, caused a national scandal. Congress, Huntington had written, was a "wild set of demagogues," who were easily bribed but hard to pin down on their promises. On May 3, 1878, in another letter to Colton, his contempt even spilled over on President Hayes. "The President signed the Sinking Fund Bill Monday. . . . *He was not big enough to veto it.*" In another passage Huntington complained of the Gould lobbyists, reporting that they had driven the going price of a congressman up to $10,000. During the Pacific Railway Investigation of 1887, Huntington blandly admitted "lending" money to any worthy legislator who found the cost of living in Washington—or in any state capital where the Southern Pacific's interests were at stake—too high to be borne without public-spirited assistance.

Early in 1881, it was apparent that Gould and Huntington were approaching a showdown. The Southern Pacific was being extended from the Colorado River to El Paso, and Huntington was combining with Texas and Louisiana railroad interests to push all the way to New Orleans, right into territory Gould regarded as his own domain.

Gould had sized up Huntington as a man who could not be bluffed, so he did not waste time on psychological warfare. He took action immediately after learning that the Southern Pacific was building track through land granted his own Texas & Pacific by Congress, and obtained an injunction in the New Mexico Supreme Court halting this intrusion.

As a diversionary measure, he also began linking together a line from Ogden to San Francisco to parallel the Central Pacific, extending a Union Pacific subsidiary, the Utah Central, westward and buying control of a feeder line, the California Central, with a right of way into San Francisco. The Utah Central and the California Central were to be joined on the Nevada state line, thus finally giving Gould an outlet to the Pacific, a dream as fervent as any Russian Czar's yearning for a warm-water port.

Huntington and his associates did not propose to take this threat lying down; competition on the approaches to San Francisco was the last thing they wanted. Their alarm was further heightened when Gould suggested to the Southern Pacific's chief rival, the Santa Fe, that they link up at El Paso, with the Texas & Pacific holding sway to the east, the Santa Fe building to the west. It was mate and checkmate on the chessboard of western railroading. Huntington, to switch metaphors, was kicking Gould in the shins to the south, but Gould had him by the throat to the north. "Their people have gone into our bailiwick," as Huntington said, "and they don't belong there."

Boldly appropriating Gould's favorite tactic of building parallel lines, or threatening to, Huntington announced that the Central Pacific would extend eastward from Ogden, right alongside the Union Pacific.

The only result would be a ruinous rate war, which would eventually cripple or ruin both contenders.

On the other hand, a settlement, with both parties turning on the Santa Fe and in effect maintaining the status quo between themselves, would make a lot more sense.

In the fall of 1881, at Huntington's New York offices, Huntington, Gould, Sage, and Dillon met to negotiate a permanent peace. On November 26, 1881, they agreed that the two systems would be joined at El Paso; Gould would renounce his ambitions of building through to the coast; Huntington would stop building a line eastward paralleling the Texas & Pacific; the revenue from through traffic to the coast would be prorated between the Texas & Pacific and the Southern Pacific. In addition, the Texas & Pacific would relinquish its land grant west of El Paso to the Southern Pacific (the government, however, later refused to permit the transfer and the land was returned to public domain). Just to show there were no hard feelings, and undoubtedly as a token of appreciation for his former opponent's hardihood, Gould conferred on Huntington the most precious boon in his possession and had him elected to the Western Union's board of directors.

From then on, Gould and Huntington entertained a healthy respect for each other, and in their dealings approached a level of wary geniality. "I know there are many people who do not like him," Huntington said of Gould, "but I will say that I always found that he would do just as he agreed to do."

He told a newspaperman of an incident growing out of the agreement that the Southern Pacific and the Texas & Pacific would pool their earnings on the traffic between New Orleans and El Paso. They met to decide on how they were to be prorated. The Texas & Pacific was entitled to about $750,000 under the agreement, but its service had been poorer and both men knew that the amount should be reduced. "In settling I called attention to the fact" that Southern Pacific was entitled to a greater share of the revenue, Huntington said, "leaving to Gould the fixing of the sum which might be proper as the share belonging to his road. Well, he studied the matter over a while and then drew his pencil through the contract, taking nothing at all. . . . Perhaps, though," Huntington added, with an acid appreciation of Gould's generally low rating with the press and public, "you had better not publish this story for the reason that it will impose too great a strain on the credulity of your readers."

Texas & Pacific stock soared with news of the agreement between Gould and Huntington. Gould took advantage of the market rise to sell some of his holdings for a quick profit-taking, as usual, but he was bullish about the prospects of continued prosperity. The New York *World*, still in his possession at the moment, predicted on December 18, 1881 that an "immense traffic" in California grains would move over the Texas & Pacific to New Orleans. Some of this optimism may have been simulated for the benefit of investors, but much of it was doubtless genuine. Between Toledo to the east and El Paso to the west he controlled much of the nation's railroad system. "His word was law throughout the vast interests in his control established in many states and territories—almost from ocean to ocean." More than 100,000 men were listed on Gould payrolls. He was at the apex of his power.

But there was trouble on the horizon, first a smudge, then a blot and then a large black cloud, as the new year turned. Commodity prices on the United States markets were higher than they had been in half a dozen years, but as the *Financial Chronicle* (January 6, 1883) later dissected the situation, "so many parties in various kinds of business, and even professional men, were engaged in carrying stocks, produce, cotton, petroleum and so forth on margin." A "movement of liquidation," said the *Chronicle*, was inevitable. The American grain harvest of 1882 was only slightly smaller than the record crops of 1880, which had encouraged the prediction of "immense traffic" on the Gould lines when the grain was moved east to market. In 1880, however, European crops had run short, while in 1882 the continent produced its largest wheat harvest in history. Miscalculating the European demand for American grain caused a panic in the inflated commodities markets, from which shock waves spread to the Stock Exchange.

For once Jay Gould and W. H. Vanderbilt were agreed— the fluttery pulse of the stock market had to be calmed, investors had to be reassured. All the leading financiers and speculators, in fact, joined in proclaiming that rumors that they were selling were dastardly lies. Vanderbilt answered accusations that he was secretly bearish by frequent predictions that stock prices would go higher in the near future.

It was left to Gould to make the most dramatic gesture of that troubled spring. One day he summoned Russell Sage, Cyrus Field, and Frank Work to his office in the Western Union Building for one of the most remarkable displays in the history of American capitalism. The three men, he solemnly told them, constituted a "select committee" to disprove two rumors being circulated about him: (1) that he was close to insolvency, and (2) that he had been unloading his securities to satisfy the banks and other creditors because his resources had been depleted by his heavy railroad building and buying programs.

"Mr. Morosini," Gould said, turning to his ultraconfidential assistant, "go to the vaults and bring out those securities."

A few minutes later, trotting back and forth between Gould's office and the vaults, Morosini began dumping armloads of railroad and telegraph stock certificates on his chief's desk.

At Gould's invitation the "select committee" riffled through the stacks of certificates.

Fifty-three million dollars worth of Missouri Pacific, Texas & Pacific, Western Union, and Manhattan Elevated stock lay before them.

"And that," Gould told them, "is only part of my holdings."

Even Russell Sage was awed by that heap of rag paper representing a dozen sizable fortunes; later he told associates that no other man in America could "make a showing like that."

To the undeceived eye of the financial commentator A. D. Noyes, however, in *Forty Years of American Finance*, "nothing . . . could better have proved the existence of liquidation than these careful efforts to disprove it." Gould actually was suffering severely from the effects of overexpanding his railroads the previous year, and was selling as discreetly as possible to reduce his obligations and cut his losses. Like many others he had misjudged and overestimated the boom of 1881. His eastern rate war with the Vanderbilt system also was costing him heavily; he was forced to dispose of his holdings in the Lackawanna, and finally, rather than lose out all around, give up his efforts to cut Vanderbilt down to size and become a major factor in eastern railroading.

In the next few years, in fact, Gould was forced to cut his losses in all directions and give up control of a number of railroads with which he had hoped to extend the Gould system. Corporate control, of course, rested not on how much money he had invested in a company but on how much influence he had over the other stockholders. The more he slipped—as, for instance, when he lost control of the New York & New England, the would-be rival to the New Haven—the less confidence he was able to muster among the stockholders of other far-flung corporations. Always prepared for all eventualities, he had decided that no matter where else he would have to pull in his horns, the Missouri Pacific, the Western Union, and the Manhattan Elevated companies would not be subject to the rise and fall of his fortunes. They were the soundest and most promising of his acquisitions, and must be passed along to his heirs. He would always be on firm footing so long as he kept those investments intact.

Losses in other sections of his railroad empire were serious, humiliating, but they were like skirmishes at far-removed outposts, nonstrategic, and could be recaptured when conditions improved. Early in 1883 his hold on the Wabash system was loosened and neither he nor Sage, who was also treading water, felt able to continue making up its deficits. The New York *Herald*, always his enemy, suggested that if its stockholders united they would be able to wrest control from Gould, especially since the Wabash was unable to meet the interest payments on its indebtedness. Gould's resourceful-

ness, however, was undiminished; he had himself appointed
receiver for the Wabash, and the United States Supreme
Court upheld the appointment, though it conceded that the
move was "without precedent." Similarly, to retain at least
partial control of the Texas & Pacific, he had the Missouri
Pacific lend it $1,250,000 to pay the interest on its debts; this
made him a creditor of his own company, and again the receivership was awarded to him. Thus his hold on two of his
more valuable properties was secured only by the most fragile
of legal bonds.

With the Union Pacific, such delaying actions simply
weren't good enough. Gould tried to impose an optimistic picture of its financial situation on the slippery surface of its
heavy indebtedness, a process something like the art of decal-
comania ordinarily practiced on Easter eggs, but bright
colors simply wouldn't distract the creditors and stockholders.
Mostly this was a matter of rigged bookkeeping, as Charles
Francis Adams, successor to Sidney Dillon as president of the
U.P., pointed out. By juggling assets, Gould was able to maintain the company's six percent dividend. Nothing, however,
could conceal the fact that the U.P. was foundering under its
burden of debt, which had only been increased by Gould's
recent expansion policies. Union Pacific stock sank from 80
to 60 in April 1884, and the Gould-Sage-Dillon triumvirate
lost control of the company. Then Adams and his new associates saw the dark side of the ledger, glimpsed the Gould
legerdemain, for once, from behind the scenes. Adams, on assuming the presidency and obtaining the company's books,
exploded in wrath over the earnings report of 1883. "They
were deceptive, they misled me and a good many others,"
Adams was quoted as saying in the *Railway Review* of September 6, 1884, "because a change in the methods of bookkeeping made the comparisons with the previous year utterly
valueless. These approximate statements were a fraud—that
is, owing to the change in bookkeeping."

Trouble in this period, late 1883 to early 1884, was coming

from all directions. Late in 1883, the Dutch bondholders in the Kansas Pacific were buzzing like a hornets' nest over the disappearance of $3,000,000 supposedly gained in the consolidation with the Union Pacific and which they charged Gould and Sage with appropriating for themselves. Their attorneys complained to the District Attorney of New York, who was urged to seek indictments before the grand jury. At this juncture the *Atalanta,* with Gould aboard, hoisted anchor for a cruise to faraway lands. It was announced that Gould was taking a long yachting trip for reasons of health. His health, as a matter of fact, did not improve until the recriminations of the Dutch bondholders died down, or were somehow appeased, and the legal climate in New York was more salubrious for the ailing financier. The press somewhat maliciously observed that this was the "longest vacation he ever took."

On his return, the Union Pacific situation had only worsened. The new threat was posed largely by the government, benign as its attitude had always been toward Gould and his fellows. Washington was aroused over reports that Gould had defied the Thurman Act of 1878, under which twenty-five percent of the net and of the gross revenue proceeding from government traffic was to be set aside to pay off the government bonds. Gould, with his scorn of governmental attempts at interference, had not done so. A longtime critic of the U.P., Senator George F. Edmunds, presented a bill which would have exacted penalties against the railroad for paying unauthorized dividends, also against any official who engineered such dividends—an arrow aimed straight at Gould.

Gould was still quick on his feet. Somehow, recognizing the wide influence of the Adams name and reputation for integrity, he persuaded Adams, who also had a wide streak of naïveté, that he should go to Washington and dissuade the Senate from going along with Senator Edmunds. Before the committee which was considering the Edmunds measure, Adams argued that the U.P.'s financial position was essentially sound and that passage of the bill would "destroy the entire value of the stock" and create a disastrous panic on Wall Street. The senators allowed themselves to be persuaded, but only on the understanding that Gould and his associates would no longer have any control over the U.P.'s affairs. The Edmunds bill, therefore, died in the committee; it could only have happened—one hopes—in 1884. And Gould was spared the embarrassment of trying to explain, possibly in the courts, why he had diverted revenues legally earmarked to retire government bonds to paying dividends. He still held a large block of U.P. stock, still secretly regarded it as "his" road—and he would be back.

At almost the same time as Adams was quelling the senatorial mutiny, Gould, in New York, was fighting off even more determined enemies who had decided to destroy him. The darkest hour of his career approached. The imperial Gould of 1881 was about to become the bankrupt Gould of 1884.

For two months, April and May, Gould sank deeper and deeper in the quicksands of speculation. Early in April, preceded by a sudden break in wheat prices, the stock market began an alarming decline, led by Gould-controlled or -influenced securities.

By the end of that month Western Union had slipped to 49, Missouri Pacific to 63, Union Pacific to 39, and the bottom had fallen out of Wabash. Gould's resources had fallen so low that he couldn't even bolster Western Union, the most valuable of the three. Both creditors and brokers carrying his accounts on margin were pressing for payment; Sage was trapped in the same bear pit, and it began to look as though only a bull movement in the market, which he had done everything possible to promote, would save him.

On May 13 and 14, a series of bankruptcies made the situation worse. The Marine and Metropolitan National Banks failed, so did several brokerages, and finally the firm of Grant & Ward, in which ex-President Grant was a partner. Grant's associate, a young trickster named Ferdinand Ward, had embezzled hundreds of thousands of dollars without Grant's knowledge and brought the firm down in ruins, finally ending the old Civil War hero's infatuation with Wall Street. Grant & Ward's collapse sent a tremor of fear running through the whole financial community and aroused fears of another panic like that of '73.

A group of bears, headed by several of Gould's bitterest enemies, was taking full advantage of these calamities, determined, once and for all, to drive Gould out of the Street. They included Henry N. Smith, his partner of twenty years ago who had predicted that Gould would end his days as an organ-grinder; Addison Cammack, James Keene, and Charles Woerishoffer. The German-born Woerishoffer, who was to die at forty, two years later, leaving a fortune estimated at eight to ten million dollars, was the current boy wonder of Wall Street and the leader of the bear movement. Keene, his wallet still flat from his last run-in with Gould, was believed to be acting in an advisory capacity.

Just after the bankruptcies, Gould was reported to have bought 30,000 shares of Western Union in three hours, and his loyal associate, Washington Connor, about the same amount on May 16. These attempts to stem the tide only fattened the bears, and Henry Smith was reported to have made $500,000 in the space of a few days.

Rumors spread that Gould was close to folding up, and the New York *Herald* inquired on May 24, "Is the load which Gould is carrying too heavy for him?" The next day, discussing Gould's position, the New York *Times* said, "An impartial view of the present crisis of his securities would indicate that the boys had not only got him under, but were walking up and down on his prostrate form." Other reports had it that Gould was "in the hole for twenty million."

One thing he hadn't lost—his nerve; somehow his nervous, sickly disposition stood up under the daily pounding, week after week of it.

Admittedly he was in a tight corner. Even his closest associates were no longer able to help him in his efforts to bolster prices. The only possible assistance would have to come from a quarter in which only a man of Gould's consummate bold-ness and clear-sightedness would think to look for it . . . his enemies, the clique of speculators who had been driving prices down . . . and they would be affected, as well he knew, not by a plea for mercy but by a very plausible threat. He shrewdly perceived that they didn't have quite enough guts to ride out the storm they had stirred up.

On the last Sunday in May, a clear beautiful morning, he boarded his yacht *Atalanta* and steamed down to Long Branch, New Jersey, the summer resort once favored by Jim Fisk, where Woerishoffer and his joyful colleagues were spending the weekend and congratulating each other that, by God, this time they had Gould trapped and a few more days of pounding at Western Union would mean the end of him.

When they heard that Gould's yacht was anchored offshore, they expected that he would come crawling, beg them to let up on their raiding.

Instead an emissary, according to Murat Halstead, came ashore bearing not a plea but an ultimatum.

Woerishoffer and his friends were shown a document which caused sweat to break out on their foreheads, although it was a seasonable spring day. It was an assignment of property executed by Gould which would throw him into bankruptcy and preserve his unencumbered holdings for his heirs. Such a step obviously would cause a far worse panic in the Street than the bears anticipated, certainly worse than they wanted. "Thus, like Samson, he stood ready to tear down the house in which they all lived."

Gould let them think it over, then himself disembarked for a parley.

Before sundown, an agreement had been reached; Woer-ishoffer and his group would pay cash for 50,000 shares of Western Union at $50 a share. This would allow Gould a breathing space and also enable his enemies, who had been selling short, to make delivery of stocks they had sold at high prices.

The Woerishoffer group was so confident they still had Gould in a bind, despite his fresh funds, that one of them was quoted the next day as saying the deal "would be as transient in its effects as a glass of brandy given to a dying man."

Actually, that "glass of brandy"—$2,500,000 in cash—did save the "dying man." He knew that the bears were short on Missouri Pacific, and he used that knowledge, plus the money received for his shares of Western Union, to trap his adversaries. Buying heavily, he boosted Missouri Pacific back up to par, a rise of almost $40, and according to Murat Halstead, "forced them to step up to his office and settle on terms of his dictation." The market slowly recovered; Gould managed to settle with his creditors, and spent the next months shoring up his shattered defenses. In what had almost happened to him, however, he discerned the eventual fate of all speculators, even the smartest. The lesson could be summed up in a two-word resolution: never again. He would conserve and consolidate. No more cruising in shark-filled waters; that was for young desperadoes on the make. Never again would he risk the millions he had acquired in the hurly-burly of speculation.

Politically as well as financially, 1884 was a disastrous year for Gould. Until then, he had not ventured on the political stage in person, preferring to work through lobbyists, campaign contributions, and back-room conferences; early in his career, as he himself testified, he had been a Republican or a Democrat depending on circumstances. Now he became a partisan in the contest between the Republican James G. Blaine and the Democrat Grover Cleveland for the Presidency.

Late in October Blaine's campaign had run into considerable difficulties, and it was obviously going to be a close election. An overly ardent pro-Republican (and Protestant) clergyman had aroused much sympathy for the Democrats by noisily linking their party to Rum, Romanism, and Rebellion. On October 29, Gould and some of his friends arranged a dinner at Delmonico's for Senator Blaine, ostensibly to "pay him tribute," more practically to raise money for a last-minute spurt of campaigning. They hoped that the press would cover the affair with no great attention to detail, but apparently they failed to reckon with the new gadfly of New York journalism, the *World*, whose circulation had shot up a hundred thousand since Pulitzer bought it from Gould.

Next morning, the whole story of the banquet, including the maneuvering behind the scenes, was spread out on the front page of the *World* under the seven-column streamer:

THE ROYAL FEAST OF BELSHAZZAR
AND THE MONEY KINGS

Underneath the flaring headline was a cartoon that also ran across the full seven columns showing Blaine, Gould, Sage, Field, and other financiers dining off "Monopoly Soup" and other delicacies, while at the foot of the dais a starving man, his shawled wife and ragged child unsuccessfully begged for a crust of bread. Leading off the story was a bulletin from Lewiston, Maine, reporting that the mills had been shut down and the Overseers of the Poor were flooded with pleas for public assistance, while a shirttail at the end of the account of the Delmonico's banquet quoted a letter from an unemployed Philadelphia moulder who complained that "my wife and six children are starving while Blaine dines at Delmonico's."

It was a gorgeous job of political propaganda, ignoring, of course, similar fund-raising banquets held by the Democrats. Down page one the headlines ran:

MAMMON'S HOMAGE
Blaine Hobnobbing with the
Mighty Money Kings
MILLIONAIRES AND MONOPOLISTS
SEAL ALLEGIANCE
A List of the Men Gathered by
Cyrus Field and Jay Gould
LUCULLUS ENJOYS HIMSELF WHILE
THE COUNTRY SORROWS
An Occasion for the Collection of
a Republican Corruption Fund
MONOPOLISTS BELIEVE IN STATESMEN WHO
CAST ANCHORS TO WINDWARD

"Delmonico's was filled with millionaires last night," the story began. "The object of the banquet was twofold—nominally to honor Mr. James G. Blaine, but really to raise a corruption fund of $500,000 with which to attempt to defeat the will of the people. . . . [Blaine] realizes where his weakness is and knows that a 'golden stream' will be more effective in some quarters than the most picturesque orators . . . every gentleman was expected to bring with him a check to be used for the guest of the evening."

The *World* naturally played up the sybaritic aspects of the affairs, the "green tropical plants . . . banks of cut flowers, glittering cut-glass chandeliers and gold-framed mirrors . . . champagne frothed and brandy sparkled like jewels. . . . All wore diamonds. . . . Jay Gould appeared comfortable in his tight-fitting pantaloons and swallowtail. . . ." Aside from the metaphoric monopoly soup, the moguls dined off Consommé à la Victoria, Timbales à la Reynière, Kingfish à la Richelieu, Filet of Beef, Terrapin à la Maryland, Canvasback Ducks, and Soufflés aux marrons.

Before the dining and speechmaking, the *World* reported, a "brief levee" was held by Senator Blaine at which his hosts

"bowed and scraped and backed as if they were in the presence of a despotic foreign potentate." Among those making
their obeisances, in addition to the chief hosts, Gould and
Field, were John F. Dillon, "formerly a judge of the United
States Circuit Court who after rendering a decision of great
service to Jay Gould immediately resigned to become the
counsel of the Gould system of railroads"; Senator Thomas
C. Platt, the Republican state leader; John Jacob Astor,
Whitelaw Reid, Horace Porter, Andrew Carnegie, H. O. Ar-
mour, Henry Clews, D. O. Mills, Chauncey Depew (president
of the New York Central and guardian of the Vanderbilt interests), Russell Sage, Washington Connor, and Elihu Root
(then United States District Attorney in New York).

After a speech in which Blaine was "obsequious to the
great Wall Street monarchs," according to the *World,* the
company adjourned to the parlors where Stephen B. Elkins,
Blaine's campaign manager, announced that Republican
National Committee funds had sunk to $30,000 and "an ur-
gent appeal was made for help." Gould and his friends, said
the *World,* pledged $500,000 to "aid Mr. Blaine in buying up
votes in Maryland, New York and Connecticut."

Gould's foray into practical politics, so vigorously publicized by the newspaper he formerly owned, along with the
"Rum, Romanism and Rebellion" blunder, may well have influenced the outcome of the election and placed Cleveland
in the White House. The banquet at Delmonico's became a
last-minute issue of great importance, particularly in New
York, whose closely contested electoral votes finally went to
Cleveland and cinched the election for him.

Before that election was over—thanks once again to the enmity of the *World* and its publisher, who considered him "one
of the most sinister figures that ever flitted bat-like across the
vision of the American people"—Gould was to have further
and more violent proof that overt activities in the political
field could be dangerous. For several days after the election
on November 4, the outcome was in doubt, largely because

the Associated Press, then controlled by Gould's Western Union, kept claiming New York for Blaine. So did the organs of his allies, Cyrus Field's *Mail and Express* and Whitelaw Reid's *Tribune.*

It wasn't until November 7, in fact, that the Associated Press conceded that Cleveland had taken New York by a margin of only 2500 votes. That day the *World,* whipping up an already frenzied public, charged that "During the past two days Gould, by false reports of election figures through his telegraph agencies, has been executing his share of the plot by preparing Republican partisans for a fraudulent claim that the vote of New York has been cast for Blaine and Logan." When the Associated Press began "correcting" its returns the following day, the *World* further charged that after Gould had been closeted with Republican state leaders he saw to it that "the Western Union manipulators began to change the style of their bulletins and claim New York for Blaine." The Wall Street rumor mill reported that Gould had "doctored" or withheld certain upstate returns so he could unload certain stocks before Cleveland, with his pledges of reform, was acknowledged to have won the election and the market had fallen accordingly. A study of Union Pacific quotations during that period shows, in fact, that prices fluctuated according to the latest reports of a Blaine victory or defeat.

Infuriated by the *World's* charges that Saturday, November 8, mobs began forming in the Park Row section and converged on the *Tribune* building, demanding that its flag be hauled down. Police, under the much-feared command of Inspector "Clubber" Williams, drove them away from the *Tribune* building, but they began forming again at the Western Union headquarters, where a man astride an electric light pole conducted a "Gould primer," with the crowd roaring the responses:

"Who buys up Presidents?"

"*Jay Gould!*"

"Who corrupts the Supreme Court?"

"*Jay Gould!*"

"Who are we after?"

"*Jay Gould!*"

The mob of several thousand then began singing the old antimonopolists' hymn, "We'll Hang Jay Gould to a Sour-Apple Tree," and shouting for Gould to show himself so he could be hanged to a lamppost, no sour-apple trees being available.

Again "Clubber" Williams was called upon to lead a night stick charge and clear Broadway of the anti-Gould partisans, but all that afternoon smaller groups of lynch-minded citizens rushed around downtown hoping to catch sight of their quarry. Meanwhile, the *World* reported, a crowd of 5000 at Republican National Headquarters was cheering boasts that Gould had "cut the wires."

All this turmoil was too much for Gould. From November 4 to 7 he had been holed up at the Windsor Hotel, across Fifth Avenue from his home. Then, as the mob spirit boiled over on Saturday, he fled to his yacht anchored at the foot of West Thirty-third Street and was safely afloat in the middle of the Hudson while the crowds were looking for him. "Jay Gould planted his anchor to windward in good season," commented the *World*, "but it is dragging in soft mud." Sometime during that harassing Saturday, deciding there was more safety and wisdom in a return to nonpartisanship, he sent a boat ashore with a telegram for President-elect Cleveland, assuring him of Gould's belief that "the country will be entirely safe in your hands." Which drew from the *World* the comment that, "That's the kind of politician Jay is."

A few days later, after the New York *Sun* reported that Gould had secretly contributed to Cleveland's campaign fund while openly backing his opponent, he was interviewed by H. D. Northrop, a reporter for the *Tribune* (and the author of *The Life and Achievements of Jay Gould*), who had obtained a note of introduction from a broker friend. Gould now proclaimed himself as disinterested in the election as some Carpathian villager. Furthermore, he denied all charges of tampering with the election results through the Western Union or the Associated Press.

"If I denied all the lies circulated about me I should have no time to attend to business," he told Northrop. "Of course there is no truth in this. I do not care one rap of my finger whether Cleveland, Blaine, Butler or anyone else has been elected. I doubt if the administration of either would imperil the prosperity of the country."

Politics, from then on, had to get along without any direct participation from Jay Gould, who had no intention of hanging from a lamppost just to butter up another Presidential candidate. The White House, after all, had a back door as well as that imposing entrance on Pennsylvania Avenue.

12. "OUT OF THE STREET"

For those who feared Gould as the most ruthless and uncannily knowledgeable of speculators, it should have been an exceedingly happy New Year. On December 31, 1885, the financial pages played up an announcement that he had decided on "permanent retirement" from Wall Street.

Some of his detractors suspected that he would be "as prolific in his retirements as Adelina Patti," the singer who proclaimed every concert tour as positively her farewell to a more or less adoring public. As if to reinforce his decision to retire, however, it was announced that Washington Connor & Co., the brokerage through which he conducted most of his trading, was dissolving itself. Gould was a special partner in the brokerage, as was his faithful G. P. Morosini, whose loyalty had been rewarded by several million dollars and an estate in Riverdale. "Between Mr. Connor, Mr. Morosini and myself," Gould said with visible pride, "there has never been an interruption of good feeling." Reluctant though his enemies may have been to believe that there was a shred of fidelity in his make-up, this seems to have been true. In the troubles of April–May 1884, Connor had backed him with his last dollar. As for Morosini, numerous attempts had been made to bribe him to betray Gould by passing along information on his activities, but all had failed.

In reply to skepticism about his retirement as a speculator, Gould said some time later, "I am out of the Street, and nothing whatever could induce me to go back to it. . . . I shall never under any circumstances be a speculator again."

His retirement, as it turned out, was genuine. Ever afterward, he spoke of speculating with the same retrospective mingling of revulsion and fascination with which a drunkard would recall his more heroic drinking bouts. He had finally come to the realization that trading on margin was gambling, with a quality no more refined or meritorious than shooting craps in an alleyway; that he had risked his most prized possessions, not to mention his family's future, in his operations in the Stock Exchange up to the spring of 1884.

Not a pang of regret was expressed at the Gould withdrawal from stock trading; on the contrary, one would have thought that eternal bliss had descended on Wall Street. Earlier the New York *Times* had declared that the Gould-controlled companies, still struggling to extricate themselves from the slump of 1884, were largely a trap for the unwary investor and were "in utter discredit." The *Times* continued, "Not one of these companies can put out a report which commands confidence; some scarcely pretend to give reports; two are bankrupt; a third is not far from it; a fourth is flourishing amid ruin with a fictitious appearance of prosperity, and its stock, while quoted at a high figure in the market, no one dares touch; the fifth, nominally controlled by the government, which built it, had contributed to our history little more than a record of scandals and corruption. Everywhere the lines run, they mark bankruptcy, fraud, deception; there is no sound spot anywhere, because far as they run to north and south and wide as they stretch from east to west, a single hand is over them all, under whose blighting shadow everything rots."

A good deal of the dry rot undermining the structure of the companies he controlled could be traced to the speculative policies which he had been following. "No man can control Wall Street," he came to realize. "Wall Street is like an ocean . . . full of currents and eddies." Experience had finally convinced him that even a man with his skill in financial navigation could not stay afloat forever on its treacherous surface.

A symptom of his new conservatism may have been noted even before his formal retirement as a Wall Street trader, when William H. Vanderbilt, the old Commodore's son, died in December of 1885. On the night he died, financial circles were fearful that the news could cause a disastrous tumbling of securities on the morrow. Late that night Cyrus Field, Russell Sage and a representative of the House of Morgan conferred with Gould in the latter's library—certainly an indication in the highest circles that he was being accepted as a responsible and conservative member of the community. The conferees decided to form a pool to buy 250,000 shares of railroad stocks the next day if there was a sharp reversal on the market. Their fears, it developed, were largely groundless and no intervention was necessary. Not long ago Gould, instead of cooperating in a plan to steady the market, would have been plotting from midnight to dawn on how to take advantage of the anticipated crisis.

On the testimony of Norvin Green, Western Union's president, Gould, the onetime lone wolf, went even farther in his efforts to save various individuals caught in a speculative squeeze. "I know that during the panic of 1884 Mr. Gould carried through many men who had gotten into financial straits," Green recalled, "although he had to sell stock to do it." Some time later, Green added, he himself was overextended and his brokers demanded that he increase his margin from ten percent to twenty because money had become tight. Gould put up Missouri Pacific bonds as security for a loan which enabled Green to extricate himself, and "never asked for collateral or interest."

Despite the tremendous power he had acquired, Green noted, Gould was always soft-spoken, unassuming, willing to listen to other men's viewpoints. He was a man of "decided views and strong will, yet he never strongly expressed them." At meetings of the Western Union board of directors, "he would sit quietly rubbing his hands while the members of the board would express their views as to what ought to be done." Then he would suggest a resolution embodying the proposals put forward by his fellow members.

Less admiring associates remarked on the fact that there was a touch of the sinister to his quietness of manner. Sometimes that unearthly stillness, that low musical voice, the deprecating gestures of his small white hands, the sudden shyness in his expressive eyes concealed a desperate purpose. "He made a suggestion," it was said of him; "and if it was presented with special gentleness there was in it the greater scope for warfare." Only in the last year or two of his life, when he was desperately ill, was he known to bluster, raise his voice or lose his temper.

Even in dealing with the representatives of organized labor he managed to remain calm, studiously polite, although he was no more generous or compassionate toward the workingman than any other large-scale employer of his time—less, if anything—and viewed unionism with the greatest repugnance. Gould's intransigence toward organized labor, in fact, gave the movement its first great impetus; yet its consequences were to be felt more severely by his fellow capitalists than by Gould himself, once he had crushed the strikes against his interests. His whole attitude toward labor could be summed up in two words: no compromise. Flexible as were his tactics in most situations, his confrontation with the rising

labor movement was marked only by his rigid determination
to crush the life out of it. There was no discoverable instance
in his career of Gould trying to work out a decent and equitable scheme of compensation for his workers. He did not even
have the excuse of a paternalistic, if somewhat hypocritical,
interest in his working force—such as some of his fellows affected—which would be warped by the crass necessity of dealing with their union representatives. Gould simply couldn't
have cared less.

By 1885, the Noble Order of the Knights of Labor had become the goblin under most capitalists' beds, especially those
involved in the railroad industry. That secret and fraternal
organization had grown so strong in the years following the
violent but unsuccessful strikes of 1877 that many tycoons
were warning that "communism and socialism" were infecting
the working classes. The New York *Sun*, rabidly antilabor, declared in a widely reprinted article that five men held absolute
power over 500,000 workingmen. "They can stay the nimble
touch of almost every telegraph operator, can shut up most
of the mills and factories, and can disable the railroads. They
can issue an edict against any manufactured goods so as to
make their subject cease buying them, and the tradesmen
stop selling them. They can array capital against labor, putting labor on the offensive or defensive, for quiet and stubborn
self-protection or for angry, organized assault, as they will."

Gould didn't give a rap if every workman in his employ
stuffed his lunch pail with Marxist tracts and his head with
radical propaganda. He simply wanted it understood that he
and his fellow railroad magnates had "made the Great West,"
and was especially proud of his "constructive labor" in the
Missouri Pacific's territory. Where would the western states
and territories be without the venturesome activities of Amer-
can capitalism? "*We* have made the country rich," he once
said in an uncommonly boastful mood, "*we* have developed
the country, coal mines and cattle raising, as well as cotton.

We have created this earning power by developing the system."

Gould's first grapple with the Knights of Labor came in 1885, when railroads throughout the country, particularly the western roads, were hit hard by the depression which followed the bear market of the spring of 1884 in which Gould narrowly escaped being trapped. Naturally the laboring force was expected to pay for the gambling losses of their corporate employers; on the Missouri Pacific, particularly, hundreds of men were discharged and wages were cut. The railroad brotherhoods and the Knights of Labor, who organized the shop workers and others not included in the brotherhoods, went out on strike when Gould refused to restore the pay cuts. He would talk with the unions' representatives—as some of his fellow magnates haughtily refused to do—but he was adamant. The Missouri Pacific was his pride and joy, and must be restored to financial health.

Led by an able and magnetic agitator named Martin Irons, the strikers succeeded in paralyzing rail traffic throughout the Southwest. Because of "violent antagonism to Gould" in most of the communities served by the Missouri Pacific, public sympathy was all on the side of the strikers, even among the middle classes generally opposed to any upheavals from below. The governors of Missouri and Kansas stepped in with offers of mediation, and the strike was finally settled, the pay cuts restored. Gould had lost his first real struggle with organized labor, largely because of public antipathy; next time he'd see to it that labor was viewed in a less favorable light. As for the courageous Martin Irons, he was black-listed, hounded from town to town by the police and private detectives (the long arm of Jay Gould?), and ended his days as a peanut vendor.

Successful strikes were exceedingly rare in the eighties, and the Knights of Labor victory over Gould brought thousands of new members. The defeat of the "strongest and wiliest of capitalists" gave them real encouragement for the first time in American unionism's brief history.

The next year, 1886, saw the Knights of Labor erupt again, this time against Gould's Texas & Pacific. Gould had obtained an agreement during the strike settlement of the previous year from Terence V. Powderly, General Master Workman of the organization, that "no strikes would be ordered until after a conference with the officers of the company." Powderly kept his promise when Gould ordered wholesale discharges on the Texas & Pacific, and informed him that the Knights of Labor would be called out unless the discharged men were returned to the payroll, the Knights were given the right to organize, and the railroad halted its practice of farming out shopwork to plants where it could be done at lower cost. Not only that, Powderly had the unprecedented impudence to demand that a $1.50 minimum wage—nine dollars a week!—be established for unskilled workers. This was really too much; Gould told the union to go ahead and strike but warned that he would sue each of its officers if the men were called out.

The Gould system, replied Powderly, "gathering in the millions of dollars of treasure and keeping them out of the legitimate channels of trade and commerce, must die. . . . I play no game of bluff or chance. . . . I speak for 500,000 organized men."

Nine thousand employes of the Texas & Pacific struck, this time with violence. Roundhouses and depots were seized, trains derailed, strikebreakers routed, railroad property worth hundreds of thousands of dollars destroyed. Throughout the Southwest commerce and industry were paralyzed. This time, Gould vowed, there would be no settlement. "I beg to say that I am yet a free American citizen," Gould wrote Powderly. "I am past forty-nine years of age. I began life in a lowly way, and by industry, temperance, and attention to my own business have been successful, perhaps beyond the measure of my deserts. If, as you say, I am now to be destroyed by the

Knights of Labor unless I sink my manhood, so be it." The letter was widely publicized.

Even Powderly apparently was appalled by the violence with which the Texas & Pacific strike erupted, and wrote Gould, "Events of the past forty-eight hours must have demonstrated the absolute necessity of bringing this terrible struggle in the Southwest to a speedy termination. You have the power, the authority and the means to bring the strike to an end. . . . You have instructed your legal counsel to proceed against every man connected with the Knights of Labor for the damages sustained since the strike began. Two weeks ago I said: 'Do not do this.' Today I say begin at once . . . we are willing to face you before the law." This letter Gould kept in his files.

Perhaps it served to stiffen his purpose, for the strike went on for months. Since Gould refused to run any trains on the Texas & Pacific because property had been damaged at the beginning of the strike, public sympathy was alienated from the strikers as hardships due to the transportation tie-up multiplied. The whole Southwest suffered from the commercial paralysis, and Gould's agents were very diligent and skillful at focusing resentment on the Knights of Labor. He was emboldened by this change in public temper to refuse all attempts at arbitration; the strikers must be starved out; the Knights of Labor must be crushed. And that was exactly what happened. Gould hired himself a new labor force in the shops, and the trains began running again, since the operating brotherhoods had not joined the strike.

Gould thus succeeded in breaking up the Knights of Labor. His own workers, furthermore, were so conclusively beaten that for many years, despite low wages, bad maintenance and the poorest of working conditions, there were no more labor troubles in the Gould railroad system.

His firmness showed his fellow capitalists how labor must be handled, and after that disastrous Texas & Pacific strike of 1886 the large industrial employers enlisted Pinkerton detectives, company spies, quickly deployed strikebreakers, and such devices as the black list, the lockout and the ironclad (antiunion) oath to keep labor disorganized and impotent.

Yet, in the end, with the slow, inexorable growth of the American Federation of Labor, such tactics as Gould pioneered were to prove self-defeating. They made unionism inevitable. Had just a little benevolence and understanding been substituted for them, the union movement might have died with the Knights of Labor. Thus, unwittingly to be certain, Gould must be reckoned one of the founding fathers of today's monolithic unions. The immaculately tailored, barbered, and manicured union executives of today, bearing no resemblance whatsoever to poor old hornyhanded Martin Irons, might well consider erecting a statue to Jay Gould and his monumental intolerance.[1]

Gould's theory on labor relations, as he expressed it before a Senate Committee on Labor and Education, had the characteristic virtue of simplicity, if not of candor.

"My idea," he blandly told the committee's hearing in Washington on the recent railroad strikes, "is that if capital and labor are let alone they will regulate each other."

Senatorial beards wagged in agreement, just as though that recommendation, considering the current potentials of capital and labor for protecting themselves against each other, was not equivalent to allowing a lion to "regulate" a lamb placed in his cage.

Seated among the bulky lawmakers, it was noted by Frank Carpenter, correspondent for the Cleveland *Leader*, Gould looked like an "insignificant pigmy," though "his income is more than five million dollars a year, or thirteen thousand dol-

[1] The workers on his New York elevated railways were no more successful in dealing with Gould. They complained of working twelve to fifteen hours a day for a daily wage of $1.75 to $2. Gould listened courteously to their grievances and agreed to the principle of a twelve-hour day. Their gratitude for cutting the workday was short-lived. He had simultaneously ordered that wages be cut.

lars a day." As Carpenter described him, "He sits with a tired look on his face, answering the questions being put to him. He speaks easily in tones as soft as a woman's, and there was nothing ostentatious or aggressive about him. A couple of his detectives sit nearby, and his lawyer is at his back to give advice when it is needed. But Gould himself answers the questions, and he exhibits no fear as he reads his denunciation of the railroad strikers with a display of feeling."[2]

Much more interesting than Gould's feelings about the men who dared to strike against his railroads, and indicative of the gullibility he felt resided in his auditors, was his straight-faced explanation of his reasons for acquiring control of the Missouri Pacific: "Railroads had got to be a sort of hobby with me—I didn't care about the money. I took the road more as a plaything to see what I could do with it."

If the Missouri Pacific was a "plaything" to distract its owner with its pretty little financial crises, striking workmen, and occasional train wrecks traceable to wretched maintenance, Gould never pretended that Western Union was anything but strictly business. There may have been a glimmer of truth in the claim that he found in railroading a rare element of romance—it was something he dreamed of as a boy, after all—but telegraphy's fascination was purely monetary. Western Union was his steadily productive bonanza, its balance sheets a constant joy to behold. A few statistics will show how it lived up to its potential. By 1900, its capital totaled almost a hundred million; it had grossed half a billion in less than half a century of existence. John Wanamaker, Postmaster General in the Harrison administration, estimated that $1000 invested in Western Union in 1858 would have brought stock dividends worth $50,000 and cash dividends worth $100,000 over a thirty-year period.

Less than any other Gould acquisition, Western Union was

[2] From the recently published collection of Carpenter's writings, *Carp's Washington*, edited by his daughter Frances.

affected by the recurring financial doldrums, and despite its much-watered stock it continued paying six percent dividends with perfect regularity. Furthermore, it had captured a large share of the transatlantic cable business. During the period in which Gould was consolidating his holdings, following the near-disaster of 1884, much of his attention was centered on maintaining Western Union's pre-eminent position. The antimonopolists were quick to point out Western Union as the most octopus-like of all the trusts, but actually it was only No. 1 in a vigorously competitive business. Throughout the country there were scores of smaller telegraph companies, some of them serving only a small section or a few cities; it wasn't until later that the industry was dominated entirely by Western Union and Postal Telegraph. Early in the decade the Southern Telegraph, the Commercial Telegraph, the Bankers & Merchants, the American Rapid Telegraph and the Mutual Union all were vigorously contending for their share of the business, in addition to the smaller companies. The Baltimore & Ohio, having retrieved control of its lines, was also an important competitor.

For several years Gould was forced to fight for Western Union's supremacy in the field while shoring up his railroad holdings and dealing out punishment to the over-ambitious unions.

Postal Telegraph assumed a particularly threatening stance just at the time Gould was staving off disaster in the spring of 1884. Fittingly enough, the company had been organized by his archenemy, James Keene, but the "Silver Fox" had lost control when he proved to be a better market gambler than he was a corporate manager.

Keene was succeeded by a much more able man from the West, John W. Mackay, one of the four Comstock Lode "bonanza kings," who proposed to run the Postal Telegraph on a business-like basis and give Western Union a run for its money. The Irish-born Mackay, who took approximately $40,-000,000 out of the Virginia City silver mines, was a quiet,

sensible, unassuming man—just the type that always gave
Gould the most trouble, because he could not be bluffed, bull-
dozed or panicked. In San Francisco it was said that "of all
the bonanza millionaires he was the only one who could be
called popular." The ultraconservative Boston *Transcript*,
whom experience had taught to be leery of financial Lochin-
vars riding out of the West, observed that the idea of Mackay
"coming to the rescue of the dear public to assist it in squeezing thirty or forty millions of water out of a modest eighty
millions of capitalization" was enough to "split the sides of
Jack Falstaff." For once the *Transcript* had looked down its
long blue nose at the wrong man; Mackay, having made more
money than he could ever use, and being levelheaded enough
to recognize the fact, had conceived rather advanced ideas of
public service, and one of his principal aims was to bring
about a reduction in rates—and his ensuing war with Gould
had exactly that effect.

Gould and Mackay were soon involved in an all-out struggle for supremacy. Western Union leased the wires of the
Mutual Union; Postal Telegraph made itself the No. 2 telegraph company in the United States during the summer of
1888 by entering into a pooling arrangement with the Bankers & Merchants Telegraph and the Baltimore & Ohio.

By then Mackay had also entered into a partnership with
James Gordon Bennett, the eccentric publisher of the New
York *Herald*, who had also become a large stockholder in the
Postal Telegraph, to break Western Union's monopolistic
grip on the cable. Mackay could not have found himself an
odder, less similar partner than Bennett. About all they had
in common was Gould's enmity, Bennett's *Herald* having for
twenty years prided itself on being Gould's most vigorous, and
often scurrilous, critic.

James Gordon Bennett "the younger" had inherited the
Herald from his father, its founder and something of a journalistic genius, in 1872. In the next half-dozen years he established a reputation for being the least predictable member of

New York and Newport society; at the same time as he was
sending Henry Stanley to find Livingstone in Africa and
equipping the ill-fated *Jeannette* Polar Expedition, he was introducing polo in America and shocking the dowagers by riding on horseback into one of Newport's most exclusive clubs.
He was something of a wild man when drinking and once
broke up a New Year's party given by his fiancée's family by
relieving himself in the fireplace, which involved him in the
last recorded duel fought in the United States. The young
lady's brother, Fred May, caught up with him a few days later
on Fifth Avenue and lashed him with a horsewhip. Bennett
and May then met on the Maryland-Delaware border under
the code duello; each fired one shot, neither of them effective,
and they were "formally reconciled after the French fashion."[3] Society, however, put him in Coventry, and he soon
exiled himself to Paris, where he established the Paris edition
of the *Herald*, and returned to America on his yacht annually
for business reasons.

Mackay and his strange partner organized the Commercial
Cable Company, it was said, because the former was angered
by the expense of cabling his expatriate wife at the Western
Union's exorbitant rates and Bennett objected to the high cost
of cabling news to his New York paper. Western Union, then
interlocked with the English cable companies, held a monopoly between Ireland and Heart's Content, Newfoundland. It
also had a pooling arrangement with competing telegraph
companies under which all messages to be cabled to Europe
had to be sent over the Western Union's wires. Between them,
Bennett and Mackay summoned up the resources to build
two new cables to Europe and sharply reduce the transatlantic rates. Western Union earnings were correspondingly
lowered.

Gould fought back with every weapon at his command—
including what turned out to be a boomerang. To all the

[3] *When James Gordon Bennett Was Caliph of Bagdad*, by Albert
Stevens Crockett.

editors of the New York newspapers except the *Herald,* he sent a bitter personal attack on Bennett, denouncing him as a lecherous expatriate, a duelist, moral leper, profligate, and drunkard. The alert managing editor of Bennett's paper got wind of the Gould statement and somehow obtained a galley proof of it from the composing room of the New York *Press.* Knowing his publisher's unconventional sense of humor, he ran the statement in full and played it up bigger than the competition, which not only pleased Bennett enormously but took all the sting out of Gould's unusually intemperate assault.

In the ensuing hostilities, the Commercial Cable slashed its rates to twenty-five cents a word, which Western Union countered by cutting to twelve-and-a-half cents. Mackay and Bennett wisely refused to follow suit, however, knowing that rate wars had been fatal to Gould competitors in the past. The Commercial Cable was so successful in its tactics, in fact, that Mackay, shortly before his death, began laying the first Pacific cable.

Meanwhile, the rate cutting between Western Union and the Postal Telegraph along their domestic systems had forced many of their smaller competitors to go out of business. Gould and Mackay-Bennett soon were alone in the field, but their rivalry had proved so costly that Western Union was passing its dividends and Postal Telegraph was close to foundering.

Finally, in 1887, both men recognized the futility of continuing their cutthroat game, beneficial though it was to the public at large. Mackay proposed a truce, and an agreement followed shortly. Both companies were to eliminate price cutting and rebates. In a sense, it was another victory for Gould; Western Union was much the stronger company and maintained its supremacy down the years, until Postal Telegraph finally gave up the struggle, leaving Western Union as the country's sole domestic telegraph company. Had it not been for Gould and his four-year war against its rivals, Western Union might not have attained today's solitary eminence. "Out of Western Union," as Julius Grodinsky has written in

Jay Gould: His Business Career, "Gould made the greatest success of his career. . . . He was aggressive at the proper time, and he was also patient and receptive in his negotiations at the proper time. He succeeded in buying or eliminating his competitors. . . . In the Western Union, Gould, contrary to the expectations of contemporaries, critics, and friends alike, was a successful man of business."

But that was only one instance, during his post-speculative career, of his ability to consolidate his holdings, to make secure what he had gained as the spoils of financial war, to turn from conquest to administration. Gradually, he re-established his control over the Wabash and the Texas & Pacific, and built up the Missouri Pacific system to a commanding position among western railroads. Bumper grain crops, in fact, caused him to overbuild the Missouri Pacific. The competition among the western roads had stimulated construction to the point where the grain-raising states looked like crazy quilts on the railroad maps. Kansas, for instance, had a thousand more miles of rail line than all the New England states put together. A typical aberration of the period, with town boosters and land sharks running wild, was the construction of a rail line from Dodge City to Montezuma, a glorified buffalo wallow which had absolutely nothing to ship anywhere. In 1888, Gould called a halt to all construction on the Missouri Pacific.

Meanwhile, he was carrying on a determined struggle with the Atchison, Topeka & Santa Fe. He had secured control of the Missouri, Kansas & Texas (the Katy), a north and south line from Hannibal, Missouri, to Fort Worth, Texas, which linked his two great east–west roads, the Missouri Pacific and the Texas & Pacific. This enabled him to tap the major share of traffic from Texas and the Indian Territory (the future state of Oklahoma). Now the Santa Fe moved to take over the Gulf, Colorado & Santa Fe which operated through the same region. In consequence, rate wars broke out between the southwestern railroad systems, and money which should have gone into maintaining and modernizing the Katy line was poured into the struggle with its rivals. Travel over the old Katy line was an experience few passengers unused to the eccentricities of western rail journeys ever forgot. On the Katy none of the rail bed was ballasted, causing the passenger cars to buck like broncos, flinging passengers into the aisles; the trains proceeded over rickety old bridges which seemed to have been fabricated from cornstalks; none of the line was fenced and cattle herds often strayed across it, interrupting service for an hour or more, and many of the "depots" were lonely little huts out in the brush with only a water tank standing nearby. It was the customers who paid heavily, in bruises, contusions, sprains and frayed tempers, for Gould's competitive spirit. Finally even he tired of the game, and in 1887 he disposed of his holdings in the Missouri, Kansas & Texas, and travel over that road soon became a less bone-crushing experience.

As Gould solidified his holdings late in the eighties, his system, including the Missouri Pacific and the Texas & Pacific and their subsidiaries, was one of the three largest in the vast territory west of Chicago, controlling approximately one-fifth of the 80,000 miles of railroad in that area. In the Southwest his only real competition came from the Southern Pacific and the Santa Fe; to the north there were the Union Pacific and the Northern Pacific systems. His domain appeared to be firmly under his control. His fortune was growing steadily with the influx of revenue from the railroads, Western Union and the Manhattan Elevated railway companies. He had proven himself to be one of the very few plungers in Wall Street history able to quit the compulsive pursuit of speculation and build its proceeds into a tremendous fortune. For him, unlike Drew, Keene, and so many other comet-like figures who vanished with a last garish burst of light in bear raids, bull uprisings, and panics, there was to be no humbled and precarious old age. He was the rare gambler with the strength of character to quit when he was ahead. Ambitions as soaring as those of his younger years still obsessed him but they were under better control and could wait upon circumstances more favorable to their accomplishment.

The time had come, considering his steadily failing health, to concern himself with the problems of succession. Although he harbored few of the superficial vanities and quietly scorned most forms of pomp, he had a strong family pride and a determination that the power and influence of the Gould name would survive after he had departed from the scene. And this vanity of the blood, so common to self-made men, who fancy that their strengths and drives, instead of being expended in their own white-hot crucibles of accomplishment, can be passed along to their descendants, was to be the costliest and most fatuous misjudgment of a generally sagacious career, so far as the fate of his fortune was concerned. He was determined to bequeath not only his vast holdings but his transcendental ambition, which was to see Gould railroads stretching in an unbroken line from the eastern seaboard to the Pacific termini; yet he could hand down only the shape, the glimmering outline of the dream that had obsessed him since youth, not the will, the cunning, the force and resourcefulness which would result in its achievement . . . if it was possible to achieve, which is doubtful.

The result was that he passed along to his heirs, with all the love and hope and tenderness of his domestic nature, a tragically foolish legacy that eventually tore his family apart and consigned his sons and daughters to years of bitter squabbling in the courts.

Although he did not subscribe to the ancient tradition of primogeniture, he designated his eldest son George both as his chief heir and his successor as head of the family. Actually there was little to choose from among his four sons; none of them had inherited his aptitude for business, his ruthlessness or his instinct in money matters. The most enterprising and imaginative, perhaps, was the youngest son, Frank, but he was only a boy in short pants. Of his two daughters, Helen had the most stability and an interest in business affairs, and

Anna evidently inherited more than a little of her father's stubbornness and ruthlessness, but one did not then invest the control of a fortune in a woman.

Somehow Gould convinced himself that the amiable George would make an able successor, would carry out his plans and conserve, if not increase, the Gould fortune. Yet George, according to his contemporaries, was equipped with few of the qualities needed for success in business; he was described as shy, unaggressive, rather unprepossessing, a trifle dull-witted. Left to his own devices he would have undoubtedly relaxed and enjoyed spending his father's money with almost as much pleasure as the elder Gould took in making it. His keenest interests were playing polo, riding to the hounds—the greatest distinction of his career was being elevated to Master of the Hounds of the Ocean County Hunt Club—and hanging around stage doors. All in all, he was splendidly endowed for one role in life, that of the rather arrogant, dim-witted New York clubman, the late Victorian playboy with a dashing actress on his arm and a gray topper on his brandy-fumed head.

Even before he reached majority, however, the malleable George was absorbing, or so his father presumed, the details of running a business empire. Most of the day was spent at his father's side. He sat in on the elder Gould's negotiations, business conferences, board meetings, and perhaps less dignified plottings and connivings. For almost ten years before his father's death, George was educated in the ways of Wall Street and the business world. Nothing his father could teach him was left untaught. How much he retained, how much he was capable of learning from this on-the-job training was another matter.

On the day George reached twenty-one, in 1885, his father called him into his office and gave him a power of attorney which would have enabled him to take over control of all his properties in the event of Gould's serious illness or death. He also gave George the combinations for all of his private safes and duplicate keys for his deposit vaults. And when his second son Edwin reached twenty-one, two years later, Gould turned over to him the same keys and combinations, and made the power of attorney a joint one, but with the understanding that George's word was to be decisive.

"My sons," Gould said proudly, "are good businessmen."

He not only acted as George's preceptor, but on occasion handed him responsibilities to be carried out on his own. During a crucial fight for control of Union Pacific a few years hence, he would assign him to the job of rounding up proxies, which he performed creditably enough. In the last years of his life, too, Gould made his eldest son "manager of the Gould enterprises," as he phrased it in his will. But the elder Gould was, of course, always looking over his shoulder, ready to pick up the pieces if George fell down on the job.

George and his father were closer, in and out of business affairs, than was usual in those times, when Papa was the frowning, heavy-handed and autocratic ruler of his household.

Together, in a proscenium box, they attended all the opening nights at Daly's Theater, their tastes running more to the popular theater than to the opera, which Mrs. Gould and her daughters favored. Out of this companionable custom developed the only critical disagreement between Gould and his wife. On the evening of November 26, 1884, a comedy titled *Love on Crutches* opened at Daly's. Its stars were John Drew and Ada Rehan, but a dark-eyed young ingénue named Edith Kingdon was the toast of Broadway when the curtain rang down that night. Miss Kingdon had a mass of dark brown hair, a beautiful profile from head to toe and the shapeliest pair of shoulders then being exposed to footlights; "there was rather a barbaric quality in her beauty," as Elizabeth Drexel Lehr wrote. By the time the ovation died down, George Gould was madly in love, and feverishly demanded an introduction of John Duff, the business manager of the theater. From then on, with his father's apparent approval, if not encouragement,

George pursued the young actress with a headlong devotion.

When George announced that he intended to marry Miss Kingdon, a most unusual note of discord was struck in the Gould household. The idea of George marrying an actress was, according to his cousin Alice Northrop Snow, "utterly distasteful, such a terrible, completely crushing blow!" to Mrs. Gould. "If she placed too much importance on 'family' and social distinctions, she simply could not help it. Steeped in old [shall we say 'Murray Hill'?] traditions, these things were inbred in her."

Jay Gould, unaccustomed as he was to opposing his wife in domestic matters, stood by his son's wishes, much as he may have privately deplored them.

Probably at Mrs. Gould's insistence, the wedding was a private one, attended only by members of the household, in an atmosphere heavy with Mrs. Gould's sorrow and disapproval.

Margaret Terry, the Gould housekeeper, described the ceremony to Alice Northrop Snow (who quoted it in her *Story of Helen Gould*) as follows:

"Your uncle surprised everyone by asking us to come down to the parlor. He simply announced, 'George is to be married.' When I reached the parlor George and Edith were there, and your uncle and aunt and the other children. The minister, Mr. Choate, performed the ceremony. I was asked to sign my name as a witness. Your aunt already had disapproved the marriage and she stood there looking as if the world had come to an end. I am sorry myself that George had to pick out an actress, but how can he be blamed? Your uncle and aunt never seemed to have the knack of bringing many young people into their home. I did feel sorry for Edith, though, too. She kept up pretty well till it was all over, then she put her head down on George's shoulder and gave way. George had his arm around her and your uncle came forward and kissed her as a sign of his blessing. He stood by George. After the ceremony two carriages drove up. George and Edith drove away in one and Mr. Choate in the other. That was all."

A few days after that depressing ceremony, her niece found Mrs. Gould still weeping over her eldest son's marriage to "that actress."

"Oh, Alice," she said, "why had this happened? What next? How do we know that Helen [her older daughter] won't fall in love with a coachman?"

The possibility of an alliance between one of her daughters and a coachman had been haunting her for weeks, ever since the daughter of her husband's confidential assistant, G. P. Morosini, had eloped with her father's coachman.

Mrs. Gould, her niece recalled, was "inconsolable" and "finally she just sat down at her desk to cry it out." Her fears actually were groundless: for all her "barbaric" beauty, Edith Kingdon Gould was a devoted wife and produced seven children—and neither of her daughters married a coachman.

Shortly after George's marriage, Mrs. Gould's health began to decline rapidly, although she was not yet fifty. Since she was suffering from an arterial disease, it would seem probable that she, too, was afflicted by the tensions of her husband's career, which penetrated every corner of that house on Fifth Avenue, and the constant fear of assailants, extortionists, lunatics and kidnapers, which had converted her home into an armed camp, with the tread of policemen always outside her door. During the winters of 1887 and 1888, frightened by her physician's report, Gould devoted himself to trying to mend his wife's health. The first winter they sailed for Naples on a liner. The *Atalanta* was waiting for them in the Italian port, and for several months they cruised the Mediterranean. During the winter of 1888 they boarded their yacht for a long cruise of the Caribbean. Mrs. Gould's health still did not improve, and that summer they took the cure at Saratoga Springs, New York, on the advice of physicians; the whole family stayed in cottages on the grounds of the United States

Hotel, and Gould had his phaeton and a team of horses sent
up from Lyndhurst.

Gould's health, too, was declining. For years he had suffered from dyspepsia, facial neuralgia, and insomnia. He
rarely slept more than a few hours a night. And now the first
symptoms of tuberculosis had been noted by Dr. Munn. His
niece Alice later wrote that he insisted that none of his immediate family, and certainly not the world at large, should
know that he was suffering from what was then the most
dreaded of diseases. "It seems incredible, but it was so. No
one must be allowed to suspect. One word, and stocks might
be affected. One word, and combinations, discovering weakness at last, might rise in concert against an economic empire
held in the precarious hollow of one man's hand."

At the end of the summer spent in Saratoga, Gould seemed
to have recovered some of his health, but Mrs. Gould was still
"so weak and listless." A few weeks after their return to New
York, she suffered the first of a series of strokes. Two more
struck her a short time later, and the doctors gave up hope.

On January 13, 1889, Helen Miller Gould died. She was
only fifty-one years old. Many times she must have been appalled, as a member of the ultrarespectable burgher class of
Murray Hill, at the more squalid aspects of her husband's
career. Her duty, as she had been taught it, however, was to
make him comfortable, to restore him to humanity, in between
his savage encounters in the financial jungle, and in this she
succeeded admirably.

PART FOUR

HEIRS AND HEIRESSES

13. A LAST FLING

IN THE early morning hours, after the partygoers had departed in their finery and before the plainer citizens ventured on their way to work, Fifth Avenue was a quiet place, its stately brownstones hidden in the shadows beyond the pools of light cast by the gas lamps. Occasionally a hansom cab would roll by with a slow clopping of weary hoofbeats. Across the avenue at Forty-seventh Street, there was a warm blaze of light from the lobby of the Windsor Hotel (soon to burn down with scores of lives lost). In that light, on the sidewalk in front of 579 Fifth Avenue, two shadowy figures could be observed, morning after morning.

One was that of a small, stoop-shouldered man, with a graying beard, sallow face, and eyes sunk deep in candle grease sockets, who would pace up and down a thirty-foot stretch of sidewalk, as circumscribed as any convict caged in his cell. He would pause only when a fit of coughing would overtake him, racking his narrow chest. He would hawk up bloody sputum, and then resume his nervous pacing. Nearby, leaning against a lamppost or the railing in front of the house, another man would always be lounging, bored and weary, but watchful; he would straighten himself up and stand on the alert whenever a hack approached or a rare stroller appeared up the block.

The two men were Jay Gould and one of the guards who attended his every waking moment.

Morning after morning, during the first years of the nineties, Gould would keep the insomniac's vigil on the sidewalk in front of his town house, hoping to exhaust himself—though he needed rest more than anything in the world—so that he could snatch a few hours sleep before daylight.

Of the few who observed those predawn pacings and prowlings, none could envy the man his millions, his useless yacht, his unseen railroads, his unknown thousands of employes.

Nor could anyone penetrate the thoughts and schemes, the fears and hopes, that must have been seething under that bald crown, glistening with tubercular sweat. As a relative said, Gould possessed a "natural uncommunicativeness." His whole life was a secret, illuminated only occasionally by his actions. All that survived him were stacks of ledgers, columns of newsprint and a mountain of ticker tape. No diaries, no packets of love letters would ever tell of his inner life.

During his postmidnight pacings in the summer of 1890, six months after his wife's death, it may be inferred that much of his thoughts were centered on the Union Pacific, in that sizable section of his mind which was given over to business. He had never abandoned the idea of regaining control of that railroad and making it the main link of a transcontinental system. Most men, given his physical ailments, would have retired years before, and sought to prolong life in Switzerland, Colorado, or some other climate more favorable to the treatment of tuberculosis, but Gould could not give up the ambition which would consume his life up to its last hours.

That summer conditions appeared to be ripening—or deteriorating, depending on the point of view—for a massive re-entry into the Union Pacific's affairs. That enormous floating debt was causing the company to founder once again, and nothing that Charles Francis Adams, its president since Gould's departure as a principal stockholder, could do seemed to stabilize its financial position. The market was falling, the banks were calling in loans, and by autumn the worst panic since that of May 1884 struck Wall Street.

Gould, on the other hand, was in splendid shape financially. Reportedly he had from $15,000,000 to $20,000,000 in cash available for immediate investment. After buying up large blocks of U.P. stock, he announced that he was willing to take over the responsibility of the railroad's management and its floating debt.

As his niece recalled, Gould was urged to undertake the reorganization of the Union Pacific against his will. He was "uncertain, undecided." But, according to this fonder version of his motives, he also felt it was his duty to rescue the poor old railroad (which had so handsomely repaid a previous rescue effort). His niece was "begging him not to consider it," she said, when the butler entered with a telegram saying "his help was vitally needed." Gould pondered it for a moment, then quietly announced, "I have decided to go ahead."

There were those in the world outside his doors who did not view his decision in such a chivalrous light.

Union Pacific stock fell at the first report that Gould was returning to control.

And its vigorously anti-Gould President Adams, who undoubtedly knew that his days were numbered, struggled desperately to keep the road out of Gould's hands. "I sought everywhere for assistance. I told the Vanderbilts they could have the property, the control of it, for practically a few millions of floating debt." The Commodore's grandsons, William K. and Cornelius II, were, however, content to reign as board chairmen of the New York Central and the Lake Shore, without risking the family fortune and pride in renewed engagements against Jay Gould. "They replied that it was more and more a settled policy that they would not move their management or interests west of Chicago."

During the last days of his term as operating head of the railroad, Adams said, he learned that its credit was being attacked "from all quarters of the West."

He described the mysterious assaults in his autobiography: "There would be something published in Chicago, and then copied in the East, attacking our credit, and then there would be an attack upon us in some Salt Lake City paper, or at Portland, Oregon, and the ball would move around the country to hit us in the back. I thought it was some attack from our rivals in the railroad business. . . .

"It was none other than the hand of Jay Gould. Of that I am satisfied. He would throw a ball against the wall in the West, and see it bound back in the East. Having me in this position with money tight, and a large floating debt, my resources failing, the western management crippled, the earnings showing poorly, where they should have shown handsomely, the Gould trap came into play.

"Finally Mr. Gould threw off the mask, and came out openly in an interview in the New York *Evening Post,* in which he attacked me, and the credit of the company, and said that as a large stockholder he was going to turn me out of office, and take the management of the company himself."

Gould, undoubtedly annoyed by his attempts to peddle control to the Vanderbilts, soon relieved Adams of the presidency and again installed Sidney Dillon in that office.

Gould spread out in other directions at the same time, buying control of the Richmond Terminal road, which operated in the southeastern states and connected with the Missouri Pacific at Memphis. He was joined on the boards of both the Union Pacific and the Richmond Terminal, and in the stock buying which preceded, by Russell Sage, now seventy-four years old but as active and acquisitive as ever. Neither man had any strongly developed talent for friendship, but common interests had brought Sage closer to Gould on a personal basis than anyone outside the family, with the possible exception of his physician, Dr. John P. Munn, and his wife. There was no doubt of his concern for Sage the day in 1891 when a man named Henry D. Norcross broke into Sage's office and threatened to explode a bomb if he didn't come across with $1,200,000. Sage thought he was just another crank and told him to go to hell, which was a tactical error. Norcross exploded his bomb, killing himself and injuring Sage. Over the protests of his family, who pointed out that another bomb thrower might be lurking near Sage's wrecked offices, Gould hastened downtown immediately to offer whatever help and comfort he could. That evening Gould hired additional detectives to watch all approaches to his house and immediately question anyone carrying a satchel which might conceal a bomb.

While Sage was recovering from the effects of that bombing, which left him with impaired hearing, Gould was seeking to extend his system to the Northwest, relatively new territory for his interests. The dominant figure in northwestern railroading was James J. Hill of the Great Northern, a brawny, two-fisted character who early had appreciated the economic potential of the northern tier of states and who had beaten out the formidable Henry Villard in a contest for supremacy in that territory. Here Gould met with a rebuff. Hill, who loved all the publicity that pictured him as the "Empire Builder of the Northwest," had no intention of sharing his domain with anyone—least of all Gould.

Sam Hill, who later told the story of the meeting between Gould and his father (as related in *They Told Barron*, by C. W. Barron, arranged and edited by Arthur Pound and Samuel T. Moore), attended the conference of the two earthshakers along with Gould's son George. "While the old men talked," as Sam Hill recalled, "we [he and George Gould] looked out of the window, but kept our ears open." Gould told Hill it was not necessary for him to take on the new construction, that he would "build and issue securities at $30,000 a mile on roads costing $15,000 a mile."

This insight into Gould's methods was received with outrage, real or feigned, on the part of Jim Hill.

He told Gould, "Our one desire is to build up the country and share in the prosperity that must follow. A railroad is a tax on the community. It has no reason for going there unless to perform a service not now provided. Give a carpenter a

dull tool and he cannot do good work. During the lifetime of
those two young men all the traffic from the coast country
will be low-grade tonnage. It will not require the old horse
and dray. We should build our railroad through and capitalize it for exactly what it costs; not a dollar more nor a dollar
less, and hope to share in the prosperity that is to follow. I
will not join you in a real estate speculation, for a real estate
speculation is not a railroad."

The curious and revolutionary theory that a railroad should
be built with consideration for its future customers—along
with the implied lecture on business ethics—only irked Gould.

"Will you take me in as a partner?" he bluntly demanded
of Hill.

"All our stockholders are partners," was the maddening
reply. "There is no inside deal. Our stock is on the exchange
and we shall be glad to have you as a partner."

Great Northern, on that basis, held no further interest for
Gould, who was always looking for exactly that "inside deal"
which gave him an edge over all other investors. Unwittingly
or not, Hill had found the one sure way of discouraging Gould
from any further interest in the project.

Shortly after Gould began his last expansion program,
J. Pierpont Morgan, extending himself somewhat from the
quietude of investment banking, organized an unofficial
federation of western railroad presidents with the aim of
eliminating the rate cutting and other ultracompetitive practices which tended to render the business unstable. Morgan
had recently succeeded in persuading the Vanderbilt interests and the Pennsylvania to agree on a halt to ruinous
competition through establishment of an advisory council
which would "establish uniformity of rates between competitive points." Morgan, of course, dominated the council. Aim-
ing at czardom, in the guise of an impartial arbitrator, he
proposed that a similar council be organized to "avoid wasteful rivalry" among the western roads. Gould, seeing which
way the wind was blowing, went even further and suggested,

in a memorandum signed by a number of the railroad presidents, that business be pooled in competitive territory, that building of parallel lines be halted for five years, and that roads failing to cooperate be black-listed. One and all agreed, in conferences held at Morgan's home, that a new and more prosperous era in railroading had been assured by such agreements. A complete reformation in "the animus of management" had been effected, the *Commercial & Financial Chronicle* declared.

Railroad men, however, had been reared in an atmosphere of distrust and it would take much knocking together of heads to make any such cooperative work.

"Think of it," Morgan marveled, somewhat prematurely, "all the competitive traffic of the roads west of Chicago and St. Louis in the control of about thirty men. It is the most important agreement made by the railroads in a long time, and it is as strong as could be desired."

A. B. Stickney, president of the Chicago, St. Paul & Kansas City, was somewhat more realistic when, only half-jokingly, he told his fellow magnates:

"I have the utmost respect for you gentlemen individually, but as railroad presidents I would not trust you with my watch out of sight."

Relaxing in a temporarily congenial atmosphere, even Jay Gould indulged in a "rare moment of levity," and according to one of Morgan's biographers[1] told a story about Daniel Drew to his fellow tycoons.

"At one time Drew went into a Methodist Church while a revival was in progress, and listened to a convert telling how sinful he had been, lying, cheating and robbing men of their money in Wall Street. Greatly interested, Drew nudged a neighbor and asked, 'Who is he, anyhow?' 'That's Daniel Drew,' was the reply."

The embittered Charles Francis Adams predicted that

[1] Lewis Corey, *The House of Morgan.*

any "gentlemen's agreement" among railroad presidents was bound to collapse for the simple reason that railroad presidents weren't gentlemen. What had always prevented the sensible administration of any railroad in a competitive situation, he believed, was the "covetousness, want of good faith, and low moral tone of railway managers. . . ."

For all his surface enthusiasm for Morgan's proposals, it may be doubted that Gould, who may have "mellowed" to some extent in the past several years as his associates claimed but who was still the supreme realist, had any real intention of keeping the faith as promulgated by "Pierpontifex Maximus" any longer than it suited his purposes. Just then he needed a cease-fire while he regrouped his forces for fresh assaults on his competitors.

Not long after those meetings in Morgan's library, the old, the free-enterprising Gould reasserted himself. His first move was to cancel an agreement between the Union Pacific and the Rock Island and St. Paul roads on the joint use of the railway bridge at Omaha. The other two roads would have to find their own way across the river, he declared, because the bridge contract was "ridiculous."

Later in 1891 the Union Pacific's longtime incubus, the floating debt, drove him to more desperate measures. The creditors began demanding payment; a new issue of $25,000,-000 in mortgage bonds failed to attract buyers, and Gould himself had to put up the money to meet the July 1 interest payments. It was necessary to secure the backing of Morgan's firm to float a new note issue of $24,000,000, from which holders of the floating debt would be paid in cash, if they insisted, or in the new notes. Gould agreed to buy $1,-000,000 worth of the new issue himself, but Morgan reportedly had to apply pressure before Gould came through with his subscription and left the banker's office looking "sulky."

During the next twelve months, heavy grain shipments from the western states to the eastern ports again aroused that "covetousness" among railway managers which Charles Francis Adams had noted with patrician distaste. Earnings on his western roads increased, but Gould was soon engaged in rate cutting wars with his rivals; it was the Union Pacific and the Missouri Pacific vs. the Santa Fe, the Rock Island and the Burlington. Huntington's Southern Pacific also was slashing its freight rates.

The law of the jungle, which Morgan had hoped to replace with more civilized procedures, had returned to western railroading. It may or may not have been precipitated by Gould, as his critics charged. Gould's motives, as his life and career came to a close, were obscure even to the most perceptive financial historians. Certainly he was driving toward some goal visible only to himself. Until then he had always been the most self-contained of men, calm and soft-spoken in the worst crises, but now his behavior became erratic. At several board meetings, it was reported, he lost his temper and shouted at his associates. One particularly violent outburst was directed at Russell Sage, presumably because Sage was slow to agree to his still venturesome plans.

He knew that death was approaching and considered that his accomplishments had still fallen short of his objectives. And nothing, not even the most persistent intimations of mortality, could persuade him to slow down, make his peace with himself (if not the world) and look back on it all with a philosophic shrug. His perpetual climate, after all, was the winter of discontent. Had he somehow succeeded in building a Gould system from New York to California, he would probably have been seized by ambitions to tunnel the Atlantic and establish connections with London and Paris. The urge to acquire was ruthless in its demands, unceasing in its appetite. During the last year or two of his life, according to Murat Halstead, Gould's income was approximately ten million a year. "Mr. Gould cannot begin to use even a small portion for his own personal use—even a small part of the interest which his dividend money alone would yield. He must reinvest it, and he does reinvest it." All of which did not prevent him from arguing with Morgan over a mere million he had promised to help anchor Union Pacific's floating debt, for which he had willingly assumed responsibility.

Philanthropy in the overwhelming Rockefeller and Ford manner had not yet come into fashion as a means of salving the conscience, pampering public opinion, and reducing the burden of all those millions. Yet, even in his few tentative essays at giving away money, Gould found himself condemned and misunderstood.

On the evening of February 23, 1892, he and his daughter Helen gave a reception for the Presbyterian Board of Church Extension. It was a fund-raising affair, at which $20,000 was subscribed. With the best of intentions, Gould slipped the chairman of the board an envelope containing a check for $10,000 after the gathering had broken up. He could hardly have arranged a less showy benefaction. Next day the news of that $10,000 check got around New York and the newspapers picked up the story. Instead of merely reporting it, several of them reacted with outrage, as though he had been caught robbing poor boxes. One called him an "ostentatious hypocrite." The Rev. Charles H. Parkhurst, who was to lead a celebrated crusade against hellish doings in the Tenderloin a few years hence, but who was then merely another publicity-hungry pulpit-pounder, was only too happy to be interviewed on the subject. Gould's gift, he said, was "an ostentatious display of wealth in the name of religion." To the Rev. Parkhurst the most important question was "where he got that money."

The millionaire's mite stirred up so much acrimony that Gould told a relative, "I guess I'm through with giving . . . it seems to cause nothing but trouble, trouble. Everything I do is purposely misconstrued. I don't care especially about myself, but it all comes back so on my family."

The constant needling of the press had finally begun to get under his skin. He asked a newspaper editor, he told H. D. Northrop, himself a newspaperman, why he was always attacked in the public prints, no matter what he did. The editor replied, according to Gould, that "there were only three or four men in the country worth abusing, and I was one of them."

Several months before his death he conceded, in another conversation, that he was the "most hated man in America," and indeed this was true. Jay Gould had become the symbol of all the evils of capitalism, the favorite whipping boy of all the crusading editors, reformers, demagogues, and professional liberals. "Their misrepresentations," as Gustavus Myers wrote, "consisted not in exaggerating his evil—that was not possible—but in singling him out as an exceptional defrauder, and in detaching him from the system which produced him and which alone could be held responsible." Certainly his fellow monopolists owed Gould an immense debt of gratitude for acting, however involuntarily, as the target of all that concentrated wrath.

Perhaps it was in recognition of that gratuitous service that the more tolerant strata of society began to relent, in the last year of his life, and accept Gould and his family as peers of their expanding realm. "The modern nobility springs from success in business," wrote Henry Clews, who thought that the American "aristocracy," though "rough-hewn" and a trifle hearty by the more effete European standards, compared favorably with the "English parchment nobility." George Gould was accepted as a member of the New York Yacht Club, which had black-balled his father. Both he and Edwin were welcomed as equals by the sons and grandsons of other "money kings." Now, their father believed, it was time to present their sister Helen, just turned twenty-one, to society.

Shortly before Christmas, 1891, the invitations went out to a reception at the Gould home on December 26:

Mr. Jay Gould

and

Miss Gould

At Home

From Three Until Seven

Society's response to these invitations was awaited with some apprehension by the Gould family. Perhaps to insure a sizable attendance at the reception, despite an anticipated number of turndowns, 3000 persons were invited to call that afternoon and evening at the Gould home, although Mrs. Astor held her guest lists down to the acceptable Four Hundred and Mrs. Vanderbilt to 1200. Delmonico's catered the supper and a Hungarian orchestra played behind a hedge of ferns, palms, holly, and mistletoe.

"Everybody in the social world was invited," observed a society editor, but they were rather slow in making their appearances. Pale and nervous, Gould stood at the head of the receiving line with his daughter, who wore a blue satin and silver brocade gown and a pearl necklace that had belonged to her mother. Helen Gould was no spoiled society beauty angling for a husband at this unofficial debut; she would, in fact, remain a spinster for many years; but she had a very pleasant face with eyes that reflected a gentle heart. A cousin said she was "excessively timid and sensitive" as a girl, and "her shyness at times was so acute that she actually suffered tortures from it."

Next in line stood Edith Kingdon Gould, her sister-in-law, whose dark beauty was enhanced by canary satin and a breath-taking array of diamonds, and who made up in assurance whatever Helen Gould lacked.

Only a trickle of guests appeared during the first few hours of the reception, according to the newspapers, and for a time it must have seemed to the Goulds, downcast and fidgeting under a bower of palm leaves, that society was once again administering a snub. Later, however, the callers passed down the line in a steady stream and it was generally conceded that the affair was a success, although not a resounding one.

Among those who attended were Mr. and Mrs. Chauncey Depew (as emissaries from the New York Central), Mr. and Mrs. William C. Whitney, Mr. and Mrs. Andrew Carnegie, Mrs. Ulysses S. Grant, the ex-President's widow; Mr. and

Mrs. Seth Low, Governor David B. Hill, Mr. and Mrs. John
D. Rockefeller, Sr., Mr. and Mrs. Henry Clews, Mr. and Mrs.
J. Pierpont Morgan, Mr. and Mrs. John D. Archbold, Mr. and
Mrs. Russell Sage, Mr. and Mrs. Abram S. Hewitt, Mr. and
Mrs. John T. Terry, Mr. and Mrs. Henry Villard, Sir Roderick
Cameron, and Mr. and Mrs. William B. Sloane. Among those
who sent their regrets were President and Mrs. Benjamin Har-
rison, Secretary and Mrs. James G. Blaine, Mr. and Mrs. John
Hay, "President" Porfirio Díaz, Secretary and Mrs. Stephen B.
Elkins, and Postmaster General and Mrs. John Wanamaker.

No Astor, no Vanderbilt, no representatives of the older
families graced the assemblage, but even without those celes-
tial presences, and even though the attendance was rather
heavily weighted with people who had to do business with
the host, the family honor was saved.

During the last year of his life, Gould still kept his hand
on the throttle of his various enterprises but referred to his
son George as their "manager." He came home early from his
offices, tried to rest and relax with his children. His second
son, Edwin, married that year, and the twenty-one-year-old
Howard was away at school, but Helen, Anna, and Frank, the
latter two still in their teens, still lived at home. His daughters
played bezique with him, and Helen read to him from Scott,
Dickens, and Twain. The only times he left the house, except
to go to his offices downtown, were on Sunday morning
strolls down Fifth Avenue (with detectives trailing at a dis-
creet distance) with Russell Sage and his wife; at Forty-
second Street they filed into the Presbyterian church and
occupied a pew together.

His greatest solace was his daughter Helen, who was his
invariable companion. According to Alice Northrop Snow, his
niece, he spent hours educating Helen in the essentials of
handling money, impressing upon her "the lesson of investing
wisely, drawing only upon interest for living expenses."

He leaned upon Helen's affectionate support "more and

more heavily," as death became a palpable presence in that rather lonely house.

To most young women, this filial duty would have become an irksome burden but Helen, according to her cousin, was not only blazingly loyal to her father, but viewed him with an intense hero-worship. All her suitors, she would say, seemed like "mere pygmies" compared to her father.

Though many of his contemporaries attributed to him all the villainies and none of the virtues in the catalogue of human character, there was considerable gallantry and spirit in the way Jay Gould lived out his last months. One of the characteristics of tuberculosis was supposed to be a marked depression, an acute melancholia, which could only aid the course of the disease. But Gould drew on some source of strength deep inside him to conceal his suffering; he refused to admit that he was beaten, and none of those around him ever heard him complain for a moment. From the outside world he even managed to conceal the fact of his desperate illness. He could face the scorn of his enemies—and no man had more—but their pity would be unbearable.

Once, sitting in the parlor with his favorite niece, he rather abruptly told her he was not "afraid to die" but he "hated to leave the younger children." Possibly he had a premonition of what their lives would be, once he was gone and all those millions fell into their hands. A super-rich orphan is not always in an enviable position, particularly one who is unprepared for the greed and envy of the world outside.

Gould seemed to realize, too late, that he had not prepared his children for the realities of the world they would live in after he died. They had certainly been overprotected, and except for the innately sensible and well-balanced Helen, none of them had acquired any measure of self-discipline. Even wealthy New Yorkers with their own quota of spoiled children raised their eyebrows at the way the Gould offspring were pampered.

It was Gould's last vain hope, reflected in the terms of his will, that somehow George, as the eldest son, would be able to take over as head of the family, and with Helen exercising whatever influence she could over her younger sister Anna, his children would grow up to the responsibility of the millions he would leave them. It was also his last and greatest folly.

14. THE EVIL MEN DO . . . .

By the end of the summer of 1892, Dr. John P. Munn, Gould's physician, knew that medicine's slender resources for fighting tuberculosis had been exhausted. Gould, at fifty-six, was a worn-out man; ever since the spring of 1884, when he was forced to fight for his financial existence and went night after night without sleeping, his health had steadily declined; the death of his wife had been a crushing blow; and he was not the sort who could be ordered to go to bed and stay there. The man probably had not had a full night's rest since early manhood. Every time a cough racked his frail body it seemed impossible that he would go on breathing. Medically speaking, he was a marvel, a triumph of mind over body.

The only encouraging clinical aspect of the case was the strong-minded patient's conviction that somehow he would come out on top, that his disease was simply another kind of bear raid which could be beaten away.

Gould, in fact, refused to take Dr. Munn's word for it that tuberculosis, particularly in his case, with a patient who would not rest or take proper nourishment, was bound to be fatal.

He read all the medical authorities on the course and treatment of the disease, consulted and cross-examined specialists in the field, as though the matter were a corporate problem which could be solved by a superior intellect. He became particularly interested in newspaper reports of a revolutionary new technique developed by Dr. Robert Koch, and even considered a trip abroad to consult with him, but he hated to leave New York and his family. Europe, to him, had always been a place to hurry home from.

Dr. Munn, presumably out of desperation, suggested that Gould get out and enjoy himself, certainly an original method of treating the disease. At the physician's promptings, Gould tried to sample some of the joys which poorer people fancied were the nightly pleasures of the rich and mighty. His face, deathly pale and emaciated under its apron-like beard, was to be seen that autumn in a number of the more fashionable places, restaurants and cafes, theaters, and Madison Square Garden. Gould did his best to enjoy himself, but it was a rather grisly and ironic spectacle. His stomach rebelled at the rich foods set before him and he had no thirst for Delmonico's costly vintages. Trying to force-feed himself with all the pleasures he had renounced or scorned in his youth, surrounded by people, most of whom detested him, who could enjoy themselves without the slightest effort, he seemed a creature of the imagination of some Greek dramatist in a particularly misanthropic mood.

Gould was not a man to waste his time on vain regrets, but in those closing months of his life he apparently realized that he had been foolish in squandering his health purely in the pursuit of money. On March 18, 1892, he had written his son George, "Do not work hard. Take plenty of outdoor exercise and plenty of air. I dare not think what would happen if anything went wrong with you. So, my dear boy, comply with the foregoing."

But for himself, hard work continued to be the only narcotic, the only solace of his existence. During Thanksgiving week, he appeared at his offices in the Western Union Building every day before the holiday. The affairs of his empire still obsessed him. At the moment his Manhattan Elevated railways were trying to impress the city with the necessity of converting historic Battery Park into a gigantic turntable for their trains, a scheme which had to be abandoned in the storm of public protest. The city still had some pride in its history and did not propose to allow the old Battery to be converted into a Gould roundhouse, not even in the name of progress.

On Thanksgiving, Dr. Munn, Gould's "medical bodyguard" as the newspapers called him, insisted that his patient accompany him on a long drive, despite the raw, blustery weather. The good doctor apparently believed that tuberculosis, as a last resort, should be confronted by a stern inhospitality. By the time they returned from the drive Gould was coughing and sneezing, had come down with a bad cold and had to be sent to bed. And there he stayed, never to arise again.

A few days later he suffered a severe hemorrhage, and members of the household were forbidden to enter his room. Dr. Munn and a staff of nurses attended him around the clock; specialists were summoned, and a screen was placed in front of the door of his room on the second floor. Dr. Munn told the family that he was a "very sick man," but the younger children, Frank and Anna, still had not been informed that their father was suffering from tuberculosis. They thought it was his stomach trouble flaring up again.

His last thoughts were centered on the only two matters that really concerned him, business and family. He knew, now, that he was dying, and he tapped his last resources to insure that neither his holdings nor his children would suffer any more than was possible from the event of his death. His son George was constantly at his bedside, listening to his last, labored instructions. George, he was convinced, would make an able chief steward of all he had wrested from the world, but he must be made to understand that he had to take control firmly and immediately, and never let it go. "I have always tried to impress upon you," as he wrote his eldest son on May 13, 1892,[1] "to take all responsibility upon the spot in everything."

A last conceit obsessed him, that the news of his death would constitute a terrible shock to Wall Street and particularly to the stocks of Gould-controlled companies. He insisted that news of his condition be withheld from the public because "the effect of rumor was never to be predicted."

Gould would not rest, in fact, until George and Helen read him the market quotations every day and he was assured that his companies' stocks were not tumbling through rumors of his approaching end. He nodded with satisfaction as each quotation was read off. It was still this world, not the shape of the one pictured by his Presbyterian minister as its inevitable successor, that absorbed him. His family always insisted, however contrary some of his actions, that Gould was a religious man and was convinced of the reality of an afterlife, but the last flickerings of his conscious mind apparently were more concerned with the Stock Exchange than the Judgment Seat.

Not until December 1, the day before his death, did any news of his condition reach Wall Street and the newspapers. That day the top head in the New York *Times* was "Is Lizzie Borden Insane?"—the alleged young murderess of Fall River, Massachusetts, who was accused of dispatching her father and mother with the "forty whacks of an ax" (actually a hatchet), was to be indicted the following day. The *Times* devoted several paragraphs to a report that Gould was "very ill." The New York *Herald* was a little more definitive, reporting "the general belief of Wall Street men that Jay Gould is a very sick man" and quoting his son Edwin as saying "His trouble is with his stomach . . . bilious attacks." The *Herald*

[1] In a letter introduced by its recipient at the lengthy court proceedings over the alleged mismanagement of the Gould estate, which was intended to show that Gould meant George to have full control of its affairs.

also noted that George J. Gould and his wife, who invariably attended the openings at Daly's Theater, had failed to appear for the première of *The Hunchback*. The *World*, skeptical as always of any news concerning Gould, informed its readers that they had a choice of rumors:

"No. 1—Jay Gould is dead.

"No. 2—Jay Gould is not dead.

"No. 3—Jay Gould is critically ill.

"No. 4—Jay Gould simply has a bilious attack."

That evening, however, the press began taking much more seriously the reports, gathering in volume, that Gould actually was near death and not merely suffering from a bilious attack.

Outside the Gould mansion the "death watch" was convened, a delegation of reporters and sketch artists from all the New York newspapers. A fair estimate of a man's importance could be gathered from the number of these journalistic sentinels who would be posted on the stoop and sidewalk of a Fifth Avenue householder who was reported to be on his deathbed. For Gould's approaching end, every morning and evening newspaper in the city was represented. Messengers carried bulletins back to their offices. Every person who entered or left the house was buttonholed and cross-examined. Servants were questioned every time they appeared out of doors. Yet the true nature of Gould's illness remained a secret. All that Dr. Munn would tell the reporters was that Gould had suffered stomach hemorrhages, which could hardly have been caused by the bilious attacks supposedly afflicting him.

All night the reporters, stamping their feet in the cold, occasionally nipping off to a nearby saloon, chattering and joking among themselves, watched the lighted window on the second floor, with the figures of doctors and nurses to be glimpsed in silhouette behind its drawn blinds.

All of the Gould children stayed at the house that night, and Russell Sage and his wife also arrived late in the evening.

The early editions of the *World* told the story, now played up at the top of page one:

JAY GOULD SO LOW
THE END IS FEARED

In the *Herald's* early editions a "member of the household" was quoted as saying that it was "doubtful he could live until morning."

By then Gould lay unconscious, the center of a typical Victorian deathbed scene, with medical attendants, family and servants all grouped around to gaze upon his waxen face and listen to his gasping reach for the breath of life, to deprive death of any vestige of privacy.

In this room, if nowhere else in the city or in the world, there was a deep and genuine sorrow; the people gathered here had never known anything but kindness in their relations with the shrunken little man, although even to them he was often a cryptic, elusive, and aloof figure completely absorbed in calculations and stratagems which they saw leaping into life only in the headlines and the denunciations of his enemies.

Shortly after 2 A.M. his eyelids fluttered and he recovered consciousness, murmuring to Dr. Munn that he wished to speak separately to each member of his household. One by one, they approached the bedside and leaned over while he clutched a hand, tried to smile, whispered a few words. First the family, then Miss Margaret Terry, the housekeeper, and all the servants. When he had said good-by to each of them, hanging onto consciousness by some last spasm of the will, his eyes closed again.

He sank back into a coma from which he never roused.

At 9:15 A.M., December 2, he died.

The newspapermen waiting outside knew that death had come when every shade in the house was lowered, every drapery drawn, and a servant appeared to place a black wreath on the door. Not until hours later, when the death certificate was presented, was it revealed that Gould had died

of phthisis pulmonalis—tuberculosis. His last secret had been
well preserved.

In a room next to the death chamber, a stock ticker had
been hooked up so that Gould could stay in close touch with
Wall Street during the last few weeks of his life. No one had
thought to turn the machine off, and it clicked away even as
the body was being laid out.

The news of his death had already reached Wall Street, and
the ticker now conveyed, in an unsentimental staccato, its
sardonic farewell to Jay Gould. Almost to the end, he had
been concerned that the shock of his death would create
something of a panic in the market, certainly that his own
stocks would fall. He needn't have troubled himself. The
ticker pronounced his fellow financiers' and investors' verdict
on his career:

> Western Union . . . . UP 2⅛.
> Manhattan Elevated . . . . UP 2¾.
> Missouri Pacific . . . . UP 1½.
> Union Pacific . . . . UP 1⅜.

Wall Street said good-by with something that would later
be called a Bronx cheer.

"No harder judgment," wrote Burton J. Hendrick in the
American Illustrated Magazine a few months later, "was ever
passed upon a departed millionaire."

Gould's death called forth large black headlines and column after column of type in the newspapers, but the city,
even Wall Street, took the news with an amazing lack of interest, considering that for years he had been the No. 1 villain
among all classes, a predator among the rich, an oppressor
among the workingmen. The *Herald* complimented Wall
Street on suppressing any "unseemly demonstrations" at the
news but noted that there was "much quiet rejoicing" on the
floor of the Exchange and in the brokerages. But "there was

no excitement whatever, and the volume of speculation was moderate. Never before did the death of a man so prominently identified with Wall Street have so little effect on the market." If his death had occurred "when he was borrowing some twenty-five million on collaterals," however, "the resulting crash would have been something for Wall Street to remember. . . . The issues with which Mr. Gould was identified were conspicuously buoyant."

In its editorial comment, the *Herald*, which had been anti-Gould for three decades, noted that Gould was "beyond criticism within the limits of the family circle. . . . But he was also a public man. . . . The example he set is a dangerous one to follow. . . . He played the game of life for keeps, and he regarded the possible ruin of thousands as a matter in which he had no concern."

Whitelaw Reid's pro-Gould *Tribune* published column after column of tributes, mostly from Gould's business associates. It was something of a revelation to the public, which had been told for years that he betrayed or destroyed everyone who crossed his path, that so many men still had reason to be grateful to him. The citizens of Memphis, for instance, recalled that Gould had telegraphed $5000 during the yellow fever epidemic of 1879. Chancellor Henry M. MacCracken of New York University, which was to receive millions from various members of the Gould family, disclosed that the dead financier had signified his intention of subscribing large sums toward its endowment fund.

The *World* and the *Times*, sternly critical for years, saw no occasion for any public manifestations of sorrow. "Ten thousand ruined men will curse the dead man's memory," said the *World*. "Convicts . . . will wonder what mental defect robbed them of such a career as Gould's. . . .

"The public had no great interest in the death of Jay Gould because Jay Gould in his life had never shown any interest in the public, except to make its franchises mills to grind money into his coffers. It is not a death that will cause any public sorrow."

In the next column, which should have given pause to any clear-sighted capitalist, was an editorial advocating an income tax. That, along with future regulation of securities, interstate commerce and trusts, was something Gould had never been forced to confront. Under the laws and regulatory agencies to come, Gould's fortune could never have flourished, nor could its founder have escaped a federal prison if he persisted in tactics which explored the outer limits of free enterprise.

"All his life," a *Times* editorial commented, "he has been knocking at the doors of State prisons without finding a single janitor who would let him in." His fortune was based on his skill at "intercepting the earnings of other people and diverting them from their original destination. . . .

"It is in our time that the 'operator' was born and Jay Gould was an operator pure and simple, although he was as far as possible from pure and as far as possible from simple. . . . No man has ever grasped the leadership of Wall Street so firmly, nor held it anything like so long."

The *Times* would concede only that Gould "never gave himself the trouble of making any false pretenses."

In England, where thousands of investors had suffered from Gould's manipulation of the railroads, from Erie onward, the press was also frankly unsorrowing. "All honour to the greatest money-maker of any age or clime," the London *News* said. "He was less a man than a machine for churning wealth." To the London *Times* he was "a disturbing element of vast and incalculable force," and the *Standard* called him a "wrecker of industries and an impoverisher of men."

Gould was entombed in high fashion. After funeral services conducted in the thronged Gould mansion on Fifth Avenue, an "endless" procession of carriages containing the high and mighty of the financial world—again excepting the Vanderbilts, the Astors, and the older New York families—followed the hearse to Woodlawn Cemetery in the Bronx. Here his wife already lay, in what was said to be the most expensive mausoleum in the United States, an Ionic temple which had cost $110,000 and was to be guarded night and day for many months. Body snatchers were then a post-mortem menace to the rich and famous; not long ago they had made off with the merchant prince A. T. Stewart. The services on that bitterly wind-swept slope overlooking the little valley of the Bronx were mercifully brief. Then, inside the mausoleum, while his children wept and watched, the box containing his oaken casket was permanently sealed, "one spoonful at a time . . . so slow . . . so unmercifully slow!" The black carriages then departed, leaving Jay Gould to his marbled glory, with a guard already pacing his rounds.

There was one possibly sinister touch to the leave-taking, according to the *Times*, whose reporter noticed a number of "unwashed, long-haired" men wearing red neckerchiefs who lurked on the fringes of the funeral throngs and "muttered and cursed." They were "Anarchists," the *Times* said, representatives of the faceless mob, unrelenting in their sullen hatred, whose eruption Gould had feared all his life.

15. A "DYNASTY" DISINTEGRATES

WHEN Jay Gould died in his fifty-seventh year, he left his six rich orphans in a position less enviable than many may have fancied. None had been properly educated, disciplined or indoctrinated in the kind of world, more dangerous than they could imagine, that they faced with their millions. He had left them, that December morning, in the fond hope that they would constitute the second generation of a dynasty; he had "something in the nature of a fixation," as a relative said, that through his children it would be possible to "recapture some of the past, to re-establish the Gould lineage," which had begun so promisingly in Colonial Connecticut and temporarily withered in the Catskill foothills. Perhaps, on the face of it, it was not so vain a hope. The astute historian Burton J. Hendrick wrote a few months after Gould's death that the "Gould dynasty promises to endure for centuries."

Perhaps if George had been less pleasure-loving, less arrogant and boneheaded, if Helen had been more understanding and less narrowly religious in her attitude toward her younger sister and brothers, if Anna had been less self-centered and willful, and if just one of the other Gould sons had shown a streak of common sense or talent, the Gould family would have become the Gould dynasty, in the manner achieved by the Rockefellers, DuPonts, and others. But if a dynasty is "the continued lordship of a race of rulers," as the dictionary has it, then Jay Gould's hopes were quickly doomed. His "dynasty," in that sense, lasted only a few years. Its members reproduced themselves with considerable fecundity, but the power and influence of the Gould fortune, the sheer weight of its holdings, were quickly reduced. A second-generation Gould was as helpless before a first-generation Harriman as William H. Vanderbilt had been before Jay himself.

At the time of his death, George was still callow at twenty-eight, Edwin better balanced and stolid at twenty-six, Helen a prim and spinsterish twenty-two, Howard about to begin sowing wild oats at twenty-one, Anna sullen and self-centered at seventeen, and Frank only fifteen.

The most stable and responsible of the six were Helen, who maintained the family home on Fifth Avenue for her younger sister and brother, and Edwin, who lived with his wife Sarah in a connecting house around the corner at 1 West Forty-seventh Street, but they were simply unable to exert any great influence over the others, all of them independently wealthy and wealthily independent.

Ten days after his death, Jay Gould's will was filed for probate. It was dated December 24, 1885, with several later codicils attached. The estate was left in trust with equal shares for all the children, but George was to receive an additional $5,000,000 for his services as "manager of the Gould enterprises." Helen, additionally, was to have the use of the house at 579 Fifth Avenue and the estate at Irvington-on-Hudson, plus $6000 a month for household expenses. His grandson Jay, son of George, was bequeathed $500,000; each of his sisters and his half brother Abraham, $25,000 plus a $2000 life annuity.

The executors and trustees were to be Daniel S. Miller (his brother-in-law), George, Helen, Edwin, and Howard Gould, with George and Helen to act as guardians for Anna and Frank. They were not to be held responsible for "any loss or depreciation" of the securities forming the trust. A majority vote of the trustees was to be required for any decisions affecting the securities held in trust, but George, in case of disagreement, was to have the controlling voice.

He tried to make certain that only descendants with the Gould blood royal would share in his estate. The trust funds left to his daughters were specifically excluded from any control by their husbands. Furthermore, none of the inheritance was to be passed along to any adopted children, or to any children resulting from a marriage which the other brothers and sisters failed to approve.

A fascinating document, revealing an intense pride of lineage and a vanity he had managed to conceal from his contemporaries, it was to prove lucrative for a whole tribe of lawyers, vexing to the courts, and tragically divisive to his heirs.

For estate purposes, the value of the inheritance was estimated at $72,000,000. Its true value was much greater. Burton J. Hendrick said conservative estimates placed it at $125,-000,000. From later court proceedings (as reported in the New York *Times,* June 1, 1927), it appeared that the various trusts held a minimum of $84,000,000, plus lands in Louisiana later sold for $12,000,000. At a very conservative approximation Gould left a hundred million to his six children, with the value of the whole estate fluctuating violently at times with the rise and fall of security values and the maladroit stewardship of George Gould.

None of his millions was left to charity or to anyone outside the family.

So the six spoiled young innocents were flung into a hectically pleasure-loving, amoral and exuberantly wasteful society with all the resources and opportunities to wreck their lives in the best tradition of the "Mauve Decade." Yet it must be said that the "conspicuous consumption" practiced in the nineties—while millions were unemployed following the Panic of '93, Coxey's Army was marching on Washington, the Molly Maguires were striking in the Pennsylvania coal fields, and William Jennings Bryan was inveighing against the "Cross of Gold"—showed a certain appreciation for the ludicrous aspects of great wealth in a time of non-taxation. To spend a million dollars then took a grandiose imagination, an almost desperate, Coal-Oil-Johnny abandon.

Never in American history was sheer extravagance, in the face of widespread poverty (the nineties were anything but gay for the majority of the people), so tauntingly and defiantly displayed. One would have thought the tumbrels were rumbling on their way to Newport, Bar Harbor, and Tuxedo Park. Some samples of high living were lovingly collected by Frederick T. Martin, himself a wealthy but more sensible man, in his *The Passing of the Idle Rich,* as well as by other social historians of the time. Mrs. Stuyvesant Fish, for instance, gave a dinner in honor of her monkey, Prince Del Drago, who was clad in white tie and tails for the occasion. The guests of C. K. G. Billings, a Chicago gas company heir, were mounted on horseback for a banquet in Sherry's fourth-floor ballroom, with two ice-packed saddlebags serving as champagne buckets for each; the wine was imbibed through rubber tubes, and scarlet-coated waiters helped the tipsy back into their saddles. A wealthy dog lover gave a banquet in honor of his pet, who was presented with a $15,000 diamond dog collar. A "poverty special" dinner, at which the guests "played poor for one night," was given by a wealthy New Yorker whose guests dined off wooden plates and drank out of rusty tin cans. Another New Yorker topped off a banquet by passing around cigarettes made of $100 bills wrapped around tobacco. Another monkey-loving society woman tucked her pet into an ivory bed and employed a valet to look after his wardrobe and grooming. A pharaoh among millionaires turned in for the night in a bedroom furnished at a cost of more than $300,000, including a $200,000 bed fashioned of ivory, ebony, and gold, a $65,000 solid-gold dressing table and a $38,000 gold washstand.

This was the atmosphere in which Jay Gould had hoped that his fortune would survive and possibly flourish, and his heirs mature in dignity and security.

And so much of the stability of that estate depended on the judgment and ability of his eldest son, who was convinced that he had inherited his father's genius as well as his money, who did not realize that he epitomized the familiar tragedy of the lackluster son of an immensely forceful father. Aside from the constant counsel and companionship of his father, George had been ill-prepared to take his place among the magnates who then dominated the American enonomy or to supervise a rail and telegraph empire whose financial power was exceeded only by the Morgan and Rockefeller interests. He had not even received a college education. By temperament, he was self-indulgent, impetuous, careless and overconfident, with a nature that alternated between moods of great enthusiasm and bleak pessimism—all of them characteristics directly opposite to what a successful financier needed. Worst of all, perhaps, he was incredibly naïve, overtrusting at times, oversuspicious at others.

After quickly but accurately sizing him up, the partner of

a great banking house[1] was said to have rubbed his hands gleefully and announced: "We are going to push George Gould off the railroad map of the United States."

George Gould's chief talent, and it was a considerable one, was for spending money. He lived on the lordliest scale of all the Goulds, with the possible exception of Anna when she was under the tutelage of her titled first husband.

His principal residence was "Georgian Court," a sprawling countryseat at Lakewood, New Jersey, where he could occupy himself playing polo with his wealthy neighbors and riding to the hounds. *Harper's Bazaar* of December 30, 1899 described it as the most magnificent estate in the country, located among sunken gardens, rampant statuary, and splashing fountains. Its main hall was 250 feet long, its walls decorated with vast murals, with a marble fireplace big enough to roast an ox and an elliptical marble and bronze staircase, which led up to thirty bedrooms and guest rooms. The furniture was Louis XIV, coated with powdered gold and covered with crimson velvet, and over it blazed an enormous chandelier with 150 cut glass pendants. George slumbered in a bed reported to have cost $25,000. Connected with this gray and white mansion was his private $250,000 playground—a court around which were built a large tanbark hippodrome, a gymnasium, a shooting gallery, a bowling alley, swimming pool, stables, and Turkish and Russian baths.

His wife Edith, in the matter of spending money, was a worthy helpmate. Her splendid throat was graced by a pearl necklace costing $500,000, and among her other trinkets were a diamond tiara and the famous "Peacock Feathers" of diamonds and emeralds, once the property of a Chinese emperor. Appearing as the Empress Catherine of Russia, at a tableau ostensibly held for sweet charity, she wore a jeweled velvet gown with a ten-foot brocade train lined with ermine. According to Elizabeth Drexel Lehr, some of her dressmaker's

[1] Quoted by Ernest Howard in *Wall Street Fifty Years After Erie.*

bills caused even her husband to "raise his eyebrows in dismay."

Something of the style of life at Georgian Court was conveyed in Mrs. Lehr's account of weekends spent there as one of Mrs. Gould's closest friends. "I was always given the 'Purple Guest Room,'" she recalled, "and slept in the enormous marriage bed which George Gould had caused to be designed for his bride. It was a particularly hideous example of the artistic ideas of the 'eighties, and I believe Marcotte had been paid a tremendous sum to embellish it with golden scrolls, lover's-knots, entwined hearts and other appropriate devices. It reared an ungraceful head somewhere near the ceiling, apparently without rhyme or reason except perhaps the better to display its lavish coating of gold.

"Edith laughed as she drew my attention to the design of the painted frieze on its centerpiece, eight cupids attending an altar of love on which hearts were melting in sacrificial flame. 'I shall never forget my feelings when I first saw it,' she said. 'I just knew I should have many children if I slept in that bed . . . and so I did!'"

Edith Gould, according to Mrs. Lehr, studied infant psychology and "searched anxiously for the slightest evidence of any special talent in her sons and daughters so that it would be developed to its fullest extent from the start. When she found five-month-old Georgie waving his arms rhythmically she instantly decided that boxing would be his future sport and as soon as he could walk had a champion boxer brought out from England at enormous cost to give him lessons." An English tennis champion was imported to coach the children, and a ballet teacher was installed at Georgian Court to give little Vivien dancing lessons. "The schoolrooms occupied a whole wing . . . the Gould children must have been among the most highly educated in the United States, for they seemed to have studied every imaginable subject. They had English, German and Italian governesses. At seventeen Vivien wrote Greek poetry, studied Latin with her brothers, and spoke five modern languages fluently."

If George Gould had been content to stay at Georgian Court and play the country gentleman, all might have gone well in the empire left by his father. But George had his own ambitions, or perhaps it would be more accurate to say he was bemused by his father's unfulfilled ones. The one will-o'-the-wisp of the elder Gould's career was the establishment of a transcontinental railroad. Even with his determination and his daring, however, he never quite managed to achieve it. He realized that to conduct the guerrilla campaigns against the Southern Pacific combine, to extend the western roads to the Pacific and the Wabash to the Atlantic, would be to risk his bottom dollar; and that thought had caused him to back off. Now George was confident that he could accomplish what his father had failed to do. Possibly, out of filial devotion, it was to round out the paternal scheme, build an enduring monument to his father. More likely, suffering under the stigma of inherited wealth, George was determined to prove that he was a better man than his masterful sire. His motivations, concealed in the murky swamp of the ego, never quite became apparent; but it was all too clear that he considered himself strong and crafty enough to oppose Harriman, Morgan, Cassatt, or anyone else who got in his way. He was "manifestly intoxicated with optimism," as a lawyer in the subsequent court fight over the Gould estate charged, and "thought he was going to double his money."

So great was his enthusiasm that, forgetting or not realizing that while his father's tactics had always been daring his strategy was invariably cautious, that the elder Gould always felt certain of his footing and made his moves one at a time, George Gould decided to expand in both directions almost simultaneously, taking the risk of a war on two fronts that has always been inadvisable in love, war, politics, or money. His war on the eastern front extended roughly from 1900 to 1903, on the western from 1901 to 1907. Where his father had often been a daring gambler, George was, simply, a reckless dunderhead. Yet he deserved credit for the courage, though it may have been the valor of ignorance, to face very long odds.

Taking on the Pennsylvania Railroad alone, with its half-century of domination over its home state's courts and politics, was an act of considerable courage. Here, however, he had the backing and encouragement of Andrew Carnegie, who declared war on the Pennsylvania in 1899, when the railroad, acting in concert with the Baltimore & Ohio, doubled all freight rates to the eastern seaboard. The railroads, Carnegie said, had "stricken out a manufacturing center," by which he meant Pittsburgh, with its annual traffic of 75,-000,000 tons. "The deliverance of Pittsburgh is my next great work," the steel master declared. It was generally believed that Carnegie, if he succeeded in ramming through a rail line to the Atlantic, would wage an all-out war on the Morgan combine of steelmakers. But first he had to free himself of reliance on the Pennsylvania, which was suspected of raising its rates at Morgan's suggestion. "Carnegie," Morgan said, "is going to demoralize the railroads just as he has demoralized steel." Thus a shadowy battle of the giant trusts was shaping up: in the back-ground, safe in their strategists' bombproofs, it would be Carnegie vs. Morgan; in the foreground, doing all the actual fighting and financial bleeding, it would be Gould vs. the Pennsylvania.

The scheme of Gould, Carnegie, and other Pittsburgh industrialists called for the extension of the Wabash into that city and the linking of a new line over the Alleghenies with the Western Maryland, terminating at Baltimore. Into this project George Gould poured all the necessary resources, refusing to flinch even when a sixty-mile stretch of line leading over the mountains into Pittsburgh cost an unprecedented $380,000 a mile. Before he was through, in fact, Gould had spent an estimated $35,000,000 on the job.

It was still necessary to obtain the city of Pittsburgh's permission to enter. For years the Pennsylvania Railroad had dominated the Common Council and most of the city government. In 1902, however, Gould money poured into Pittsburgh to support a "reform" ticket—one, that is, sympathetic to his designs—and the entry of the Wabash was made the principal issue of the municipal election. Gould's slate won; the new Common Council approved his plans for the Wabash, and at the same time his lobbyists in Washington secured passage of a bill to permit the construction of a new railroad bridge over the Monongahela. Newspapers said this legislative maneuvering and electioneering cost him $12,000,000.

Alexander J. Cassatt, the hardheaded and hot-tempered president of the Pennsylvania, reacted violently. Gould had to be punished for playing Othello to Carnegie's Iago. The Pennsylvania president ordered his crews to rip out 60,000 poles carrying 1500 miles of Western Union wire along his right of ways. Even J. P. Morgan was appalled at this vandalism. "I don't like George Gould," Morgan said, "but I do not like a man who destroys $5,000,000 worth of vested property."

Thus Gould had become embroiled in a bitter, hopeless battle with the Pennsylvania, which could result only in both parties damaging themselves. Carnegie and Morgan soon made peace after their own fashion, with the former selling his interests to the Morgan combine for $492,000,000, a price considerably jacked up, it may be believed, by Gould's witless service as Carnegie's cat's-paw.

Meanwhile, Gould was also engaged in dubious battle out West. With the Wabash system reaching from the Mississippi to the Atlantic, however rickety some of its connections, the Missouri Pacific should be extended from Colorado to the Pacific, Gould believed. The Gould system would then be the first and only line to stretch from coast to coast.

Only one of the flaws in this scheme, but indubitably the most critical, was that it conflicted with the equally ambitious plans of Edward H. Harriman and his supporters in eastern banking houses. And Harriman was a self-made man, brilliant and audacious in his operations as Jay Gould himself had been. Harriman, one of six children of a Long Island clergyman whose parishioners paid him $200 annually, had gone to work as an office boy in a brokerage at fourteen. Eight years later he was able to borrow enough money to buy a seat on the Exchange and open his own brokerage. He began speculating, with considerable success, in railroad stocks, and when the market panicked in 1893 he was able to buy enough stock in Union Pacific, which had tumbled into insolvency, to assume a dominating position in that railroad's affairs, superseding the Gould interests. By this time he had shown sufficient potential as a juggler of railroad securities—again in the Jay Gould pattern, but with more subtlety and discretion, both qualities being required now in dealing with an increasingly watchful, antitrust federal government—to catch the eye of Wall Street's financial rulers. The banking house of Kuhn, Loeb & Company decided to back him in his ventures, and Harriman was on his way.

At first George Gould and Edward Harriman were, ostensibly, friends and allies. It was a measure of Gould's naïveté, in fact, that he considered the endlessly striving Harriman an "intimate friend." This one-sided friendship prevented Gould, actually, from achieving his ambition to reach the Pacific. When Collis Huntington died in 1900, Gould had the opportunity (and the resources) to buy out his interests in the Southern Pacific, a purchase which would have cleared his way to the coast. He told his associates, however, that buying the Southern Pacific would be "disloyal" to his friend Harriman. Uninhibited by such considerations, Harriman then bought control of the Southern Pacific himself—and when Gould hopefully suggested that Harriman sell him half-interest he was coldly rejected.

Even George Gould could see now that Harriman was more interested in establishing a dictatorship over the country's railroads, with the help of Kuhn, Loeb & Co., than in furthering any personal friendships. Very well, he would proceed on his own. He was "not afraid of Harriman or the devil," still secure in the belief that the Gould name and the Gould millions conquered all. Furthermore, he would rock Harriman back on his heels while devoting his usual attention to fox hunting, theatergoing, polo playing and all the other relaxations essential to the good life; no gentleman could be expected to spend ungodly hours grubbing about in offices, sitting in on board meetings, rounding up proxies and conniving with self-important little men who fancied they had a vested interest in one's affairs. As one observer wrote, he "developed the habit of suddenly going to Europe and leaving nobody with authority to make a business move. . . . His entourage developed into a petty court, constantly filled with jealousies, bickerings and scandal-mongerings."

It seemed quite simple to Gould: he would push the Missouri Pacific to San Francisco and let Harriman and the New York bankers protest their heads off. Just to make sure that there would be no objections from Washington, he contributed $500,000 from the Gould estate (as was revealed in 1922 during court proceedings over his management) to Theodore Roosevelt's campaign fund.

The Missouri Pacific already operated as far as Pueblo, Colorado, where it connected with the Denver & Rio Grande, which was a Gould-controlled line. He would build westward from Denver; the Western Pacific, his own creation, would extend his system to the Pacific Coast, and passengers and freight could travel all the way from Baltimore to San Francisco without once leaving a Gould-operated train. The prospect of having his Central Pacific paralleled by the Western Pacific threw Harriman into a rage, and he was said to have warned Gould, "If you build that railroad, I'll kill you."

But Gould had been dreaming and boasting to his sycophantic "entourage," and not looking ahead to the day when money got tight and stocks would fall, when the Gould enterprises, with their peculiar financing and their tendency to drain off profits as fast as they came in, would inevitably be engulfed by a sea of red ink. Jay Gould had always prepared for such a day and was an expert at retaining control by having himself appointed as receiver for any failing company. His son, however, was seriously overextended in expanding the Wabash and building the Western Pacific. When the squeeze came in 1907, with another panic in Wall Street and banks calling in their loans, Gould railroads were thrown into receivership, the Kuhn-Loeb and Rockefeller interests took over the Wabash and the Denver & Rio Grande, and he had to abandon all hope of ever operating a coast-to-coast railroad system. He also lost control of the Missouri Pacific, the star in the Gould diadem, as well as of Western Union and Manhattan Elevated. Financial columnists referred to him as "the sick man of Wall Street." Gould was dead, long live Harriman!

After forty-five years of striking terror in the hearts of fellow speculators, investors, and business rivals, the House of Gould was no longer a power in the Street. As Burton J. Hendrick analyzed it in *McClure's Magazine* of March 1912, the Goulds lost control of their domain "because, like the Vanderbilts, they have attempted to do two incompatible things—live lives of idleness and luxury, and at the same time control great enterprises. . . . The complex forces controlling modern industrialism have proved too much for them." Furthermore, the Harriman-Kuhn-Loeb combination "had all the essential qualities that the Gould family conspicuously lacked." The Gould estate had been cut approximately in half. In another several years it would lose its last remaining bit of influence in the railroads. Enough money was left to allow the heirs and heiresses to live in luxury, though possibly with fewer steam yachts and country houses, but the Gould fortune was no longer large enough to exercise any considerable authority in financial affairs. George Gould, his wings clipped to the nub, had to content himself with less weighty matters.

. . . While still posing as head of the family, George had managed to interfere effectively in his younger sister's happiness. Anna, who was nineteen at the time, fell in love with an actor named Frank Woodruff, a decent enough fellow judging by his behavior, but without the social cachet that George desired for his sister. They became engaged, but George, as Anna's guardian, insisted that the relationship be broken off. "From the very beginning he refused his consent," according to Elizabeth Drexel Lehr. "Anna said she would marry without it, renounce riches for love. Then Frank Woodruff unselfishly stood aside. . . . He could not allow her to sacrifice herself for him." In this bit of meddling, George conveniently ignored the fact that he had married into the theater himself. A titled husband was all the rage for American heiresses, and Anna must do her share in enhancing the Gould name.[2]

So the sulky young woman was packed off to Paris a few months later, in 1894, to stay with Miss Fanny Reed, a formidable lady whose *salon* served as a bridge between French and expatriate American society. The younger of the Gould sisters was no great beauty. Like her father, she was small, sallow, self-centered, determined to have her own way. Fortunately, she also inherited her father's expressive dark eyes. While she rebelled at her sister Helen's stern watchfulness over her conduct, she also was deeply suspicious of worldliness, particularly in men. She had little tact, an abrupt manner, and had been thoroughly spoiled; bitterness over the frustrated romance with Frank Woodruff only added to the resentment visible in all her photographs as a young woman.

[2] Actually, between money-hungry European noblemen and American social butterflies, there wasn't much choice for a girl entering the marriage market. Mrs. Lehr recalled that her husband, Ward McAllister's successor as Mrs. Astor's social arbiter, told her immediately after they were married, "Do you imagine that I am the type of man who would let himself be influenced by any woman's attractions, least of all yours? Let me tell you once and for all that love of woman is a sealed book to me. I have not wanted it, or sought it, and I never shall . . . I married you only because the only person on earth I love is my mother. I wanted above everything else to keep her in comfort. Your father's fortune will enable me to do so."

Yet it was a typical product of the fashionable *faubourgs*, of the ultrasophisticated Parisian society, who won her reluctant approval at Miss Reed's gatherings . . . a deceptively dainty worldling who bore the title of Count Marie Ernest Paul Boniface de Castellane. Count Boni, poseur, duelist, roué and gambler, was penniless at twenty-eight, and his only hope of living in the style to which his family had become accustomed long before the French Revolution was to marry an heiress. He was a slender, elegantly turned-out fellow with golden hair and a waxen complexion, so doll-like in appearance that an uncouth American subsequently named him "Powder Puff." Anyone who called him that to his face, however, was likely to be invited to share a brace of pistols at dawn, and Count Boni had already won several duels.

He found Miss Gould something less than fascinating—"excessively shy, childish, a trifle malicious," as he recorded his first impression in his embittered memoir[3]—but reports of her enormous trust fund persuaded him that she would make the ideal wife. So brazenly mercenary was his pursuit of Anna and her fortune that, as Elizabeth Eliot has written in *Heiresses and Coronets*, "his behavior and his motives were compared unfavorably with those of a 'gentleman' who was alleged to have taken a dowry of $10,000 from the father of his colored bride and then, in Richmond, Virginia, sold her for what would seem to have been the poor price of $300."

Count Boni's courtship proceeded so promisingly that George Gould and his wife came over to inspect him and give their approval. Before the year was out, he spent his last centime on passage to America to "complete my conquest of this charming daughter of the New World." He stopped off in England, where his friend the Marchioness of Anglesey (the American-born Mary Livingston King) warned him that he didn't understand Americans, that American girls made "elusive wives," and that Anna Gould's "soft exterior hides a will

[3] *How I Discovered America.*

of iron. She is essentially the child of her father." Good advice, but Count Boni was in no position to take it; he was staking everything on a wealthy marriage, and it had to be arranged quickly. On arrival in New York he borrowed enough money from a fellow Frenchman to keep him going while he pursued Anna Gould.

The high-born suitor was not particularly impressed with the Goulds, their tastes, their possessions or their style of living; nor was he particularly comfortable under the critical scrutiny of Helen Gould and her mentor, Mrs. Russell Sage. At the town house on Fifth Avenue he was appalled by the "bead curtains" and a "bronze monstrosity of a floor lamp" with a "tumor-like shade." Mrs. Sage "took an instant dislike of me," and Helen, who "had the lowest opinion of men," viewed him with the utmost suspicion until he decided to "enact the role of the virtuous curate" and Helen's "smile was more encouraging."

Helen, he observed, "dressed like a deaconness," would not permit wine to be served at her table (not even to a Frenchman!), and was so mistrustful of the male sex that her household was staffed entirely by female servants. The "bevy of pretty parlor maids," he also noted, was "not at all displeasing to the roguish eye of Frank Gould," two years younger than Anna and still in his older sister's custody.

Anna, he said, announced that she wouldn't marry him because "I don't like foreigners and I won't live out of America."

Then Anna found that Helen was spying on her, Count Boni related, and "from that moment Anna seriously considered me in the light of a husband." He helped his cause along by flirting with other millionaire's daughters. "I was not disposed to allow her to retain the idea that foreigners were not sympathetic to other American beauties."

Helen insisted that they accompany her to Lyndhurst for Christmas, but life was so unbearably dull under its Gothic towers that Anna wired her brother George to invite her to

Georgian Court, and soon Anna and Boni were "bidding good-bye to Helen and Holiness."

George, playing the role of fox-hunting squire to the hilt, was no great improvement over Helen. Practically all of the Georgian Court offended the Count's aesthetic eye. He was distressed by the quantity of black, white, brown, and gray bearskins strewn over the steps of the monstrous elliptical staircase. The gilded piano in the main hall looked like "a sea monster." They dined off gold plate, of course, and the walls of the dining room were hung with jade-green silk to match Edith Gould's eyes. Worst of all, perhaps, the statuary striking attitudes all over the Gould gardens was wrought of *cement.*

Boni, who had a sharp eye for the ridiculous, except as it pertained to himself, told of a fox hunt he was cajoled into joining which ended when the quarry was run to earth in the sunken garden and found to have wrapped himself around the neck of a statue of Venus de Milo. The incident, to Boni, seemed to epitomize the farcical quality of country life among the American millionaires.

At the end of July 1894, the George Goulds, some of their friends, Anna and Boni took off for Montreal in the Goulds' private Pullman car. There Boni proposed and Anna accepted, but with a proviso that would have chilled a less purposeful suitor. When he suggested that she become a Catholic, he said, she replied that "I will never become a Catholic, because if I were to do so I should not be able to divorce you, and if I were not happy I would not remain your wife a moment longer than was necessary." Even the blasé Boni was taken aback by the discovery that "every American girl only thinks of marriage in connection with divorce." Marriage, though not its vows, was sacred to Boni.

Marrying a Gould, he found, was a practical as well as a romantic affair. He had to sign a marriage settlement, "the dominant idea of the Gould family being to keep the Gould fortune in America: it was nothing short of an obsession with them, and it was responsible for much of the injustice and bitterness which I was destined to experience later at their hands." Anna retained "full control of her fortune," and though he admittedly ran through five and a half of her millions, she "allowed me to spend her money of her own free will."

They were married March 4, 1895, in a ceremony performed by a Monsignor Corrigan at the Gould town house. Anna wore a $6000 lace veil from Paris which she frugally converted later into a bedspread. Boni's fragile, disdainful mother was imported for the occasion, and looked, her son said, "like an ancestral portrait purchased by a millionaire," standing among the swarthy, half-awed and half-mistrustful tribe of Goulds.

Not many months passed before the Goulds learned that their suspicions were justified, and that acquiring a genuine French aristocrat for grafting on the family tree could be almost as expensive as George's dabbling in high finance. Boni's unsuccessful operations at the gaming table, the society gossip sheet *Town Topics* tolerantly remarked, should be forgiven on the ground that "he is not yet accustomed to the handling of ready cash."

Since Boni believed that it was his duty to show Anna how to live on the grand scale, he exerted himself heroically to spend her money. He bought Gobelin tapestries by the acre, old masters, town and country houses. They lived in a mansion on the Avenue Bosquet while a pink marble palace modeled on the Trianon was being built, a construction job that took, in fact, about half of their married life to complete. In celebration of Anna's twenty-first birthday, and, incidentally, the end of George's irksome guardianship, with a consequent further loosening of the purse strings, Boni arranged a fete which he promised would re-create the good old days at Versailles, with a 200-man orchestra, eighty ballet dancers, fireworks, sixty scarlet-liveried footmen, and 80,000 Venetian lamps made specially for the occasion at Murano. The "bluest blood of France" contributed its presence, the fete went off beautifully, yet "it might have been *anywhere* and *anything*," Boni complained, "so far as Anna was concerned." A short time later he bought the historic Château de Grignan, and now the Gould family was becoming restive over his expenditures. Buying Grignan, he said, "unfortunately added fuel to the fire of the hostility they now displayed" and the Gould brothers particularly were "vexed that the family fortunes should be wasted in such a manner."

Undismayed by his brothers-in-law and their refusal to understand the duties of a nobleman with a rich wife, Boni proceeded to buy the largest pleasure craft he could find afloat —not a mere steam yacht but, as the New York *Herald* of December 8, 1900 described it, "a three-masted full-rigged ship with auxiliary steam engines." The *Valhalla* was "so large that she has sometimes been mistaken for an old warship. She costs $150,000 a year to keep in service and carries a crew of 130 men. She was refitted most luxuriously after her purchase by the Castellanes in 1897."

Even the Gould fortune, it developed, could not support Boni's expensive whims. By 1900 his creditors were closing in from all directions. A Paris banker demanded seizure of the *Valhalla* on the grounds that Boni owed him 750,000 francs. An art dealer brought suit for several million francs in the high courts. George Gould refused him any help, and Boni found himself treading the edge of a volcano, as he said, "the volcano in this case being the activities of the Gould advisers."

Anna, furthermore, was growing increasingly unsympathetic and reproachful—not about the money so much as his affairs with other women. His gallantries, Boni confessed, were the "orange peel" on which he was to slip. Anna had the curious American attitude that a man was supposed to be literally faithful unto death. As Boni described his downfall, Anna "would defend me and my misdoings to others, but she would never defend them to herself. . . . She never forgave me for having 'lived' before I married her. . . . Life became impossible. Anna saw a rival in every woman."

Coupled with jealousy, he said, was the fact that "her infernal pride made her believe she was superior to everybody, and that the universe was at her disposal."

It wasn't enough that he fathered three beautiful sons, Boni, George, and Jay, nicknamed Pittipat, Tippytoe, and Tittymouse; she expected him to be at her side constantly, displaying a spaniel-like devotion for the benefit of their friends.

He never could understand her intense self-centeredness, her assumption that she lived in the dead-calm eye of the storms in the world around her. Once, on a cruise to Constantinople aboard the *Valhalla*, the craft was buffeted by one of the Sea of Marmora's sudden storms. Boni and his guests huddled together in the *salon*, certain she was going to break up. Some time later Boni noticed that Anna was missing. Searching the battered and careening vessel, he finally found her seated in her cabin, calmly polishing her collection of pearls with sea water.

A cloud no bigger than a hungry cousin subsequently appeared on Boni's horizon. His first cousin, the Duc de Talleyrand-Périgord, later the Prince de Sagan, came down to visit them at Marais, one of their country estates. Talleyrand announced, perhaps a little too casually, that he just happened to be in the neighborhood and decided to pay them a call. Later Boni had reason to suspect that his cousin's visit was more in the nature of a reconnaissance. "Little did I dream when I entertained this angel unawares, that he would eventually own Marais and—incidentally—marry my wife." Perhaps Boni should have been forewarned by the Talleyrands' expertness at wooing American heiresses; the Duke's brother had married Helen Morton, daughter of the wealthy banker Levi Morton, and other members of that prolific branch of the family had carried off a startling number of wealthy American girls.

From then on relations between Boni and Anna froze into

hostility; during the last few years they were barely on speaking terms. There were rumors that Anna had discovered an interesting packet of letters in Boni's safe, although he later denied this. One day in January 1906, Anna and their three children disappeared from the pink marble palace on the Avenue de Bois. When Boni returned home at dusk, he found the place in utter darkness; the electricity had been cut off, the servants paid and sent away . . . and Count Boni, once again, was on his own.

Hoping for a reconciliation, Boni waited patiently to hear from Anna but "the Goulds mustered their forces and blackened my reputation still further," with the result that Anna demanded a divorce.

Anna remarried in 1908, her choice being Boni's first cousin. In Parisian society it was generally agreed that Anna chose the Duc de Talleyrand for her second husband largely because it would greatly annoy her first and thus afford her a measure of revenge for Boni's infidelities and extravagances. Boni had spent approximately $800,000 a year during their marriage. This time George Gould objected to another French nobleman being brought into the family with his expensive tastes, and that may have been another reason for Anna to accept the Duke. He was a great improvement over Boni, at any rate, and fathered two more of Anna's children. She had a limited capacity for contentment, but it appeared to have been reached in her second marriage.

George Gould meanwhile was not stinting himself, despite the fact that the estate had been cut in half by his misadventures in railroad financing. His social position seemed to have been enhanced by his downfall as a financier; perhaps society had only been waiting for a Gould to prove himself mortal in money matters. He and Edith regularly received invitations to the Astor Ball, and only the Vanderbilts withheld their approval. The Goulds gave the most lavish cotillions in town, with dancing, champagne suppers, and breakfasts at dawn.

In 1910, when they announced the engagement of their daughter Marjorie to Anthony J. Drexel, Jr., their guests at the cotillion were given solid-gold souvenirs, rings and charms for the women, scarfpins for the men.

Even more elaborate were the celebrations attending the marriage of their demurely beautiful daughter Vivien. By this time George had recovered sufficiently from his experiences with Count Boni to permit another transatlantic experiment with the nobility. Vivien had met a young British Army major named Jack Beresford while touring Europe. They fell in love, but his suit was not encouraged until his elder brother died suddenly and he succeeded to the title of Lord Decies.

For this marriage, heralded as the "most brilliant of all these Anglo-American unions," George laid on all the fripperies his money and position could command. Harry Lehr led the cotillion at the announcement of the engagement, at which the lady guests were given gold vanity boxes. Two hundred and twenty-five seamstresses worked on the bride's trousseau; the wedding cake was decorated with electric lights and cupids emblazoned with the Decies coat of arms (a fair sample of Edwardian excessiveness), and the bride's present from her parents was a diamond coronet, which, it should be said, she wore with a more regal air than most Goulds could manage. Judging from photographs and the testimony of her contemporaries, Vivien was the beauty of the family, with old Jay's darkly magnetic eyes.

The wedding at St. Bartholomew's on February 6, 1911, attracted all the public interest, and perhaps a bit more, that the Goulds could wish. Several gallant American males objected to yet another heiress being carried off to corrupt and perfidious Europe. "Cad that you are," one fellow addressed the groom, "you are here to marry an American girl for a fortune that was made in America." The anonymous writer warned that "well-devised plans" had been set in motion to prevent the marriage "regardless of the cost." John Madison Turner, who identified himself as a member of the Virginia aristocracy, challenged the Englishman to a duel. Lord Decies, considering the challenge beneath the dignity of an officer of His Majesty's Seventh Hussars, commented that the only weapons he would consider were chocolate éclairs at ten paces.

Thousands pushed their way into the area around the church, watched from surrounding rooftops, climbed lampposts and telephone poles, and massed around the barriers erected by the police to keep all those without invitations a block away. A group of women broke through the police lines somehow, raced for the church, and were happily snatching up baskets of flowers when the Gould forces launched their counterattack. A squad of private detectives held in reserve at the rear of the church went into action and rushed the women into the street with more vigor than sentiment. The crowds cheered. Inside the church, as the bride glided down the aisle on her father's arm, the more privileged created an equally vulgar scene, jumping up on the pews and digging their elbows into each other's ribs for a glimpse of that celebrated wedding gown. More than one lady conveniently fainted, and more than one gentleman's gray topper was stove in, before order was restored and Vivien Gould was pronounced the wife of the fifth Lord Decies.

Shortly after she was established at the ancestral seat, Lady Vivien proceeded to make the old home statelier by installing new paneling for which the contractors, overstimulated by the scent of all those Gould millions, charged $25,000 more than was considered proper. Old Jay would have approved of his granddaughter: she promptly took them to court. The judge, after inspecting the premises, agreed that the contractors had overcharged, remarking that "I could hear the plug being pulled in the water closet while I was sitting in the drawing room."

The George Goulds were much less pleased with the marriage of their son Kingdon, who fell in love with a Signorina Annunziata Camille Maria Lucci, who was proud and beautiful . . . and one of his mother's servants. Mrs. Lehr was having tea with Mrs. Gould one day at the Georgian Court when the Italian girl was summoned and informed by her employer that she must not take the young man's attentions too seriously.

"You think he not love me? You are wrong. I will marry him . . . I will marry him!" Signorina Lucci cried out.

Mrs. Gould "tried to reason with her . . . warned her that Kingdon was only trying to learn Italian," but the girl would not listen and had to be discharged. A few days later the mother learned that she was mistaken, when Kingdon and his brother Jay drove into New York and met Signorina Lucci at St. Bartholemew's. No other Goulds were present, and there were no mob scenes such as attended Vivien's wedding, but Kingdon married the girl of his choice. The marriage, incidentally, was fruitful and enduring.

Maternal sensibilities received another blow a short time later when, on January 31, 1921, a Mrs. Richard Blum filed a $500,000 suit against Kingdon Gould charging that he had breached his promise to marry her and had even "paid for the employment of detectives who obtained evidence on which she obtained a divorce."

As a whole, the Gould family, with its marriages and divorces, its scandals and recriminations, climaxed finally by the long court fight over George's management of the estate, provided in its accumulated legal papers a documentary serial on the corrosion of a second generation fallen, with little guidance or preparation, into great wealth.

George Gould, now a portly and middle-aged man about town whose affairs had largely been taken over by lawyers and trust companies, strayed from the straight and narrow in the winter of 1913–14. One night he attended the opening of a musical comedy, *The Girl in the Film*, destined to close a few performances later, without his wife. "This was an era," as Dixon Wecter has written in *The Saga of American Society*, "when many plutocrats waited with orchids at stage doors—

though, unlike Gould, they often married the homely daughters of their business partners." George's speculative eye, roving the buxom chorus line, was attracted by a young actress named Guinevere Jeanne Sinclair, who played bits in some of the sketches. At the curtain call, it was said later, George simply tossed his card over the footlights to Miss Sinclair, and a meeting was arranged. Soon afterward he established her on an estate in the Westchester suburb of Rye, and in his will he acknowledged that he had fathered her three children, born in 1915, 1916, and 1922. His first wife died on November 13, 1921. Six months later he married Miss Sinclair. One year after that he contracted pneumonia while they were abroad and died in a villa at Mentone on May 16, 1923.

With the exception of his sedate brother Edwin, who took Sarah Shrady as his bride a few months before his father's death and stayed married to her, the marital lives of Jay Gould's sons followed an eccentric pattern. Howard led the typical Edwardian playboy's life on his Long Island estate, and later he settled in England after his name cropped up on a list of contributors to the personal welfare fund of the blackmailing publisher of a gossip sheet. He was married to an actress named Viola Clemmons, whom he subsequently divorced on charges of infidelity, naming Colonel William (Buffalo Bill) Cody, who cut a mighty swath through English society while touring with his Wild West show, as the corespondent. Much later he married Margarete Fosheim, a Viennese stage star, but divorced her in 1947.

The liveliest of the Gould sons was Jay's youngest, Frank, who died in 1956 at the age of seventy-nine. There were glimmers of promise to his career, had it not been complicated by so much inherited money. The only member of his family to undergo a formal education, apparently at Helen's insistence, he was a member of the Class of 1899 at New York University. According to the university's records, he was "a special student in engineering and sciences at the University Heights campus." While still an undergraduate, he presented the school with a costly machine to measure stress and tension in building materials. The university, in fact, has been greatly assisted through the years by endowments from the Gould family, and in a rather worthy sense bears the Gould seal much more distinctively than any of the great corporations it once controlled. N.Y.U., the Goulds' one large-scale experiment with philanthropy, has received a total of $8,000,000 through the years. Frank gave it $1,500,000 for construction of a student center bearing his name, twice made $1,000,000 contributions to its general endowment fund, and shortly before his death gave $2,000,000 toward completion of the engineering and science center at University Heights. His sister Helen was an equally generous contributor, financing the Gould Memorial Library, the Hall of Fame, and the Gould Dormitory. The university also acquired the old summer home at Irvington-on-Hudson after Helen's death.

While still in his twenties, Frank Gould showed signs of his father's genius at promotion and acquisition. Just when his older brother was losing his battles with Harriman and the Pennsylvania, Frank was quietly building a small business empire for himself. From 1902 on, he began buying up electric traction and power companies in Richmond and other Virginia cities. He organized a combine known as the Virginia Railway and Power Company, which was capitalized at $42,-000,000, and for a time gloried in doing something on his own. "When I was young," he once complained, "I was never let to do what I wanted to do." Before he was thirty, realizing that making more money simply for money's sake was futile for a man in his position, he gave up direct supervision of his Virginia interests, which were finally sold in 1925 and became known as the Virginia Electric Power Company.

Of all the Gould children, Frank put his money to the most imaginative use, eventually becoming known as the "croupier de luxe of the Riviera." Before settling down abroad, he tried to distract himself with several marriages, membership in twenty-seven different clubs, and building a block-long private riding hall on Fifty-seventh Street. But America bored him. In 1913 he expatriated himself and became one of the more dashing and productive members of the international set. In time, "M'sieu Goolt" as the French called him, a familiar sight on the roads of the Riviera as he roared around in his Hispano at reckless speeds, helped to pioneer the resort coasts of France and make them a gilded haven for the care-worn rich. He was credited with "making" Juan-les-Pins between Nice and Cannes as well as Bagnoles-de-l'Orne in Normandy. He created the most luxurious and glamorous of the Riviera casinos, the Palais de la Méditerranée, which as a French magazine said "neither the Caesars nor the Bourbons could have built." In the Twenties he was not only the "World's Gambling Czar," as the New York *Sun* called him, but the owner of one of Europe's finest racing stables, a Norman stud farm, a chocolate factory, a paper mill, an auto-body plant and a string of hotels. To sojourning Americans, in particular, Frank Jay Gould, with his devilish eye and his rakish mustache, was the epitome of sophistication and trans-atlantic glamour, the incredible offshoot of a grubby little father.

His marital life was fittingly spiced with variety. His first wife was the eighteen-year-old Margaret Kelly, who divorced him on charges of misconduct. A young actress named Edith Kelly, no relation to her predecessor, was his second wife. She also divorced him, and made certain she would linger in his memory by suing him, on various pretexts, a total of thirteen times between 1918 and 1929. His third and final wife was Florence LaCaze, the daughter of a French newspaper editor, whom he married in 1923.

The kindliest, the best-intentioned and undoubtedly the happiest of the Gould children was Helen, who created her own gentle world of deserving orphans, of jungle heathen waiting to be saved, worshipful social workers, fund-raisers and dominies of all sects and schemes. Helen had a mission in life, and worked endlessly, if sometimes a trifle oddly, at improving the lot of others less fortunate.

It was remarkable that this unceasing concern for humanity was not stamped out of her, as it would have been in a person of lesser faith or with even the narrowest streak of cynicism, by the crooks, cranks, and pretenders of all varieties who lurked constantly on the fringes of her life. Almost every mail, according to her cousin, Alice Northrop Snow, "contained some kind of threat" against her life. Others begged for everything from mortgage payments to baby grand pianos. Still others invariably began, "I saw your beautiful face in the paper and fell in love at once," and proposed marriage at the earliest possible date. A particularly nasty and troublesome threat to her peace of mind, if not her fortune, was the claim of an upstate New York woman that Jay Gould had married her in 1853 (when he was seventeen), had fathered her daughter, and that she was entitled to a share in the estate. The plotter rigged up a fairly convincing case out of perjured testimony, until her witnesses fell apart under the relentless cross-examination of Elihu Root, an attorney for the Gould estate. The woman, it was subsequently revealed, had made a profitable specialty of threatening suit against wealthy heirs and was convicted of blackmail.

Unsoured by these opportunists, Helen Gould spent much of her time searching out students who needed help in finishing their education, foreign missions which needed funds, and causes, ranging from temperance to distributing the Bible in every land under the sun, which required bolstering. She traveled constantly in her private railroad car on her investigations, a shy, prim little woman indefatigably bent on spreading enlightenment. In one year, besides all the standard charities she contributed to, she was financing the distribution of wholesome literature to soldiers stationed in China and sailors in the Philippines, sending two missionaries into French Equatorial Africa, endowing twenty-six Y.M.C.A. branches through the United States, building the Jay Gould

Reformed Church in Roxbury, New York, organizing a "crusade against Mormonism," and combating the inroads of Mohammedanism by sending several hundred thousand Bibles to the Middle East. That year she also bought the first ten Edison "talking machines" and donated them to the Army, one of them somehow reaching the Philippine jungle outpost of a young cavalry captain named John J. Pershing, who put it to good use impressing Moro chiefs with its amazing sounds. Her benefactions penetrated to the farthest corners of the earth, and drink-sodden men in the remotest tropical ports were likely to have temperance tracts published by Helen Gould pressed into their trembling hands.

Twenty years after her father's death, she was still unmarried, content with a life of good works. In the fall of 1912, while en route to a Y.M.C.A. convention in Chicago, her train collided with a buckled freight. In the course of rescue work, she met a fellow passenger, Finley J. Shepard, assistant to the president of the Missouri Pacific, who had once been introduced to her on the platform on a Y.M.C.A. meeting in Denver. Their ages, tastes, and temperaments were strikingly similar, and a most circumspect and touchingly tentative courtship ensued. The next year, at the age of forty-four, Helen married her suitor. It was a very happy marriage, although she was "so dreadfully disappointed" they could not have children. "I would go to death's door for a baby," she said.

In her late forties, Mrs. Shepard adopted four children from orphanages, one of whom was found on the steps of St. Patrick's Cathedral. She also raised Frank's two daughters by his first marriage. Remembering all too well how her brothers and sisters had been spoiled, she did not propose to allow the children in her care to think that money materialized out of thin air, which was just as well considering that the four orphans she adopted, under the terms of her father's will, could not share in any part of his inheritance. As Celeste Andrews Seton wrote in her memoir *Helen Gould Was My*

Mother-in-Law, the children received allowances of fifty cents a month, of which twenty cents had to be placed in the Sunday-school collection and twenty cents in the church collection, leaving each child with ten cents a month to spend as he chose.

In her determinedly placid life, the most bitterly disturbing intrusion was the long court fight over the estate initiated by her sister Anna and brother Frank.

The Goulds fought it out in the courts from 1916 to 1927, when a settlement was finally reached after what was said to have been the costliest litigation in U.S. legal history, and after several members of the family had been hopelessly estranged from each other. Helen, a relative said, was particularly aggrieved when "criticisms, recriminations and wounded feelings effected a rift in the family. . . . It was a hurt that left a permanent scar."

In 1919, three years after they instituted suit, Frank and Anna succeeded in having George removed as chief executor and trustee of the estate. Edwin was jointly charged with neglect as the second most decisive factor in the administration of the trusts, and Helen and Howard were accused of approving of their actions.

Attorneys for the two younger children humiliated George by mocking his pretensions as a business genius. One of them charged that George, believing he had inherited his father's talents, "launched forth as a great railroad magnate" with "bombastic flourishes" and succeeded only in bringing down a shower of bankruptcy proceedings, receiverships, and reorganizations that lost the family control of the Wabash, the Missouri Pacific, the Texas & Pacific, and subsidiary lines. George's derelictions, it was charged, cost the estate upwards of $25,000,000.

In answering these accusations, George did not scruple to call for a washing of family linen on the public record. Anna's suit, he said, was motivated by his objections to her various romances and marriages; Frank had concealed his second marriage from George, as titular head of the family, until long after the event. As early as 1896, immediately after her marriage to the expensive Count Boni, Anna had started objecting to "investments by Helen and myself as her guardians." George denied, furthermore, that he engineered the purchase of the Denver & Rio Grande by the Missouri Pacific as "part of a transcontinental scheme" but maintained that the "welfare of the Missouri Pacific seemed to demand it."

If his younger brothers and sisters had been more interested in the general welfare of the estate, George claimed, the Gould interests would not have been thrown to the wolves during the Panic of 1907. For several years before the crash, he maintained, he had sought their assistance in bolstering the finances of the Gould-controlled railroads but "Edwin was interested in other investments, Howard was improving a large estate on Long Island, Frank was interested in racing, Helen was interested in her charities, and Anna's income was tied up by the creditors of her husband."

By the time he died in 1923, George was "no longer on speaking terms" with several members of the family. Two years later the courts ordered that the four older children turn over $20,000,000 to Frank and Anna's trust funds, out of the $50,000,000 which Referee James O'Gorman found had been lost to the estate through George's ineptitude.

In the New York Supreme Court on June 1, 1927, the long contest was finally ended when Justice John M. Tierney approved a settlement by which the trustees distributed $16,-000,000 among the six trust funds established by Jay Gould. Henceforth the estate would be administered by four trust companies. Its value, despite the losses incurred by George Gould's misadventures, was estimated at a total of $66,500,-000, having been newly inflated by the booming stock market of the twenties. And the New York legal profession, to whom Jay Gould's affairs had been pie in the sky for almost seventy years, took a huge final bite out of the estate. Some fifty lawyers were awarded a total of $2,703,000 in the settlement, including the strait-laced Samuel Seabury's half a million as one of Frank Jay Gould's attorneys. But there was still enough left for Jay Gould's surviving children, grandchildren and great-grandchildren to live comfortably and maintain their social position, now greatly enhanced by so many links to the European aristocracy, off the money wrested by the founder of the fortune in endeavors ranging from battling over a backwoods tannery to managing the coup which resulted in the capture of the Western Union.[4]

Thus ended the morality play of a nineteenth century capitalist. Its ending struck a note of tragic irony pleasing, perhaps, to those who were impressed by Biblical injunctions against storing up earthly treasure. The stress and turmoil of his career cut short both his own life and that of his wife, and its preoccupations prevented him from educating his children in the essentials of avoiding the pitfalls which must lie before them. Those he loved the most he inadvertently hurt the most.

His more or less subtle rewards, measurable only to himself, were the great private joy of acquisition, the fierce pleasures of financial combat, the skillfully dissimulated satisfaction he must have known while making his name feared and hated. One remembers his odd little smile as a schoolboy when the teacher punished his tormentors, when he preferred the tattletale's unpopularity to not, somehow, coming out on top. Not once in all the storms of adverse public opinion did he ever doubt, apparently, that the game was worth the candle.

It is far too late in the day to feel much moral indignation over the waxworks villain his contemporaries made of him.

[4] When Howard, the last surviving son of Jay Gould, died in New York on September 13, 1959, his estate totaled $62,745,000 and was left to twenty-eight relatives. Howard Gould, eighty-eight when he died, had maintained a seat on the New York Stock Exchange since 1898, the second oldest on the exchange, but his rare trading activities never caused a tremor of fear in Wall Street that another Gould was about to wreak havoc.

His victims, like those of any confidence man, were mostly destroyed through their own greed—aside from that ephemeral horde of widows and orphans summoned up by their critics to haunt all financial adventurers. "He was the scapegoat of the unsuccessful," as Julius Grodinsky has written. The worst that can be said of him is that he was no better than his fellow entrepreneurs, in a time when the nation was moving west, partly on rails he built, over the graves of an aboriginal race destroyed with a cold calculation by a generation of conquerors. His great sin was that he hit his generation where it hurt the most, in the pocketbook, and that he never bothered to apologize for it—not even to himself.

His villainies emerge from the welter of old headlines only as picturesque symptoms of a time so uncomplicated that one man could draw to himself a hatred now reserved for nations.

THE END.

BIBLIOGRAPHY

Adams, Charles Francis, Jr., and Adams, Henry, *Chapters of Erie*, New York, 1886.

Adams, Henry, *The Education of Henry Adams*, Boston, 1918.

Amory, Cleveland, *Who Killed Society?*, New York, 1960.

Andrews, Wayne, *The Vanderbilt Legend*, New York, 1941.

Barrett, James W., *Joseph Pulitzer and His World*, New York, 1941.

Barron, C. W. (arranged and edited by Arthur Pound and Samuel T. Moore), *They Told Barron*, New York, 1930.

Barrus, Dr. Clara, *John Burroughs, Boy and Man*, New York, 1922.

Beer, Thomas, *The Mauve Decade*, New York, 1926.

Bruce, Robert V., *1877: Year of Violence*, Indianapolis, 1959.

Carpenter, Frank G., *Carp's Washington*, New York, 1960.

Clews, Henry, *Fifty Years in Wall Street*, New York, 1908.

Corey, Lewis, *The House of Morgan*, New York, 1930.

Crapsey, Edward, *The Nether Side of New York*, 1872.

Crockett, Albert Stevens, *When James Gordon Bennett Was Caliph of Bagdad*, New York, 1926.

De Castellane, Marquis Boni, *How I Discovered America*, New York, 1924.

Eliot, Elizabeth, *Heiresses and Coronets*, New York, 1959.

Fuller, Robert H., *Jubilee Jim*, New York, 1928.

Gould, Jay, *History of Delaware County*, Roxbury, N.Y., 1856.

Grodinsky, Julius, *Jay Gould: His Business Career, 1867–1892*, Philadelphia, 1957.

Halstead, Murat, and Beale, J. Frank, *The Life of Jay Gould*, New York, 1892.

Harlow, Alvin F., *Old Wires and New Waves*, New York, 1936.

Holbrook, Stewart H., *The Age of Moguls*, New York, 1953.

Howard, Ernest, *Wall Street Fifty Years After Erie*, Boston, 1923.

Jones, Theodore F., *New York University, 1832–1932*, New York, 1933.

Josephson, Matthew, *The Robber Barons*, New York, 1934.

Lehr, Elizabeth Drexel, *King Lehr and the Gilded Age*, Philadelphia, 1935.

Lewis, Oscar, *The Big Four*, New York, 1938.

Lord, Walter, *The Good Years*, New York, 1960.

Lundberg, Ferdinand, *America's Sixty Families*, New York, 1937.

McAllister, Ward, *Society As I Have Found It*, New York, 1890.

Martin, Frederick T., *The Passing of the Idle Rich*, New York, 1911.

Martin, M. J., *Jay Gould and His Tannery* (a pamphlet), Scranton, 1945.

Medbery, James K., *Men and Mysteries of Wall Street*, Boston, 1870.

Minnigerode, Meade, *Certain Rich Men*, New York, 1927.

Myers, Gustavus, *History of the Great American Fortunes*, New York, 1909.

Northrop, H. D., *Life and Achievements of Jay Gould*, Philadelphia, 1892.

Noyes, Alexander D., *Forty Years of American Finance*, New York, 1898.

O'Connor, Richard, *Hell's Kitchen*, Philadelphia, 1958.

Riegel, Robert E., *The Story of the Western Railroads*, New York, 1926.

Seitz, Don C., *The Dreadful Decade*, Indianapolis, 1926.

——, *The James Gordon Bennetts*, Indianapolis, 1928.

——, *Joseph Pulitzer: His Life and Letters*, New York, 1924.

Seton, Celeste Andrews (as told to Clark Andrews), *Helen Gould Was My Mother-in-Law*, New York, 1953.

Snow, Alice Northrop (with Henry Nicholas Snow), *The Story of Helen Gould*, New York, 1943.

Strong, George T. (edited by Allan Nevins and Milton Halsey Thomas), *The Diary of George Templeton Strong*, New York, 1952.

Swanberg, W. A., *Jim Fisk*, New York, 1959.

Trottman, Nelson, *History of the Union Pacific*, New York, 1923.

Villard, Henry, *Memoirs of Henry Villard*, Boston, 1904.
Wecter, Dixon, *The Saga of American Society*, New York, 1937.
White, Bouck, *The Book of Daniel Drew*, New York, 1910.
White, Trumbull, *The Wizard of Wall Street*, Philadelphia, 1893.
Worden, Helen, *Society Circus*, New York, 1936.

REPORTS OF VARIOUS INVESTIGATING COMMITTEES

Report of the Committee on Railroads, New York State Senate, January 14, 1869.
Report of the Special (Hepburn) Committee, New York State Assembly, 1879.
Congressional Record, Vol. XVII, 49th Congress, First Session, 1885–86.
House Report No. 31, 41st Congress, Second Session, 1870.
Report of the Select Committee, New York State Assembly, 1873.
United States Pacific Railway Commission (50th Congress, First Session), published in Washington, 1887.

MAGAZINES

American Illustrated
Financial Chronicle
Fortune
Harper's Bazaar
Harper's Weekly

Literary Digest
The Nation
Town and Country
Town Topics
World's Work

NEWSPAPERS

Boston *Herald*
    Transcript
New York *Dramatic Mirror*
    Evening Post
    Herald
    Journal
    Mail and Express
    Press

Sun
Times
Tribune
World
Philadelphia *North American*
    Press
St. Louis *Post-Dispatch*
San Francisco *Chronicle*

INDEX